Talk Like **TED**

Carmine Gallo, bestselling author of *The Presentation Secrets of Steve Jobs*, is the communications coach for the world's most admired brands. A former anchor and correspondent for CNN and CBS, Gallo is a popular keynote speaker who has worked with executives at Intel, Cisco, Chevron, Hewlett-Packard, Coca-Cola, Pfizer, and many others and writes the *Forbes.com* column 'My Communications Coach'. He lives in Pleasanton, California, with his wife and two daughters.

Visit www.talkliketed.com and www.carminegallo.com.

Praise for *Talk Like TED*:

'The premise of this book, that TED talks provide great examples and lessons, is a magnificent insight. Then Carmine's execution of this premise is even better. This book will make you a much better speaker'
Guy Kawasaki, former chief evangelist of Apple
and author of *APE: Author, Publisher, Entrepreneur*

'Inspire, motivate and persuade any audience! That's what Carmine Gallo helped me do and now he can help you, too, in *Talk Like TED*. Your success depends on your ability to pitch and present your vision, ideas, and proposals. Learn to deliver like a pro'
Darren Hardy, publisher and founding editor of *SUCCESS* magazine

'In this book, Gallo performs magic: he shows us exactly what makes the world's greatest talks so great. Through story, detail, insight, and passion, Gallo gives us secrets we can apply to our own presentations so that people actually want to hear us talk'
Dan Roam, author of *The Back of the Napkin* and *Show and Tell*

ALSO BY CARMINE GALLO

The Apple Experience:
Secrets to Building Insanely Great Customer Loyalty

The Power of foursquare:
7 Innovative Ways to Get Customers to Check In Wherever They Are

The Innovation Secrets of Steve Jobs:
Insanely Different Principles for Breakthrough Success

The Presentation Secrets of Steve Jobs:
How to Be Insanely Great in Front of Any Audience

Fire Them Up!: 7 Simple Secrets to: Inspire Colleagues,
Customers, and Clients; Sell Yourself, Your Vision, and Your
Values; Communicate with Charisma and Confidence

10 Simple Secrets of the World's
Greatest Business Communicators

The Storyteller's Secret: How TED Speakers and
Inspirational Leaders Turn Their Passion Into Performance

Talk Like **TED**

THE 9 PUBLIC SPEAKING SECRETS
OF THE WORLD'S TOP MINDS

Carmine Gallo

PAN BOOKS

First published 2014 by St Martin's Press

First published in the UK 2014 by Macmillan

This edition published 2017 by Pan Books
an imprint of Pan Macmillan
20 New Wharf Road, London N1 9RR
Associated companies throughout the world
www.panmacmillan.com

ISBN 978-1-5098-6739-4

7 8 9

A CIP catalogue record for this book is available from the British Library.

Printed and bound by CPI Group (UK) Ltd, Croydon, CR0 4YY

Visit **www.panmacmillan.com** to read more about all our books
and to buy them. You will also find features, author interviews and
news of any author events, and you can sign up for e-newsletters
so that you're always first to hear about our new releases.

To Vanessa, with love and gratitude

CONTENTS

ACKNOWLEDGMENTS

A great presentation requires a team of people who offer their advice, input, and skill. Writing and publishing a book is no different. It is very much a team effort.

The team at St. Martin's Press is truly exceptional. My editor, Matt Martz, shared my passion for the topic right from the beginning. We were on the "same page" throughout the entire process. His guidance, feedback, and judgment helped me structure *Talk Like TED* into a narrative that I believe the reader will find informative, instructive, inspiring, and entertaining. I also wish to thank the many others at St. Martin's Press who share my enthusiasm for this project. This is certainly not an exhaustive list, but I'd like to extend a special shout-out to: Sally Richardson, Dan Weiss, Laura Clark, Michelle Cashman, Mariann Donato, Michael Hoak, Kerry Nordling, Christy D'Agostini as well as Robert Allen and the dedicated team at Macmillan Audio.

Roger Williams, my literary agent and managing director at New England Publishing Associates, is more than a colleague. He's a trusted friend, advisor, and mentor. Roger, thank you for your continued guidance and inspiration.

My speaking agents at BrightSight Group, Tom Neilssen and Les Tuerk, deserve special recognition. They've inspired me to share my ideas through keynote presentations at a wide range of conferences, meetings, and events. I'm forever grateful for their wonderful friendship and guidance. BrightSight itself relies on the work of an exceptional team of passionate experts and I thank each and every one of them—Cynthia Seeto, Christine Teichmann, Jeff Lykes, Michele DiLisio, and Marge Hennessy.

Carolyn Kilmer, Community Manager at Gallo Communications, is a big fan of TED presentations and enthusiastically dived into the research. She watched countless presentations to help categorize the talks, subjects, and techniques. Carolyn's work helped to give structure to the vast amounts of material we had to analyze.

I'm especially proud of the deep science behind every technique. Each of these techniques are effective because they are based on how the brain works and how it processes and remembers information. My friend Danny Mourning is an attorney and former graduate research assistant in the field of communications. Danny was a sounding board and often pointed me in the right direction, putting me directly in touch with research professors or introducing me to novel academic papers on related subjects. Danny has an incredible passion for communicating ideas and I thank him for his insight.

The most important recognition must be reserved for my wife, Vanessa Gallo. Vanessa worked tirelessly to support the content of this book. She conducted exhaustive research, edited the manuscript prior to submission, and viewed hours of TED presentations. Her writing and editing expertise was invaluable. Vanessa's background as an instructor in psychology at San Francisco State Universtiy also helped us to analyze the speakers for their body language, gestures, and verbal delivery. Vanessa's unwavering belief in this topic and the value of these ideas fueled my passion and enthusiasm every day. How she juggles the management of our business and caring for our daughters, Josephine and Lela, is beyond me. Yet she does everything masterfully. She is truly my inspiration.

Special thanks to my family for their support: Tino, Donna, Francesco, Nick, Ken, and Patty. My mother, Giuseppina, will always have a special place in my heart along with my departed father, Franco, who taught me about faith, courage, and determination.

Ideas Are the Currency of the Twenty-first Century

"I'm a learning machine and this is the place to learn."

—TONY ROBBINS, TED 2006

IDEAS ARE THE CURRENCY OF the twenty-first century. Some people are exceptionally good at presenting their ideas. Their skill elevates their stature and influence in today's society. There's nothing more inspiring than a bold idea delivered by a great speaker. Ideas, effectively packaged and delivered, can change the world. So, wouldn't it be amazing to identify the exact techniques shared by the world's greatest communicators, watch them deliver jaw-dropping presentations, and apply their secrets to wow your audiences? Now you can, thanks to a world famous conference that posts its best presentations for free on the Internet—TED (Technology, Education, Design), a scientific analysis of hundreds of TED presentations, direct interviews with TED's most popular speakers, and my personal insights gleaned from years of coaching inspiring leaders of the world's most admired brands.

Talk Like TED is for anyone who wants to speak with more confidence and authority. It's for anyone who delivers presentations, sells products and services, or leads people who need to be inspired. If you have ideas worth sharing, the techniques in this book will help you craft and deliver those ideas far more persuasively than you've ever imagined.

In March 2012, civil rights attorney Bryan Stevenson delivered a talk to 1,000 people attending the annual TED conference in Long Beach, California. He received the longest standing ovation in TED history, and his presentation has been viewed nearly two million times online. For 18 minutes Stevenson held the audience spellbound by appealing to their heads and their hearts. The combination worked. Stevenson told me that the attendees that day donated a combined $1 million to his nonprofit, the Equal Justice Initiative. That's over $55,000 for each minute he spoke.

Stevenson did not deliver a PowerPoint presentation. He offered no visuals, no slides, no props. The power of his narrative carried the day. Some popular TED speakers prefer to use PowerPoint to reinforce the impact of their narrative. In March 2011, professor David Christian launched a movement to teach "Big History" in schools after delivering a riveting 18-minute TED talk backed by visually engaging slides and intriguing graphics. "Big history" teaches students how the world evolved and its place in the universe. Christian's presentation, which covers 13 billion years of history in 18 minutes, has been viewed more than one million times.

Christian and Stevenson have seemingly different presentation styles and you will hear from both of them in this book. One tells stories, the other delivers mountains of data with image-rich slides, yet both are captivating, entertaining, and inspiring because they share nine secrets. They understand the science and the art of persuasion.

After analyzing more than 500 TED presentations (more than

150 hours) and speaking directly to successful TED speakers, I've discovered that the most popular TED presentations share nine common elements. I've also interviewed some of the world's leading neuroscientists, psychologists, and communications experts to gain a better understanding of why the principles that underlie these elements work as well as they do. Best of all, once you learn the secrets these communicators share, you can adopt them and stand out in your very next pitch or presentation. These are techniques I've used for years to coach CEOs, entrepreneurs, and leaders who have invented products or run companies that touch your life every day. While you may never speak at an actual TED conference, if you want to succeed in business you'd better be able to deliver a TED-worthy presentation. It represents a bold, fresh, contemporary, and compelling style that will help you win over your audience.

IDEAS WORTH SPREADING

Richard Saul Wurman created the TED conference in 1984 as a onetime event. Six years later it was reinvented as a four-day conference in Monterey, California. For $475, attendees could watch a variety of lectures on topics covering technology, education, and design (TED). Technology-magazine publisher Chris Anderson purchased the conference in 2001 and relocated it to Long Beach, California in 2009. In 2014, the TED conference begins a run in Vancouver, Canada, reflecting its growing international appeal.

Until 2005 TED was a once-a-year event: four days, 50 speakers, 18-minute presentations. In that year, Anderson added a sister conference called TEDGlobal to reach an international audience. In 2009, the organization began granting licenses to third parties who could organize their own community-level TEDx events. Within three years more than 16,000 talks had been delivered at TEDx events around the world. Today there are five TEDx events organized every day in more than 130 countries.

Despite the astonishing growth in the conference business, TED speakers were introduced to a much larger global audience through the launch of TED.com in June 2006. The site posted six talks to test the market. Six months later the site only had about 40 presentations, yet had attracted more than three million views. The world was and still is clearly hungry for great ideas presented in an engaging way.

On November 13, 2012 TED.com presentations had reached *one billion* views, and are now being viewed at the rate of 1.5 million times per day. The videos are translated into up to 90 languages, and 17 new viewings of TED presentations start every second of every day. According to Chris Anderson, "It used to be 800 people getting together once a year; now it's about a million people a day watching TED Talks online. When we first put up a few of the talks as an experiment, we got such impassioned responses that we decided to flip the organization on its head and think of ourselves not so much as a conference but as 'ideas worth spreading,' building a big website around it. The conference is still the engine, but the website is the amplifier that takes the ideas to the world."[1]

The first six TED talks posted online are considered classics among fans who affectionately call themselves "TEDsters." The speakers included Al Gore, Sir Ken Robinson, and Tony Robbins. Some of these speakers used traditional presentation slides; others did not. But they all delivered talks that were emotional, novel, and memorable. Today TED has become such an influential platform, famous actors and musicians make a beeline to a TED stage when they have ideas to share. A few days after accepting the Oscar for best picture, *Argo* director Ben Affleck appeared at TED in Long Beach to talk about his work in the Congo. Earlier in the week U2 singer Bono delivered a presentation on the success of antipoverty campaigns around the world. When celebrities want to be taken seriously, they hit the TED stage.

Facebook COO Sheryl Sandberg wrote her bestseller *Lean In* after her TED presentation on the subject of women in the workplace went viral on TED.com. TED presentations change the way people see the world and are springboards to launch movements in the areas of art, design, business, education, health, science, technology, and global issues. Documentary filmmaker Daphne Zuniga attended the 2006 conference. She describes it as "a gathering where the world's top entrepreneurs, designers, scientists and artists present astonishing new ideas in what can only be described as a Cirque Du Soleil for the mind."[2] There's no event like it, Zuniga says. "It's four days of learning, passion, and inspiration . . . stimulating intellectually, but I never thought the ideas I heard would move my heart as well." Oprah Winfrey once put it even more succinctly: "TED is where brilliant people go to hear other brilliant people share their ideas."

THE PRESENTATION SECRETS OF STEVE JOBS

I'm in a unique position to analyze TED presentations. I wrote a book titled *The Presentation Secrets of Steve Jobs*, which went on to become an international bestseller. Famous CEOs are known to have adopted the principles revealed in the book, and hundreds of thousands of professionals around the world are using the method to transform their presentations. I was flattered by the attention, but I wanted to reassure readers that the techniques I explored in *Presentation Secrets* were not exclusive to Steve Jobs. The Apple cofounder and technology visionary just happened to be very good at putting them all together. The techniques were very "TED-like."

In the book I make the point that Steve Jobs's famous commencement speech at Stanford University in 2005 was a magnificent illustration of his ability to captivate an audience. Ironically, the commencement speech is one of the most popular videos on

TED.com. While it's not officially a TED talk, it contains the same elements as the best TED presentations and has been viewed more than 15 million times.

"Your time is limited, so don't waste it living someone else's life.[3] Don't be trapped by dogma—which is living with the results of other people's thinking," Jobs told the graduates. "Don't let the noise of others' opinions drown out your own inner voice. And most important, have the courage to follow your heart and intuition. They somehow already know what you truly want to become." Jobs's words spoke directly to the type of people who are moved by TED presentations. They're seekers. They're eager to learn. Discontent with the status quo, they are looking for inspiring and innovative ideas that move the world forward. With Steve Jobs, you learned the techniques from one master; in *Talk Like TED* you get them all.

DALE CARNEGIE FOR THE TWENTY-FIRST CENTURY

Talk Like TED digs far deeper into the science of communication than almost any book on the market today. It introduces you to men and women—scientists, authors, educators, environmentalists, and famous leaders—who prepare and deliver the talk of their lives. Every one of the more than 1,500 presentations available for free on the TED Web site can teach you something about public speaking.

When I first started thinking about writing a book on the public speaking secrets of TED talks, I thought of it as *Dale Carnegie for the Twenty-first Century*. Carnegie wrote the first mass market public-speaking and self-help book in 1915, *The Art of Public Speaking*. Carnegie's intuition was impeccable. He recommended that speakers keep their talks short. He said stories were powerful ways of connecting emotionally with your audience. He suggested the use of rhetorical devices such as metaphors and analogies. Three-quarters of a century before PowerPoint was invented Carnegie was talking about using visual aids. He understood the importance of enthusiasm, practice, and strong delivery to move people. Everything Carnegie recommended in 1915 remains the foundation of effective communication to this day.

While Carnegie had the right idea, he didn't have the tools available today. Scientists using fMRI (functional magnetic resonance imaging) can scan people's brains to see exactly what areas are being activated when a subject performs a specific task, such as speaking or listening to someone else. This technology and other tools of modern science have led to an avalanche of studies in the area of communication. The secrets revealed in this book are supported by the latest science from the best minds on the planet, and they work. Is passion contagious? You'll find out. Can telling stories actually "sync" your mind with that of the person listening to you? You'll discover the answer. Why does an 18-minute presentation trump a 60-minute one? Why did video of Bill Gates releasing mosquitoes into an audience go viral? You'll learn the answer to those questions, too.

Carnegie also lacked the most powerful tool that we can use to learn the art of public speaking: the Internet, which wouldn't be commercialized until 40 years after Carnegie's death. Today, thanks to the availability of broadband, people can watch videos on TED.com and see the world's best minds deliver the presentations of their lives. Once you learn these nine secrets, read the interviews with popular TED speakers, and understand the science behind it all, you can turn to TED.com to see the presenters in action using the skills you've just read about.

WE'RE ALL IN SALES NOW

The most popular TED speakers give presentations that stand out in a sea of ideas. As Daniel Pink notes in *To Sell Is Human*, "Like it or not, we're all in sales now."[4] If you've been invited to give a

TED talk, this book is your bible. If you haven't been invited to give a TED talk and have no intention of doing so, this book is still among the most valuable books you'll ever read because it will teach you how to sell yourself and your ideas more persuasively than you've ever imagined. It will teach you how to incorporate the elements that all inspiring presentations share, and it will show you how to reimagine the way you see yourself as a leader and a communicator. Remember, if you can't inspire anyone else with your ideas, it won't matter how great those ideas are. Ideas are only as good as the actions that follow the communication of those ideas.

TALK LIKE TED **IS DIVIDED** into three parts, each revealing three components of an inspiring presentation. The most engaging presentations are:

- EMOTIONAL—**They touch my heart.**

- NOVEL—**They teach me something new.**

- MEMORABLE—**They present content in ways I'll never forget.**

EMOTIONAL

Great communicators reach your head and touch your heart. Most people who deliver a presentation forget the "heart" part. In chapter 1 you'll learn how to unleash the master within by identifying what it is that you are truly passionate about. You will read about research—never published in the popular press—that explains why passion is the key to mastering a skill like public speaking. Chapter 2 teaches you how to master the art of storytelling and why stories help your listeners get emotionally attached to your topic. You'll learn about new research that shows how stories actually "sync" your mind to those of your audience, allowing you to create far deeper and more-meaningful connections than you've ever experienced. In chapter 3 you will learn how TED presenters exhibit body language and verbal delivery that is genuine and natural, almost as if they are having a conversation instead of addressing a large audience. You'll also meet speakers who spent 200 hours rehearsing a presentation and learn how they practiced. You will learn techniques to make your presence and delivery more comfortable and impactful.

NOVEL

According to the neuroscientists I've interviewed, novelty is the single most effective way to capture a person's attention. YouTube trends manager Kevin Allocca told a TED audience that in a world where two days of videos get uploaded every minute, "Only that which is truly unique and unexpected can stand out." The brain cannot ignore novelty, and after you adopt the techniques in this section, your listeners will not be able to ignore you. In chapter 4 we explore how the greatest TED presenters engage their audiences with new information or a unique approach to an area of study. Chapter 5 is about delivering jaw-dropping moments, highlighting those speakers who carefully, consciously design and deliver "wow" moments their audiences are still talking about years later. Chapter 6 addresses the sensitive but important element of genuine humor—when to use it, how to use it, and how to be funny without telling a joke. Humor is unique to each presenter and it must be incorporated into your personal style of presenting.

MEMORABLE

You may have novel ideas, but if your audience cannot recall what you said, those ideas don't matter. In chapter 7 I explore why the 18-minute TED presentation is the ideal length of time to get your point across. And yes, there's science to back it up. Chapter 8 covers the importance of creating vivid, multisensory experiences so your audience can recall the content more successfully. In chapter 9 I emphasize the importance of staying in your own lane, the ultimate key to being a genuine, authentic speaker whom people feel they can trust.

Each chapter features a specific technique shared by the most popular TED speakers along with examples, insights, and interviews with the people who delivered the presentations. I've also included "TEDnotes" throughout each chapter: specific tips that will help you apply the secrets to your very next pitch or presentation. In these notes you will find the name of the speaker and the title of his or her presentation so you can search for it easily on TED.com. In each chapter we'll also explore the science behind the featured secret—why it works and how you can apply the technique to take your presentations to a higher level. In the last 10 years we've learned more about the human mind than we've ever known. These findings have profound implications for your very next presentation.

LEARN FROM THE MASTERS

In *Mastery* author Robert Greene argues that we all have the ability to push the limits of human potential. Power, intelligence, and creativity are forces that we can unleash with the right mind-set and skills. People who are masters in their field (e.g., art, music, sports, public speaking) have a different way of seeing the world. Greene believes the word *genius* should be demystified because we have "access to information and knowledge that past masters could only dream about."[5]

TED.com is a gold mine for those who want to attain mastery in the area of communications, persuasion, and public speaking. *Talk Like TED* will give you the tools and show you how to use them to help you find your voice and maybe even your fortune.

Better-than-average communicators are generally more successful than other people, but great communicators start movements. They are remembered and revered by their last names alone: Jefferson, Lincoln, Churchill, Kennedy, King, Reagan. Failure to communicate effectively in business is a fast road to failure. It means startups won't get funded, products won't get sold, projects won't get backing, and careers won't soar. The ability to deliver a TED-worthy presentation could mean the difference between enjoying acclaim and toiling in hopeless obscurity. You're still alive. That means your life has purpose. You were meant for greatness. Don't sabotage your potential because you can't communicate your ideas.

At TED 2006, motivational guru Tony Robbins said, "Effective leaders have the ability to move themselves and others to action because they understand the invisible forces that shape us."[6] Passionate, powerful, and inspiring communication is one of those forces that moves and shapes us. A new approach to solving long-standing problems, inspiring stories, intriguing ways of delivering information, and standing ovations are known as "TED moments." Create those moments. Captivate your audience. Inspire them. Change the world. Here's how . . .

PART I

Emotional

The key part of the TED format is that we have humans connecting to humans in a direct and almost vulnerable way. You're on stage naked, so to speak. The talks that work best are the ones where people can really sense that humanity. The emotions, dreams, imagination.

—CHRIS ANDERSON, CURATOR, TED

Unleash the Master Within

Passion is the thing that will help you create the highest expression of your talent.

—LARRY SMITH, TEDx, NOVEMBER 2011

AIMEE MULLINS HAS 12 PAIRS of legs. Like most people she was born with two, but unlike most people Mullins had to have both legs amputated below the knee due to a medical condition. Mullins has lived with no lower legs since her first birthday.

Mullins grew up in a middle-class family in the middle-class town of Allentown, Pennsylvania, yet her achievements are far from ordinary. Mullins's doctors suggested that an early amputation would give her the best chance to have a reasonable amount of mobility. As a child Mullins had no input into that decision, but as she grew up she refused to see herself as or to accept the label most people gave her—"disabled." Instead, she decided that prosthetic limbs would give her superpowers that others could only dream of.

Mullins redefines what it means to be disabled. As she told

comedian and talk-show host Stephen Colbert, many actresses have more prosthetic material in their breasts than she does in her whole body, "and we don't call half of Hollywood disabled."

Mullins tapped her superpower—her prosthetic limbs—to run track for an NCAA Division One program at Georgetown University. She broke three world records in track and field at the 1996 Paralympics, became a fashion model and an actress, and landed a spot on *People* magazine's annual list of the 50 Most Beautiful People.

In 2009 the 5'8" Mullins stood on the TED stage at 6'1" the height she chose for the occasion. Mullins picks different legs to suit the event. She uses more-functional limbs for walking the streets of Manhattan and more-fashionable ones for fancy parties.

"TED literally was the launch pad to the next decade of my life's exploration,"[1] said Mullins. Mullins believes her TED appearance began a conversation that profoundly changed the way society looks at people with disabilities. Innovators, designers, and artists outside the traditional prosthetic medical community were inspired to see how creative and lifelike they could make legs. "It is no longer a conversation about overcoming deficiency. It's a conversation about potential. A prosthetic limb doesn't represent the need to replace loss anymore . . . So people that society once considered to be disabled can now become the architects of their own identities and indeed continue to change those identities by designing their bodies from a place of empowerment . . . it is our humanity, and all the potential within it, that makes us beautiful."

Mullins's determination made her a world-class athlete; her passion won the hearts of the TED audience.

Secret #1: Unleash the Master Within

Dig deep to identify your unique and meaningful connection to your presentation topic. Passion leads to mastery and your presentation is nothing without it, but keep in mind that what fires you up might not be the obvious. Aimee Mullins isn't passionate about prosthetics; she's passionate about unleashing human potential.

Why it works: Science shows that passion is contagious, literally. You cannot inspire others unless you are inspired yourself. You stand a much greater chance of persuading and inspiring your listeners if you express an enthusiastic, passionate, and meaningful connection to your topic.

IN OCTOBER 2012, CAMERON RUSSELL told a TEDx audience, "Looks aren't everything."[2] Cliché? Yes, if it had been delivered by anyone else. Russell, however, is a successful fashion model. Within thirty seconds of taking the stage Russell changed her outfit. She covered her revealing, tight-fitting black dress with a wraparound skirt, replaced her eight-inch heels with plain shoes, and pulled a turtleneck sweater over her head.

"So why did I do that?" she asked the audience. "Image is powerful, but also image is superficial. I just totally transformed what you thought of me in six seconds."

Russell explained that she's an underwear model who has walked runways for Victoria's Secret and has appeared on the covers of fashion magazines. While Russell acknowledges that modeling has been good to her—it paid for college—she's also keenly aware that she "won the genetic lottery."

Russell showed the audience a series of before-and-after photos. The "before" photos revealed what she looked like earlier in the day of a photo shoot and the "after" photos displayed the final ad. Of course the two photographs didn't look at all alike. In one photo, Russell—16 years old at the time—was seductively posed with a young man whose hand was placed in the back pocket of her jeans (Russell had never even had a boyfriend at the time of the shoot). "I hope what you're seeing is that these pictures are not pictures of me. They are constructions, and they are constructions by a group of professionals, by hairstylists and makeup artists and photographers and stylists and all of their assistants and preproduction and postproduction. They build this. That's not me."

Russell is a master of her craft—modeling. But modeling is not what she's passionate about. She's passionate about raising self-esteem in young girls, and that's why she connects with her audience. Passion is contagious. "The real way that I became a model is I won a genetic lottery, and I am the recipient of a legacy, and maybe you're wondering what is a legacy. Well, for the past few centuries we have defined beauty not just as health and youth and symmetry that we're biologically programmed to admire, but also as tall, slender figures, and femininity and white skin. And this is a legacy that was built for me, and it's a legacy that I've been cashing in on."

Russell's looks made her a model; her passion made her a successful speaker.

Russell and Mullins were given a platform because they are masters in their fields, but they connect with their audiences because they are passionate about their topics. What fuels a speaker's passion does not always involve their day-to-day work. Russell didn't talk about posing for photographs, and Mullins didn't talk about competing in track and field. Yet each gave the talk of her life.

The most popular TED speakers share something in common with the most engaging communicators in any field—a passion, an obsession they must share with others. The most popular TED speakers don't have a "job." They have a passion, an obsession, a vocation, but not a job. These people are called to share their ideas.

People cannot inspire others unless and until they are inspired themselves. "In our culture we tend to equate thinking and intellectual powers with success and achievement. In many ways, however, it is an emotional quality that separates those who master a field from the many who simply work at a job,"[3] writes Robert Greene in *Mastery*. "Our levels of desire, patience, persistence and confidence end up playing a much larger role in success than sheer reasoning powers. Feeling motivated and energized, we can overcome almost anything. Feeling bored and restless, our minds shut off and we become increasingly passive." Motivated and energized speakers are always more interesting and engaging than bored and passive ones.

I'm often asked to work with CEOs on major product launches or initiatives, helping them to tell their brand stories more effectively and persuasively. I travel around the world to visit brands such as Intel, Coca-Cola, Chevron, Pfizer, and many other companies in nearly every product category. In any language, on any continent, in every country, those speakers who genuinely express their passion and enthusiasm for the topic are the ones who stand apart as inspiring leaders. They're the ones with whom customers want to conduct business.

For years I started with the same question during my coaching sessions with a client—what are you passionate about? In the early stage of building a story, I don't care about the product as much as I care about why the speaker is fired up about the product or service. Howard Schultz, the founder of Starbucks, once told me he wasn't passionate about coffee as much as he was passionate about "building a third place between work and home, a place where employees would be treated with respect and offer exceptional customer service." Coffee is the product, but Starbucks is in the business of customer service. Tony Hsieh, the founder of online retailer Zappos, isn't passionate about shoes. He told me he's passionate about "delivering happiness." The questions he asks himself are: How do I make my employees happy? How do I make my customers happy? The questions you ask will lead to a very different set of results. Asking yourself, "What's my product?" isn't nearly as effective as asking yourself, "What business am I really in? What am I truly passionate about?"

Tony Hsieh is so passionate about customer service and employee engagement, he is a sought-after speaker at events and conferences around the world (he has to turn down far more requests than he accepts). Since many speakers are bone-dry because they have no passionate attachment to the topic, watching an enthusiastic speaker is as refreshing as drinking ice-cold water in the desert.

WHAT MAKES YOUR HEART SING?

Recently I've started to change the first question I ask of my executive clients who want to become better communicators. In his last major public presentation, Steve Jobs said, "It's the intersection of technology and liberal arts that makes our hearts sing." So today I've replaced "What are you passionate about" with "What makes your heart sing?" The answer to the second question is even more profound and exciting than the former.

For example, I worked with a client in the agribusiness community of California. He headed an association of strawberry growers, an important crop for the state. Here's how he answered my questions:

Question 1: What do you do? "I'm the CEO of the California Strawberry Commission."

Question 2: What are you passionate about? "I'm passionate about promoting California strawberries."

Question 3: What is it about the industry that makes your

heart sing? "The American dream. My parents were immigrants and worked in the fields. Eventually they were able to buy an acre of land and it grew from there. With strawberries, you don't need a lot of land and you don't need to own it; you can lease it. It's a stepping stone to the American dream."

I'm sure you'll agree that the answer to the third question is much more interesting than the first two. What makes your heart sing? Identify it and share it with others.

TEDnote

WHAT MAKES YOUR HEART SING? Ask yourself, "What makes my heart sing?" Your passion is not a passing interest or even a hobby. A passion is something that is intensely meaningful and core to your identity. Once you identify what your passion is, can you say it influences your daily activities? Can you incorporate it into what you do professionally? Your true passion should be the subject of your communications and will serve to truly inspire your audience.

THE HAPPIEST MAN IN THE WORLD

Matthieu Ricard is the happiest man in the world, and he's not happy about it. In 2004 Matthieu Ricard temporarily left the Shechen monastery in Kathmandu to teach a TED audience in Monterey, California the habits of happiness.

According to Ricard, happiness is a "deep sense of serenity and fulfillment." Ricard should know. He's not just pleased with his life. He's really, really happy. Scientifically, he's off-the-charts happy. Ricard volunteered for a study at the University of Wisconsin, Madison. Research scientists placed 256 tiny electrodes on Ricard's scalp to measure his brain waves. The study was conducted on hundreds of people who practice meditation. They were rated on a happiness scale. Ricard didn't just score above average;

the researchers couldn't find anything like it in the neuroscience literature. The brain scans showed "excessive activity in his brain's left prefrontal cortex compared to its right counterpart, giving him an abnormally large capacity for happiness and a reduced propensity towards negativity."[4]

Ricard isn't all that happy about being labeled the happiest man in the world. "In truth, anyone can find happiness if he or she looks for it in the right place,"[5] he said. "Authentic happiness can only come from the long-term cultivation of wisdom, altruism, and compassion, and from the complete eradication of mental toxins, such as hatred, grasping, and ignorance."

Ricard's presentation, "The Habits of Happiness," attracted more than two million views on TED.com. I believe Ricard's presentation was well received because Ricard radiates the joy of someone who is deeply committed to his topic. Indeed, Ricard told me, "These ideas are dear to me not only because they brought me a lot of fulfillment, but because I am convinced that they can bring some good to society. I am particularly passionate to show that altruism and compassion are not luxuries, but essential needs to answer the challenges of our modern world. So, whenever I am asked to join a conference, I am glad to do so and be able to share my ideas."[6]

Successful speakers can't wait to share their ideas. They have charisma and charisma is directly associated with how much passion the speaker has for his or her content. Charismatic speakers radiate joy and passion; the joy of sharing their experience and passion for how their ideas, products, or services will benefit their audiences. "I believe that the best way to communicate with anyone is to first check the quality of your motivation: 'Is my motivation selfish or altruistic? Is my benevolence aimed at just a few or at the great number? For their short-term or their long-term good?' Once we have a clear motivation, then communication flows easily," says Ricard.

Amazingly, if your motivation is to share your passion with your audience, it's likely that you'll feel less nervous about speaking in public or delivering that all-important presentation in front of your boss. I asked Ricard how he remains calm and relaxed in front of large audiences. Ricard believes that anyone can talk him- or herself into feeling joy, bliss, and happiness when they choose to do so. It all comes down to your motivation. If your only goal is to make a sale or to elevate your stature, you might fail to connect with your audience (and you'll place a lot of pressure on yourself). If, however, your goal is more altruistic—giving your audience information to help them live better lives—you'll make a deeper connection and feel more comfortable in your role. "I am very happy to share ideas, but as an individual I have nothing to lose or to gain," said Ricard. "I don't care about my image, I have no business deal to cut, and I am not trying to impress anyone. I am just full of joy to be able to say a few words about the fact that we vastly underestimate the power of transforming the mind."

WHY YOU WILL FAIL TO HAVE A GREAT CAREER

If you're not happy and passionate about the work you do, you might fail to have a great career, and if you're not having a great time at a great career, it will be harder for you to generate enthusiasm through your presentations. That's why career, happiness, and the ability to inspire people are connected.

The topic of career success consumes University of Waterloo economics professor Larry Smith. Smith is frustrated with today's college students. He's upset because most college students will pursue specific careers for the wrong reasons—money, status, etc. According to Smith, those students will fail to have great careers. The only way to have a great career, says Smith, is to do what you love. Smith channeled his frustration into an inspiring, passionate, and humorous TEDx lecture, "Why You Will Fail to Have a Great Career."

I spoke to Smith about the popularity of his TED presentation, which at the time of our discussion had been seen more than two million times. The reaction surprised him. Smith agreed to do the talk at the request of his students. Since his classes are usually three hours long, he took it as a personal challenge to distill his ideas into 18 minutes. It was hugely popular because the audience sees a speaker with unbridled passion and a sense of urgency that makes his lecture riveting. Smith's presentation was essentially 30 years of pent-up frustration reaching a boiling point. "Wasted talent is a waste I cannot stand,"[7] Smith told me. "My students want to create technology. I want them to create really 'kick-ass' technology. I want them to be passionate about what they're doing."

Smith's premise is simple. There are plenty of bad jobs, he says. Those "high-stress, blood-sucking, soul-destroying" jobs. Then there are great jobs, but very little in between. Smith says most people will fail to land a great job or enjoy a great career because they are afraid to follow their passion. "No matter how many people tell you that if you want a great career, pursue your passion, pursue your dreams . . . you will decide not to do it." Excuses, he says, are holding people back. His advice? "Find and use your passion and you'll have a great career. Don't do it and you won't."

Smith was one of the most inspiring TED presenters I've met though I have to admit that I may be a little biased. I've been preaching the same gospel since the day I changed my plan to go to law school and pursued a career in journalism instead. At first I didn't earn nearly as much as I would have in the legal profession, and I certainly had some doubts about my chosen career path. Following your passion takes courage, especially if you don't see the results as quickly as you'd like. My life is vastly different today than it was in those early years, and I enjoy sharing my ideas with audiences around the world. Best of all, I don't feel as though I "work." Writing these words, watching these presentations, studying the science behind them, interviewing famous speakers, and sharing their thoughts with you is a joyful experience for me. Above all, I've learned that those who are joyful about their work often make the best public speakers.

> "You've got to follow your passion. You've got to figure out what it is you love—who you really are. And have the courage to do that. I believe that the only courage anybody ever needs is the courage to follow your own dreams."   —Oprah Winfrey

In his TEDx lecture Smith cited Steve Jobs's famous commencement speech at Stanford University in 2005 when Jobs encouraged the students to pursue the path they really love. "Your work is going to fill a large part of your life, and the only way to be truly satisfied is to do what you believe is great work. And the only way to do great work is to love what you do. If you haven't found it yet, keep looking. Don't settle. As with all matters of the heart, you'll know when you find it. And, like any great relationship, it just gets better and better as the years roll on. So keep looking until you find it. Don't settle."

Smith agrees with Jobs, but believes the advice often falls on deaf ears. "It doesn't matter how many times you download Steven J.'s Stanford commencement address, you still look at it and decide not to do it," Smith told the TED audience. "You're afraid to pursue your passion. You're afraid to look ridiculous. You're afraid to try. You're afraid you may fail."

After spending a quarter century in journalism, writing, speaking, and communications, I can tell you without hesitation that the most inspiring presentations are delivered by people such as

Larry Smith, Aimee Mullins, and most of the other speakers you'll meet in the chapters that follow. They share a deep well of experience and a passionate commitment to sharing their ideas to help others succeed.

TEDnote

ACCEPT HAPPINESS AS A CHOICE. What is one challenge you have been faced with recently? After identifying your challenge, list three reasons why this challenge is an opportunity. You see, happiness is a choice, an attitude that is contagious, and your state of mind will positively affect the way your listeners perceive you. Matthieu Ricard told me, "Our natural state of mind, when it is not misconstrued under the power of negative thoughts, is perfection. It is essential to inspire hope and confidence, since it is what we lack most and need most in our times."

THE NEW SCIENCE OF PASSION AND PERSUASION

Passion and public speaking are intimately connected. French philosopher Denis Diderot once said, "Only passions, great passions, can elevate the soul to great things." Successful leaders throughout history have speculated that passions—great passions—can elevate the soul. Today science proves them right. Neuroscientists have discovered—and have been able to quantify—why passionate people like TED speakers and great leaders inspire, energize, and influence other people.

Before we can create and deliver more-passionate presentations, we need to understand what passion is and why it works. For ten years Pace University management professor Melissa Cardon has made passion her passion. In her breakthrough study "The Nature and Experience of Entrepreneurial Passion," Cardon, along with four research colleagues from prestigious universities, found that passion plays a critical role in an entrepreneur's success. For one thing, passion mobilizes a person's energy and enhances his commitment to a goal. But passion does so much more. According to Cardon, "Entrepreneurial passion catalyzes full-blown emotional experiences, complete with engagement of brain and body responses."[8]

Cardon began her research by developing a definition for *entrepreneurial passion*. The common definition of *passion* simply didn't lend itself to academic studies and measurement. Passion is typically defined as "strong amorous feelings" or "sexual desire"; not exactly the kind of passion Cardon was interested in pursuing as an academic study. Yet "passion" is thrown around constantly as a critical component of success and, I would argue, is a critical element of all inspiring presentations.

What exactly does it mean to have a passion for something and, more important, how can people harness their passion to improve their odds of success in life, business, and public speaking? Cardon's challenge was to identify what passion means, what it does, and how to measure it. Academically, if you can't measure something you cannot quantify what it actually does. In order to establish passion as a robust area of study, Cardon had to develop a definition most scholars could agree on. Today, Cardon's definition of entrepreneurial passion (EP) is generally accepted in the academic literature: "A positive, intense feeling that you experience for something that is profoundly meaningful for you as an individual."

Cardon says that passion is something that is core to a person's self-identity. It defines a person. They simply can't separate their pursuit from who they are. *It's core to their being.* "Passion is aroused not because some entrepreneurs are inherently disposed to such feelings but, rather, because they are engaged in something that relates to a meaningful and salient self-identity for them."

Cardon's analysis helps explain why the most popular TED speakers connect with their audiences: they speak about topics that are salient to their self-identity. Take urban environmental consultant Majora Carter, for example. Carter's oldest brother served in Vietnam but was gunned down near their home in the South Bronx. Poverty, hopelessness, and racial divides made Carter who she is—a passionate advocate for urban renewal. Her experience defined her, and it defines her work. According to TED.com, "Carter's confidence, energy and intensely emotional delivery make her talks a force of nature." For Majora Carter, raising the hopes of those who have lost hope is core to who she is.

Entrepreneurship is core to Sir Richard Branson's identity. In 2007 Branson told a TED audience, "Companies are all about finding the right people, inspiring those people, and drawing out the best in people. I just love learning and I'm incredibly inquisitive and I love taking on the status quo and trying to turn it upside down."[9] Building companies like Virgin Atlantic that challenge the status quo is core to who he is. I spent a day with Richard Branson on April 22, 2013. I had been invited to accompany him on the inaugural flight of Virgin America's new route from Los Angeles to Las Vegas. On the ground and in the air, Branson was all smiles as he enthusiastically talked about customer service and how it makes the difference in the success of his brand.

Branson and Carter are engaged in activities that are intensely associated with their role identities in a profoundly meaningful way. And it's that passion that plays a critical role in their career successes and their success as communicators, according to Cardon.

"People who are genuinely passionate about their topic make better speakers. They inspire their audiences in ways that nonpassionate, low-energy people fail to do," Cardon told me. "When you are passionate about something you can't help yourself from thinking about it, acting on it, and talking about it with other people." Cardon says that investors, customers, and other stakeholders are "smart consumers": they know when a person is displaying genuine passion and when he or she is faking it. It's very difficult—nearly impossible—to electrify an audience without feeling an intense, meaningful connection to the content of your presentation.

PASSION—WHY IT WORKS

The next step for Cardon was to identify why passion matters. She found that passion leads to important behaviors and outcomes. Cardon, along with dozens of other scientists in the field, has discovered that passionate business leaders are more creative, set higher goals, exhibit greater persistence, and record better company performance. Cardon and her colleagues also found a direct correlation between a presenter's "perceived passion" and the likelihood that investors will fund his or her ideas.

Professors Melissa Cardon, Cheryl Mitteness (Northeastern University), and Richard Sudek (Chapman University) performed a remarkable experiment and published their results in the September 2012 issue of the *Journal of Business Venturing*. The researchers set out to understand the role that passion plays in investor decision-making.

The business pitch is one of the most critical presentations in business. Without funding, most ventures would never get off the ground. Companies like Google and Apple would never have changed our lives if it hadn't been for charismatic, passionate leaders who grabbed the attention of investors. Is passion the only criteria on which Apple and Google investors based their funding decision? Of course not. Did the perceived passion of the founders (Steve Jobs, Steve Wozniak, Sergey Brin, and Larry Page) play a role in the investors' ultimate funding decision? It certainly did.

The setting for Cardon's study was one of the largest angel investor organizations in America, Tech Coast Angels, based in Orange County, California.[10] Since 1997, the group of individual investors has invested more than $100 million in nearly 170 companies. The sample involved investors who did not invest as a group—they made their decisions independently.

From August 2006 through July 2010, 64 angel investors screened 241 companies. The screening involved a 15-minute PowerPoint presentation and a 15-minute question-and-answer session (later you'll learn why 15 to 20 minutes is the ideal length of time to make a business pitch).

Forty-one (17 percent) of the companies were eventually funded. The startups fell into 16 categories including software, consumer products, medical devices, and business services. Using a five-point scale, angel investors were asked to assess the passion and enthusiasm of the presenter by evaluating two items: "The CEO is passionate about the company" and "The CEO is very enthusiastic." The researchers controlled for other factors such as market opportunity, relative risk, and revenue potential, thereby isolating passion as one factor in the funding decision. Isolating passion allowed the researchers to quantify the role it played and they discovered that passion did indeed play a very important role in the ultimate success of a business pitch.

Investors based their judgment of the entrepreneur's potential on 13 criteria and were asked to rank each one in order of importance to their final decision. The strength of the opportunity and the strength of the entrepreneur were the most prized criteria, ranking numbers one and two. "Perceived passion" came in third, well above such criteria as the entrepreneur's education, style, startup experience, or age.

The researchers concluded, "Our findings provide evidence that perceived passion does make a difference when angels evaluate the funding potential of new ventures . . . perceived passion involves enthusiasm and excitement, and is distinct from how prepared or committed an entrepreneur may be to their venture . . . perceived passion does appear to matter to equity investors."

Cardon's research is essential for helping us understand why some TED presentations become Internet sensations and, more important, how to unleash our own public speaking potential.

"Carmine, you know the old adage we tell college students that they never listen to—do what you love? Well, it's true," says Cardon. "If you're starting a company in an area that you think will make you rich, but you don't enjoy that product, industry, or anything about it—that's a mistake." Cardon believes it's also a mistake to believe that you can influence and inspire others by speaking about a topic that you don't love—that is not core to your identity.

A FRONT-ROW SEAT TO HER OWN STROKE

Few TED speakers have as deep an emotional connection to their topic as neuroanatomist Jill Bolte Taylor (Dr. Jill), a national spokesperson for the Harvard Brain Tissue Resource Center, which partly explains why her presentation is one of the most popular TED talks of all time.

One morning Dr. Jill awoke to a pounding pain behind her left eye, the kind of sharp jolt you might feel with an ice-cream headache. If only it had been as innocuous as a bite of ice cream. The headache got worse. Dr. Jill lost her balance and soon realized her right arm was completely paralyzed. A blood vessel had ruptured in her head. She was having a stroke—the vessels in the left side of her brain were literally exploding.

Dr. Jill considered the stroke a stroke of luck. You see, Dr. Jill is a neuroanatomist, specializing in the postmortem investigation of the human brain as it relates to severe mental illness. "I realized, 'Oh my gosh! I'm having a stroke! I'm having a stroke!' The next thing my brain says to me is, 'Wow! This is so cool! How many brain scientists have the opportunity to study their own brain from the inside out?'"[11] she told a TED audience in March 2008.

Dr. Jill's stroke transformed her physically and spiritually. The stroke was severe, leaving her unable to speak or move. It took years of rehabilitation before she was able to recover partially. She didn't give the TED presentation until eight years after her stroke.

Dr. Jill's spiritual awakening was profound. She connected to the world—and to others—in a way that she had never experienced in her "left -brain" world, where she saw herself as separate from the wider universe. Without the chatter of her left brain and her inability to feel where her body began and ended, her "spirit soared free." She felt part of an expansive universe. In short, she had reached Nirvana. "I remember thinking, there's no way I would ever be able to squeeze the enormousness of myself back into this tiny little body."

Dr. Jill's stroke changed her life, as did her TED presentation. "My Stroke of Insight," a presentation based on her book of the same title published in 2008, has been viewed more than 10 million times. As a direct result of the presentation, Dr. Jill was chosen as one of *TIME* magazine's 100 Most Influential People for 2008. In January 2013, Dr. Jill explained the transformative impact of the presentation for a blog on the Huffington Post. "Within weeks of delivering that talk in 2008, my life changed and the repercussions still resonate loudly in my world. My book, *My Stroke of Insight*, has been translated into 30 languages. *TIME* and *Oprah's Soul Series* came calling. I've traveled to Europe, Asia, South America, Canada; I've crisscrossed the states. And in February 2012, I took a trip to Antarctica with Vice President Al Gore, 20 scientists, and 125 global leaders who care deeply about climate."[12]

Dr. Jill had a great career, as Larry Smith would say, because she discovered and pursued her life's calling, well before the traumatic event that would make her an inspiring speaker. Dr. Jill became a brain scientist because her brother had been diagnosed with schizophrenia. "As a sister and later, as a scientist, I wanted to understand, why is it that I can take my dreams, I can connect them to my reality, and I can make my dreams come true? What is it about my brother's brain and his schizophrenia that he cannot connect his dreams to a common and shared reality, so they instead become delusion?"

I spoke to Dr. Jill about her presentation style—how she builds the story, practices it, and delivers it. Dr. Jill's advice to educators and communicators: tell a story and express your passion. "When I was at Harvard, I was the one winning the awards," Dr. Jill told me. "I wasn't winning the awards because my science was better than anyone else's. I was winning the awards because I could tell a story that was interesting and fascinating and it was mine, down to the detail."

Dr. Jill's deep connection with her topic cannot be separated from her riveting ability to communicate with passion and, ultimately, change the way her listeners see the world. If you find your topic fascinating and interesting and wonderful, it's more than likely your audience will, too.

YOUR BRAIN NEVER STOPS GROWING

Thanks to the study of neuroplasticity, scientists are finding that the brain actually grows and changes throughout your life. The intense repetition of a task creates new, stronger neural pathways. As a person becomes an expert in a particular area—music, sports, public speaking—the areas of the brain associated with those skills actually grow.

"We all get better at what we do if we do it repeatedly,"[13] according to Dr. Pascale Michelon, adjunct professor at Washington University in St. Louis. Michelon told me about research that has been conducted on everyone from taxi drivers to musicians. Compared to bus drivers, London taxi drivers had a larger hippocampus in the posterior region of the brain. The hippocampus has a specialized role in developing the skill used to navigate routes, whereby the bus drivers' hippocampi was understimulated because they drove the same route day after day. Scientists also found that the gray matter involved in playing music (motor regions, anterior superior parietal and inferior temporal areas) was highest in professional musicians who practiced one hour a day, intermediate in amateur musicians, and lowest in nonmusicians. Learning a new skill and repeating the skills over and over builds news pathways in the brain.

Michelon believes these studies also apply to people who speak repeatedly on topics they're passionate about. "The brain areas involved in language—the areas that help you talk and explain ideas more clearly—these brain areas become more activated and more efficient the more they are used. The more you speak in public, the more the actual structure of the brain changes. If you speak a lot in public, language areas of the brain become more developed."

Compelling communicators, like those TED presenters who attract the most views online, are masters in a certain topic because of the inevitable amount of devotion, time, and effort invested in their pursuit, which is primarily fueled by fervent passion.

SECRETS OF INFECTIOUS PERSONALITIES

Psychologist Howard Friedman studies the most elusive of qualities: charisma, a concept closely tied with passion. In *The Longevity Project*, Friedman reveals the astonishing results of a groundbreaking study on the subject.

First, Friedman devised a questionnaire meant to categorize low-charisma individuals and high-charisma people. The survey includes questions such as, "When I hear great music my body automatically starts moving to the beat,"[14] or, "At parties, I'm the center of attention," and, "I am passionate about the job I do." The respondents had a range of options from "not very true" to "very true." The average score was 71 points (top scorers registered about

117 points). The study separated the magnetic personalities from the wallflowers. Friedman calls it the Affective Communications Test (ACT), intended to measure how well people can send their feelings to others. Friedman, however, took it one step further.

Friedman chose dozens of people who scored very high on the test and others who scored very low. He then gave them a questionnaire and asked them how they felt at the moment. High scorers and low scorers were then placed in a room together. They sat in the room for two minutes and couldn't speak to one another. After the time was up they were asked to fill out another questionnaire to gauge their mood. Without saying a word, the highly charismatic individuals were able to affect the mood of the low charismatics. If the highly charismatic person was happy, the low charismatic would report being happier, too. It did not, however, work the other way around. Charismatic people smiled more and had more energy in their nonverbal body language. They exuded joy and passion.

Friedman's study showed that passion does indeed rub off on others. People who did not communicate emotionally (little eye contact, sitting stiffly, no hand gestures) were not nearly as capable of influencing and persuading others as high charismatics.

PASSION IS CONTAGIOUS, LITERALLY

Ralph Waldo Emerson once said, "Nothing great has ever been achieved without enthusiasm." Professors Joyce Bono at the University of Minnesota and Remus Ilies at Michigan State University have proved Emerson right. The business-school professors conducted four separate studies with hundreds of participants to measure charisma, positive emotions, and "mood contagion."

The researchers found that "individuals who are rated high on charisma tend to express more positive emotions in their written and spoken communications."[15] Positive emotions include passion, enthusiasm, excitement, and optimism. Bono and Ilies also discovered that positive emotions are contagious, lifting the moods of the participants in the audience. Participants who listened and watched positive leaders in person and on video experienced a more positive mood than those who watched leaders rated low for positive emotions. Further, positive leaders were perceived as more effective and therefore more likely to persuade their followers to do what they want their followers to do.

"Results of our study clearly indicate that leaders' emotional expressions play an important role in the formation of followers' perceptions of leader effectiveness, attraction to leaders, and follower mood. Our results also suggest that charismatic leadership is linked to organizational success because charismatic leaders enable their followers to experience positive emotions. More importantly, our results indicate that the behavior of leaders can make a difference in the happiness and well-being of the followers by influencing their emotional lives."

It's been said that success doesn't lead to happiness; happiness creates success. The most popular TED speakers reflect the truth of that aphorism. How you think—the confidence you have in your expertise, the passion you have for your topic—directly impacts your communications presence. Thoughts change your brain chemistry, shaping what you say and how you say it.

> "When you are inspired by some great purpose, some extraordinary project, all your thoughts break their bonds. Your mind transcends limitations, your consciousness expands in every direction, and you find yourself in a new, great, and wonderful world. Dormant forces, faculties, and talents become alive, and you discover yourself to be a greater person by far than you ever dreamed yourself to be."
> —Patanjali, an Indian teacher often called the Father of Yoga.

When you're passionate about your topic—obsessively so—the energy and enthusiasm you display will rub off on your listeners. Don't be afraid to express yourself—your authentic self. If you're inspired like Dr. Jill, share it. If you're frustrated like Larry Smith, say so. If you're happy like Matthieu Ricard, express it.

TEDnote

INVITE PASSIONATE PEOPLE INTO YOUR LIFE. Starbucks founder Howard Schultz once told me, "When you're surrounded by people who share a collective passion around a common purpose, anything is possible." Identifying your passion is one step, but you must share it, express it, and talk about what motivates you with the colleagues, clients, and other people in your life. Most important, link yourself with others who share your passion. Leaders use passion as a hiring criteria. Richard Branson hires people with the Virgin attitude: they smile a lot, are positive and enthusiastic. As a result, they are better communicators. It's not enough to be passionate yourself. You must also surround yourself with people who are passionate about your organization and the field in which they're working. Your ultimate success as a leader and communicator will depend on it.

500 TEDSTERS CAN'T BE WRONG

Richard St. John was on a plane on his way to a TED conference when a teenager sitting next to him, curious about his work, asked, "What really leads to success?" St. John didn't have a good answer, but he had a good idea—he would ask the successful leaders attending and speaking at the TED conference. He interviewed 500 TEDsters over the next decade and uncovered the traits that made them ultra-successful. St. John revealed his findings in a three-minute presentation at TED Monterey, 2005.

In a presentation viewed more than four million times,

St. John delivered "The 8 Secrets of Success." The number-one "secret"? You got it—passion. "TEDsters do it for love; they don't do it for money,"[16] St. John said.

In his book by the same title, St. John writes about Mullins, whom I opened this chapter with, "Passion has enabled Aimee Mullins to set running records, even though she's missing two essential limbs for running—legs . . . she's well named since 'Aimee' comes from the French word 'love' and it's a big reason for her success on the track and in life. No wonder she says, 'If it's your passion then inevitably you'll succeed.'"

WANT TO HELP SOMEONE? SHUT UP AND LISTEN

Dr. Ernesto Sirolli, founder of the Sirolli Institute and a world-renowned economic-development expert, learned the hard way that *we* is a more powerful word than *I*. Sirolli, who got his start in sustainable development by doing aid work in Africa in the early 1970s, told a TEDx audience in 2012 that what many "experts" knew about sustainable development has turned out to be wrong.

At the age of 21, he worked for an Italian NGO and "every single project that we set up in Africa failed."[17] Sirolli's first project was to teach villagers in southern Zambia to grow tomatoes. "Everything in Africa grew beautifully. We had these magnificent tomatoes . . . we were telling the Zambians, 'Look how easy agriculture is.' When the tomatoes were nice and ripe and red, overnight, some 200 hippos came out from the river and they ate everything. [Laughter] And we said to the Zambians, 'My God, the hippos!' And the Zambians said, 'Yes, that's why we have no agriculture here.' [Laughter]

"'Why didn't you tell us?' 'You never asked.'"

If you want to help someone, shut up and listen. That's what Sirolli learned from his early experience in sustainable agriculture. "You never arrive in a community with any ideas," he said. Instead, he recommends, capture the passion, energy, and imagination of the people living in that community.

As we've discussed, passion is the foundation of success in business, in careers, and in public speaking. As it turns out, passion is the crucial ingredient of success in Sirolli's work, too. "You can give somebody an idea. If that person doesn't want to do it, what are you going to do? The passion that the person has for her own growth is the most important thing. The passion that that man has for his own personal growth is the most important thing. And then we help them to go and find the knowledge, because nobody in the world can succeed alone. The person with the idea may not have the knowledge, but the knowledge is available." You're reading this because you have a passion for personal growth. You've probably mastered (or are close to mastering) the topic on which you speak. Don't be afraid to share your excitement. It will rub off on your audience.

> "It is our experience that the very best executives are the ones who are the most passionate about what they do."
> —Ron Baron, billionaire investor

Secret #1: Unleash the Master Within

I can teach you how to tell a story. I can teach you how to design a gorgeous PowerPoint slide. I can even teach you how to use your voice and body more effectively. Effective stories, slides, and body language are important components of a persuasive presentation, yet they mean little if the speaker isn't passionate about his or her topic. The first step to inspiring others is to make sure you're inspired yourself. The simplest way to identify that which you are truly passionate about is to ask yourself the question I raised earlier in the chapter: "What makes my heart sing?" Once you discover that which makes your heart sing, the stories you tell, the slides you use, and the way you deliver your content will come to life. You will connect with people more profoundly than you ever thought possible. You will have the confidence to share what you've learned as a true master. That's when you'll be ready to give the talk of your life.

2

Master the Art of Storytelling

"Stories are just data with a soul."

—BRENÉ BROWN, TEDx HOUSTON 2010

BRYAN STEVENSON'S GRANDMOTHER WAS THE end of every argument in his family's household. She was also the beginning of a lot of arguments! Above all, she taught Stevenson about the power of identity. Stevenson is a civil rights attorney and the executive director of the Equal Justice Initiative, a nonprofit group that provides legal representation to poor defendants who have been denied fair treatment in the criminal justice system. Stevenson won a landmark Supreme Court case that barred states from imposing mandatory life sentences without parole on juveniles convicted of a felony. The justices ruled five-to-four that such sentences were unconstitutional, violating the Eighth Amendment ban on cruel and unusual punishment.

In September 2011, the Roosevelt Institute awarded Stevenson a Freedom Medal for his work in the area of social justice. A representative from the TED conference was in the audience and asked Stevenson to give a presentation at the March 2012 event in Long Beach. Stevenson told me he didn't know much about TED at the time and was inclined to turn down the invitation because he had two Supreme Court cases to argue at the end of March. His staff "went ballistic" and told Stevenson that he had to speak at TED. Stevenson is glad he did. The TED audience was so inspired by Stevenson's presentation they donated a combined $1 million to his nonprofit.

Over the course of 18 minutes, Stevenson held the audience spellbound as he told stories of several people who had influenced his life: his grandmother, Rosa Parks, and a janitor. Stevenson began with a story about his grandmother's parents, who were born into slavery, and the experience of how slavery shaped the way she saw the world. She had 10 children, and it was difficult for Stevenson to find time with her. One day, when Stevenson was eight or nine, his grandmother walked across the room, took him by the hand, and said, "Come on, Bryan. You and I are going to have a talk."[1] Stevenson said he would never forget the discussion that happened next.

> She sat me down and she looked at me and she said, "I want you to know I've been watching you." And she said, "I think you're special." She said, "I think you can do anything you want to do." I will never forget it. And then she said, "I just need you to promise me three things, Bryan." I said, "Okay, Mama." She said, "The first thing I want you to promise me is that you'll always love your mom." She said, "That's my baby girl, and you have to promise me now you'll always take care of her." Well I adored my mom, so I said, "Yes, Mama. I'll do that." Then she said, "The second thing I want you to promise me is that you'll always do the right thing even when the right thing is the hard thing." And I

thought about it and I said, "Yes, Mama. I'll do that." Then finally she said, "The third thing I want you to promise me is that you'll never drink alcohol."

Well I was nine years old, so I said, "Yes, Mama. I'll do that." [Laughter]

A few years later, Stevenson was in the backwoods near his house with two of his siblings who insisted that he take a sip of beer. Stevenson pushed back and said he didn't feel right about it. "And then my brother started staring at me. He said, 'What's wrong with you? Have some beer.' Then he looked at me real hard and he said, 'Oh, I hope you're not still hung up on that conversation Mama had with you.' And when I asked him what he was talking about said, 'Oh, Mama tells all the grandkids that they're special.'"

2.1: Bryan Stevenson, speaking at TED 2012. Courtesy of James Duncan Davidson/TED (http://duncandavidson.com).

(Laughter.)

I was devastated.

(More laughter.)

Stevenson lowered his voice and said, "I'm going to tell you something I probably shouldn't. I know this might be broadcast broadly. But I'm 52 years old, and I'm going to admit to you that I've never had a drop of alcohol. I don't say that because I think that's virtuous; I say that because there is power in identity. When we create the right kind of identity, we can say things to the world around us that they don't actually believe makes sense. We can get them to do things that they don't think they can do."

The audience, most of whom had been laughing at Stevenson's story about his grandmother, suddenly grew silent as they took in his words. He was reaching their minds, but he could do that only after he had touched their hearts.

Secret 2: Master the Art of Storytelling

Tell stories to reach people's hearts and minds

Why it works: Bryan Stevenson, the speaker who earned the longest standing ovation in TED history, spent 65 percent of his presentation telling stories. Brain scans reveal that stories stimulate and engage the human brain, helping the speaker connect with the audience and making it much more likely that the audience will agree with the speaker's point of view.

BREAK DOWN THE WALL WITH STORIES

Stevenson spoke for five minutes before he introduced his first statistics about how many people are incarcerated in U.S. prisons and the percentage of those who are poor and/or African-American. Data supported his thesis, but a story took up the first one-third of his presentation. It wasn't just any story, either. Stevenson purposely chose to tell a story that made it easy for his audience to connect with him on a personal and emotional level.

"You have to get folks to trust you,"[2] Stevenson told me. "If you start with something too esoteric and disconnected from the lives of everyday people, it's harder for people to engage. I often talk about family members because most of us have family members that we have a relationship to. I talk about kids and people who are vulnerable or struggling. All of those narratives are designed to help understand the issues."

Stevenson talks to many people who have made up their minds to disagree with him well before he says a word. Narrative—storytelling—can help break down the wall between him and the people he needs to persuade. Stevenson says he tells stories to engage judges, jurors, and other decision makers who are inclined to disagree with his perspective. Stevenson has discovered that narrative is the most powerful way to break down resistance.

Stevenson's TED talk is a brilliant example of storytelling because he connected each story to the central theme of "identity." His last story involved a janitor whom he'd met briefly on his way to a court appointment. Once inside court, the conversation between Stevenson and the judge got especially heated. Stevenson picks up the story.

Out of the corner of my eye, I could see this janitor pacing back and forth. He kept pacing back and forth. And finally, this older black man with this very worried look on his face came into the courtroom and sat down behind me, almost at counsel table. About 10 minutes later the judge said we would take a break. And during the break there was a deputy sheriff who was offended that the janitor had come into court. And this deputy jumped up and he ran over to this older black man. He said, "Jimmy, what are you doing in this courtroom?" And this older black man stood up and

Ben Affleck: Director's Notes

Actor/director Ben Affleck considers Stevenson's presentation among his favorite TED talks. Affleck has seen many presentations, lectures, and talks about social justice, yet it was Stevenson's conversation—and it was more of a conversation than a formal presentation—that left an indelible impression on Affleck. "Human rights lawyer Bryan Stevenson shares some hard truths about America's justice system . . . these issues, which are wrapped up in America's unexamined history, are rarely talked about with this level of candor, insight and persuasiveness."[3]

—Ben Affleck

he looked at that deputy and he looked at me and he said, "I came into this courtroom to tell this young man, keep your eyes on the prize, hold on."

Stevenson concluded the presentation by telling the TED audience that they cannot be fully evolved human beings until they care about human rights and basic dignity. "Our visions of technology and design and entertainment and creativity have to be married with visions of humanity, compassion, and justice. And more than anything, for those of you who share that, I've simply come to tell you to keep your eyes on the prize, hold on." Stevenson's audience rose to their feet because his stories had connected with them. He had touched their souls.

When I spoke with Stevenson, I said, "Your subject is sensitive, controversial, and complex," and I asked him, "How much of your success do you owe to the effective communication of your story?"

"Almost all of it. There are so many presumptions that will condemn the clients I care about, so my task is to overcome the narratives that have evolved. Almost all of what we're trying to do turns on effective communication. You need data, facts, and analysis to challenge people, but you also need narrative to get people comfortable enough to care about the community that you are advocating for. Your audience needs to be willing to go with you on a journey."

In my interview with Stevenson he validated the core concept in my communications coaching—storytelling is the ultimate tool of persuasion. Brands, as well as individuals, who tell stories—emotional and genuine stories—connect with their customers and audiences in far deeper and more-meaningful ways than do their competitors. Stevenson's observation should give you confidence, too. Many business professionals are intimidated to tell personal stories in a PowerPoint presentation, especially if the content contains data, charts, and graphs. But if Stevenson, a speaker who successfully argues cases in front of Supreme Court justices, can find power in stories, then the rest of us should take a cue from his experience.

POWER IN PATHOS

Stevenson has pathos. The Greek philosopher Aristotle is one of the founding fathers of communication theory. He believed that persuasion occurs when three components are represented: ethos, logos, and pathos. Ethos is credibility. We tend to agree with people whom we respect for their achievements, title, experience, etc. Logos is the means of persuasion through logic, data, and statistics. Pathos is the act of appealing to emotions.

Bryan Stevenson's presentation contained 4,057 words. I analyzed those words and assigned them into each of the three categories. If Stevenson talked about his work in prisons, I placed that sentence or paragraph in the category Ethos. When Stevenson delivered statistics, I added those sentences to the category Logos. If Stevenson told a story, I placed the content under Pathos. The results are shown in the pie chart in figure 2.2.

2.2: Pie Chart: Percentage of Ethos, Logos and Pathos, represented in Bryan Stevenson's TED 2012 presentation. Created by Empowered Presentations @empoweredpres.

As you can see, Ethos made up only 10 percent of Stevenson's content, and Logos only 25 percent. Pathos made up a full 65 percent of Stevenson's talk. Remarkably, Stevenson's talk has been voted one of the most "persuasive" on TED.com. To "persuade" is defined as influencing someone to act by appealing to reason. Emotion doesn't appear in the definition, yet without the emotional impact of stories, Stevenson's talk would have failed to have the influence it's had.

You simply cannot persuade through logic alone. Who says so? Some of the most logical minds in the world.

TEDnote

HOW DO YOU USE ARISTOTLE'S COMPONENTS OF PERSUASION?
Take one of your recent presentations and categorize the content into one of the three categories we just covered: Ethos (credibility),

Logos (evidence and data), and Pathos (emotional appeal). How does your pathos stack up against the rest? If your emotional appeal is minimal, you might want to rethink your content before you give this presentation again, like adding more stories, anecdotes, and personal insights.

YOUR BRAIN ON STORIES

Dale Carnegie believed in the power of stories to inspire audiences. "The great truths of the world have often been couched in fascinating stories," Carnegie wrote. Carnegie once said, "The ideas I stand for are not mine. I borrowed them from Socrates. I swiped them from Chesterfield. I stole them from Jesus. And I put them in a book. If you don't like their rules whose would you use?"

Many of the ideas in this book do not belong to me. They do not belong to TED. They do not belong to the awe-inspiring speakers who gave the presentations. The techniques work because they are based on how the human mind works; how it processes and recalls information and how that information gets stamped in our brains. Carnegie based his advice on intuition. Today we have brain scans to prove him right. Scientists using functional MRI (fMRI) images have studied brain activity by tracking changes in blood flow. In the last 10 years we've learned more about the human brain than in all of the combined years humans have been on Earth, and much of that research has direct implications for those who seek to excel in the area of public speaking and communications.

STORIES PLANT IDEAS AND EMOTIONS INTO A LISTENER'S BRAIN

In a darkened conference room on the campus of Princeton University, someone is watching a Charlie Chaplin movie to give the rest of us a deeper insight into how the brain processes information.

Uri Hasson, assistant professor of psychology at Princeton, is the psychologist conducting the experiment for the Princeton Neuroscience Institute.

Hasson's experiments include activities such as watching movies or listening to stories while his subjects are connected to fMRI machines to study their brain waves. Hasson wants to learn how the brain processes complex information. Hasson and his colleagues have discovered that personal stories actually cause the brains of both storyteller and listener to sync up. *Sync up* is my term; Hasson calls it "brain-to-brain coupling."

Hasson and his colleagues recorded the brain activity of a speaker telling unrehearsed stories. Next, they measured the brain activity of the person listening to the story and asked the listener to fill out a detailed questionnaire to measure comprehension. The results are among the first of their kind in the area of neuroscience. The researchers found that the speaker's and the listener's brains "exhibited joint, temporally coupled, response patterns."[4] To put it simply, "The listener's brain responses mirrored the speaker's brain responses." There was actually a mind-meld between the speaker and the listener.

Hasson chose a graduate student to be the speaker. Lauren Silbert told a personal story about going to her prom. Researchers scanned her brain and the brains of the 11 students who were listening. The same parts of everyone's brain showed "activation," meaning a deep connection between the person doing the talking and the person doing the listening. It also suggested that everyone in the room—all the listeners—was experiencing a similar response! The "coupling" did not occur when the listeners were told a story in Russian, a language they didn't know.

"When the woman spoke English, the volunteers understood her story, and their brains synchronized. When she had activity in her insula, the region in the brain responsible for emotion, the listeners did too. When her frontal cortex lit up, so did theirs. By simply telling a story, the woman could plant ideas, thoughts, and emotions into the listeners' brains,"[5] reports Hasson.

Researchers have discovered that our brains are more active when we hear stories. A wordy PowerPoint slide with bullet points activates the language-processing center of the brain, where we turn words into meaning. Stories do much more, using the whole brain and activating language, sensory, visual, and motor areas.

Hassan's findings are profoundly important for anyone who needs to deliver a presentation with the intent of influencing behavior. If stories trigger brain-to-brain "coupling," then part of the solution to winning people over to your argument is to tell more stories.

STORIES ARE JUST DATA WITH A SOUL

In June 2010, Brené Brown delivered the talk "The Power of Vulnerability" at TEDx Houston. As a research professor at the University of Houston, Brown studies vulnerability, courage, authenticity, and shame. It's a pretty big subject area to squeeze into 18 minutes, yet Brown did it so well that her presentation has been viewed more than seven million times. Brown began her presentation with a short anecdote.

> A couple of years ago, an event planner called me because I was going to do a speaking event. And she called, and she said, "I'm really struggling with how to write about you on the little flier." And I thought, "Well, what's the struggle?" And she said, "Well, I saw you speak, and I'm going to call you a researcher, I think, but I'm afraid if I call you a researcher, no one will come because they'll think you're boring and irrelevant." And I was like, "Okay." And she said, "But the thing I liked about your talk is

you're a storyteller. So I think what I'll do is just call you a storyteller."[6]

Brown said the "insecure" part of her was hesitant to adopt the title because she was a serious academic researcher. However, she eventually warmed to the idea. "I thought, you know, I am a storyteller. I'm a qualitative researcher. I collect stories; that's what I do. Maybe stories are just data with a soul. And maybe I'm just a storyteller." As Brown suggests, we're all storytellers. You're telling stories every day. In a business presentation, you're telling the story behind your campaign, company, or product. In a job interview, you're telling the story behind your personal brand. In a marketing pitch, you're telling the story about your idea. Yes, we're all storytellers and we're telling stories in business each and every day.

I'll never forget the one time I received a severe reprimand from my professor at the Medill School of Journalism at Northwestern. I had returned from an assignment empty-handed. "There was no story," I told my instructor. He got so angry that I thought he would blow a blood vessel in his forehead. "There's always a story!" he yelled. I always recall that encounter when I hear someone say, "I don't have a story." Sure you do. There's always a story. All you have to do is look, and if you look hard and smart enough, you'll be sure to find a good one.

> "We all love stories. We're born for them. Stories affirm who we are. We all want affirmations that our lives have meaning. And nothing does a greater affirmation than when we connect through stories. It can cross the barriers of time, past, present and future, and allow us to experience the similarities between ourselves and through others, real and imagined."[7]
> —Andrew Stanton, writer of "Toy Story," TED February 2012

THREE SIMPLE, EFFECTIVE TYPES OF STORIES

Inspiring communicators and the best TED presenters stick to one of three types of stories. The first are personal stories that relate directly to the theme of the conversation or presentation; second are stories about other people who have learned a lesson the audience can relate to; third are stories involving the success or failure of products or brands.

Personal Stories

Stories are central to who we are. The most popular TED presentations start with a personal story. Recall the touching stories Bryan Stevenson told about his grandmother and the janitor who gave him an energizing piece of advice: "keep your eyes on the prize." The ability to tell a personal story is an essential trait of authentic leadership—people who inspire uncommon effort. So, tell personal stories. What are your fondest memories of a loved one? You probably have a story to tell about that person. My daughters enjoy hearing stories of their grandfather (their "nonno") who was held captive in World War II, how he tried to escape, and how he and my mom eventually emigrated to America with $20 in their pocket. Stories like this one are central to our identity as a family. I'm sure it's the same for you.

If you're going to tell a "personal" story, make it personal. Take the audience on a journey. Make it so descriptive and rich with imagery that they imagine themselves with you at the time of the event.

A Burn Unit Inspires a Career and a Groundbreaking Presentation

Professor of psychology and behavioral economist at Duke University and bestselling author Dan Ariely develops clever studies to demonstrate why people make predictably irrational decisions. His interest in the subject started in the burn unit with his personal story. "I was burned very badly. And if you spend a lot of time in hospitals, you'll see a lot of types of irrationalities. And the one that particularly bothered me in the burn department was the process by which the nurses took the bandage off me,"[8] Ariely told a TED audience in 2009.

In graphic detail he explained how bandages could be ripped off quickly or slowly. If you're like most people—and Ariely's nurses—you probably assume it's better to strip off the bandages quickly to get the pain over with. It took the nurses one hour to rip off the bandages. Ariely, in massive pain, pleaded with the nurses to take two hours instead of one, making the pain less intense. The nurses said they knew best and Ariely had to endure the pain.

Ariely left the hospital three years later (70 percent of his body had been burned) and entered a Tel Aviv University. There he examined the question of how to take bandages off burn patients. "What I learned was that the nurses were wrong. Here were wonderful people with good intentions and plenty of experience, and nevertheless they were getting things wrong predictably all the time. It turns out that because we don't encode duration in the way that we encode intensity, I would have had less pain if the duration would have been longer and the intensity was lower."

Ariely also uses a very effective storytelling technique—unexpectedness. In *Made to Stick*, Dan and Chip Heath reveal several elements of a "sticky" idea, one that people remember. According to the Heaths, "The most basic way to get someone's attention is this: Break a pattern."[9] Curiosity and mystery are powerful ways to get our attention. For evidence, the Heaths cite George Loewenstein's work at Carnegie Mellon University. "Curiosity, he says, happens when we feel a gap in our knowledge . . . gaps cause pain. When we want to know something but don't, it's like having an itch that we need to scratch. To take away the pain, we need to fill the knowledge gap. We sit patiently through bad movies, even though they may be painful to watch, because it's too painful not to know how they end."[10]

Ariely's personal story is made more effective because its outcome is unexpected. Tell personal stories, but choose them carefully. A personal experience that led to an unexpected result often makes for a particularly compelling story.

Mom's Personal Fiscal Cliff

Personal stories grab attention in nearly every communications format—presentations, social media, and television interviews. I started my journalism career in 1989, the last year Ronald Reagan was in office. Reagan was called the Great Communicator because he could wrap his message in a story. When I left day-to-day journalism to start my own communications practice, I remembered the quality that gave Reagan his charisma—his ability to tell a story.

Today I give CEOs and politicians the same advice: if you want to be quoted, tell a story, and the more personal the better. It works nearly every time. For example, in December 2012, the U.S. media was obsessed about the "fiscal cliff," a combination of automatic spending cuts and tax increases that would have gone into effect had lawmakers failed to reach a budget deal. A new member of Congress called me about one hour before a scheduled television interview. He wanted to run some messages by me. All I heard were "talking points" so I politely suggested he tell stories instead. We decided that he should tell a story about his mother, a nurse, and how the fiscal cliff would impact her. The congressman told the story, the reporter aired the story, and the politician used it for every one of his subsequent interviews. Sometimes the congressman was successful in getting his talking points across; other times he was not. His mother, however, always made the cut.

People love stories. Business professionals rarely tell personal stories, which is one reason why they make such an impact when they do. Today when I coach CEOs for press interviews or major presentations, I always encourage them to incorporate a personal story. Reporters and bloggers who cover the event include the story nearly every time. No technique is 100 percent guaranteed, but telling personal stories comes close.

Stories about Other People

Sir Ken Robinson, a PhD and thought leader in the area of creativity and innovation in education and business, says schools kill creativity. Millions of people clearly agree with him or have found his argument so provocative that they feel compelled to view and share his 2006 TED talk. It's the most popular TED talk of all time (14 million views at the time of this writing). I'm fascinated by Robinson's presentation because he uses no PowerPoint, no visuals, no props, yet he still connects with the audience. He does it through the skillful use of analysis, data, humor, and storytelling.

Schools That Nurture (Not Undermine) Creativity

Robinson's most intriguing and gripping story does not involve himself. Its central character is someone whom Robinson had interviewed. Her name was Gillian Lynne, and few in the audience had ever heard of her. They had, however, heard of her work. Lynne was the choreographer behind *Cats* and *Phantom of the Opera*. Robinson asked Lynne how she had become a dancer. She said that when she was going to school in the 1930s, her school administrators believed she had a learning disorder because she couldn't concentrate and was always fidgeting. "I think now they'd say she had ADHD. Wouldn't you? But this was the 1930s, and ADHD hadn't been invented at this point. It wasn't an available condition. People weren't aware they could have that,"[11] Robinson said dryly as the audience laughed.

Robinson continued the story with Lynne's visit to a specialist whom her mother had brought her to see. After listening to Lynne and her mother for about 20 minutes, the doctor told Lynne that he would like to speak to her mother privately. "But as they went out of the room, he turned on the radio that was sitting on his desk. And when they got out of the room, he said to her mother, 'Just stand and watch her.' And the minute they left the room, she said, she was on her feet, moving to the music. And they watched for a few minutes, and he turned to her mother and said, 'Mrs. Lynne, Gillian isn't sick; she's a dancer. Take her to a dance school.'" Lynne did go to dance school. She had a career at the Royal Ballet, met Sir Andrew Lloyd Webber, and has been responsible for choreographing some of the greatest musicals in the history of theater.

Robinson uses the story as a setup to the conclusion of his presentation and to reinforce his theme: "What TED celebrates is the gift of the human imagination. We have to be careful now that we use this gift wisely and that we avert some of the scenarios that we've talked about. And the only way we'll do it is by seeing our creative capacities for the richness they are and seeing our children for the hope that they are. And our task is to educate their whole being, so they can face this future."

Robinson's call to "educate their whole being" would be hard for the audience to fully comprehend had he not told the story of Gillian Lynne. Abstractions are difficult for most people to process. Stories turn abstract concepts into tangible, emotional, and memorable ideas.

A TED-worthy Preacher Tells Stories from the Pulpit

Lakewood Church pastor Joel Osteen has never given a TED talk, but he gives a TED-worthy performance every week to 40,000 people who attend his sermons in person and another seven million who watch him on television.

In TED fashion, Osteen always begins a sermon with a theme. He started one sermon, "I want to talk to you today about how 'Yes Is in Your Future.'[12]. He followed with a short anecdote about a friend of his. The friend had been working hard for years. One day a supervisor retired and several people were up for the job. Osteen's friend had seniority and had been faithful to the company, yet he was turned down for the promotion in favor of a younger and less-experienced person. The friend felt cheated but "he didn't get bitter or quit doing his best." Two years later, a senior vice president retired and Osteen's friend got the promotion he deserved. "His position now is many levels higher than that old supervisor position," Osteen said. "You might be in a 'no' right now but favor is coming. Healing is coming. Promotion is coming. Say to yourself, 'I'm not going to get stuck in a no. I know a yes is coming.'"

After establishing pathos with the audience, Osteen turned to logos and shared the following statistics with the audience. He said that 90 percent of all first businesses fail. Ninety percent of all second businesses succeed, yet 80 percent of business owners never try a second time. "They failed to realize that they were a few 'no's' away from seeing their business succeed."

Osteen followed the statistics with many more stories. Characters included biblical figures, people who attended Lakewood services, historical personalities (Albert Einstein failed 2,000 times), and his own mother, who was seated in the front row. Osteen told one story about a friend with a reasonably successful small business. The friend wanted to expand and went to the bank he had been doing business with for years. He had a business plan and proven results. The bank turned him down. A second bank turned him down. "Ten banks, then twenty banks . . . you'd think he'd get the message," Osteen said. "Thirty banks turned him down. Then another one. Thirty-one banks said no. Then bank number thirty-two came along and said, 'We like your idea. We'll take a chance on you.' When God puts a dream in your heart, you know you're going to succeed. Every 'no' means you're one step closer to 'yes.'"

Personal stories are stories about yourself, but they can also be stories about other people with whom the audience can empathize. Osteen shares a quality with popular TED speakers: they are masters at creating empathy. Empathy is the capacity to recognize and feel emotions experienced by somebody else. We put ourselves in the shoes of the other. We've seen how stories can help us "experience" someone else's emotions. Some famous neuroscientists believe we are hardwired for empathy, that it's the social glue that holds society together. In a presentation you can create empathy by talking about yourself *or* someone else.

> "The truthful, inside story of almost any man's life—if told modestly and without offending egotism—is most entertaining. It is almost sure-fire speech material."   —Dale Carnegie

Stories about Brand Success

When I give a keynote presentation I tell personal stories, stories about other individuals whom I know personally, have interviewed, or have read about, and stories of brands that have successfully leveraged the business strategy I'm discussing.

I'm always looking for stories for my columns and presentations. I find them everywhere. I walked onto a Virgin America plane, talked to the pilots, and was surprised to learn that they monitor the brands' Twitter feed. That led to a story about brands that use social media to have conversations with their customers. When I stayed at a Ritz-Carlton hotel, I asked a waiter why he gave me a free appetizer. He said, "I'm empowered to deliver a great customer experience." That led to several stories on employee engagement and customer service. I walked into an Apple Store and discovered that employees are trained to walk a customer through five steps that either lead to a sale or promote brand loyalty. That experience led not only to a story, I wrote an entire book about it. Brand stories are everywhere.

Popular blogger and TED speaker Seth Godin also tells brand stories and does so brilliantly. In February 2003 Godin taught the TED audience how to get their ideas to spread. The video became a hit and has attracted more than 1.5 million views. U2 lead singer Bono said it was his favorite TED presentation. "Describing a revolution in media in the most unrevolutionary terms, this talk is an understatement,"[13] said Bono. "Godin is a smart, funny dude."

A Smart, Funny Dude with a Story to Tell

Godin tells three stories that support his theme: smart marketers promote their products differently; ordinary is boring. Godin persuasively argues that the riskiest thing to do is "be safe," or average, and he uses short and simple stories to do it.

In a story about Wonder Bread, Godin tells the audience:

This guy named Otto Rohwedder invented sliced bread, and he focused, like most inventors did, on the patent part and the making part. And the thing about the invention of sliced bread is this—that for the first 15 years after sliced bread was available no one bought it; no one knew about it; it was a complete and total failure. And the reason is that until Wonder came along and figured out how to spread the idea of sliced bread, no one wanted it. That the success of sliced bread, like the success of almost everything we've been talking about at this conference, is not always about what the patent is like, or what the factory is like—it's about can you get your idea to spread, or not.

In another story Godin showed a photo of a famous Frank Gehry–designed building. "Frank Gehry didn't just change a museum; he changed an entire city's economy by designing one building that people from all over the world went to see. Now, at countless meetings at, you know, the Portland City Council, or who knows where, they said, we need an architect—can we get Frank Gehry? Because he did something that was at the fringes."

Finally, here is how Godin told the story behind Silk soymilk: "Silk. Put a product that does not need to be in the refrigerated section next to the milk in the refrigerated section. Sales tripled. Why? Milk, milk, milk, milk, milk—not milk. For the people who were there and looking at that section, it was remarkable. They didn't triple their sales with advertising; they tripled it by doing something remarkable."[14]

Godin's stories all feature brands that are remarkable. The next time you see Silk or Wonder Bread in the grocery store, you'll think differently about the brand and about the messages you use to stand out in the marketplace of ideas.

Larger companies are discovering that stories put a human face on an otherwise faceless conglomerate. Tostitos, Taco Bell, Domino's Pizza, Kashi, McDonald's, and Starbucks are turning to commercials that highlight farmers who grow the ingredients behind their products. People are more engaged with products when they know where those products come from and if they get to know the real people behind those products. The Lush chain of soap stores puts a small picture of a real employee on each product—the faces are those of people who actually made the product. Lush believes that every product has a story. There's a reason why many successful brands spend millions on advertising that includes real faces, real people, and real stories. It works.

A Rich Man's Convenience and a Poor Man's Lifesaver

Every product has a story, as does every startup entrepreneur who built those products. Twenty-one-year-old Ludwick Marishane of Cape Town, South Africa, was named the 2011 global student entrepreneur of the year all because he didn't want to take a bath. Marishane invented DryBath, the world's first non-water-based bath-substitute lotion.

If Marishane crafted an elevator pitch for his invention it would go something like this: "DryBath is the world's first and only bath-substituting skin gel. You apply it to your skin and you don't need to bathe." What's missing? The why and the what. Why did he invent it and what's the benefit of it? Stories fill in the blanks.

At TED Johannesburg in May 2012, Marishane told a story to explain the why and the what. "I grew up in Limpopo, in a little town called Motetema. Water and electricity supply are as unpredictable as the weather and growing up in these tough situations, at the age of 17, I was relaxing with a couple of friends of mine in winter and we were sunbathing. The Limpopo sun gets really hot in winter. As we were sunbathing, my best friend next to me says, 'Man, why doesn't somebody invent something that you can just put on your skin and then you don't have to bathe?' As I sat, I thought, 'Man, I would buy that!'"[15]

Marishane went home, conducted research, and found "shocking" statistics. He learned that over 2.5 billion people in the world do not have proper access to sanitation, 5 million of whom are in South Africa. Horrible diseases thrive in these environments. For example, trachoma blinds 8 million people every year. "The shocking part about it is that all you have to do to prevent being infected with trachoma is wash your face," Marishane said. With nothing but a cell phone and very limited access to the Internet, Marishane did the research and wrote a 40-page business plan. Four years later he received a patent and DryBath was born. Its value proposition: "DryBath is a rich man's convenience and a poor man's lifesaver."

Every brand, every product, has a story. Find it and tell it.

What is a story? Jonah Sachs offers this definition in *Winning the Story Wars*: "Stories are a particular type of human communication designed to persuade an audience of a storyteller's worldview. The storyteller does this by placing characters, real or fictional, onto a stage and showing what happens to these characters over a period of time. Each character pursues some type of goal in accordance with his or her values, facing difficulty along the way, and either succeeds or fails according to the storyteller's view of how the world works."[16] Sachs believes that in the battlefield of ideas, marketers have a secret weapon—a well-told story. Sachs says that contemporary audiences are so bombarded by messages that they are more resistant and more skeptical than at any other time in history. However, "These same audiences, when inspired, are willing and able to spread their favorite messages, creating a massive viral effect for those who win their love."

Gladwell, Happiness, and Spaghetti Sauce

At the Monterey TED conference of February 2004, *The Tipping Point* author, Malcolm Gladwell, told a simple story about Howard Moskowitz, a man who became famous for reinventing spaghetti sauce. The title of the presentation was "Choice, Happiness, and Spaghetti Sauce."

The story went like this. Campbell's Soup approached Moskowitz to help the company make a spaghetti sauce that would compete against Ragu, the dominant sauce of the 1970s and 1980s (Campbell's made Prego). It seems as though Prego was struggling despite being a higher-quality product. Moskowitz worked with the company to create 45 varieties of spaghetti sauce. He brought them on the road to have average consumers taste-test each one.

> If you sit down, and you analyze all this data on spaghetti sauce, you realize that all Americans fall into one of three groups. There are people who like their spaghetti sauce plain; there are people who like their spaghetti sauce spicy; and there are people who like it extra-chunky. And of those three facts, the third one was the most significant, because at the time, in the early 1980s, if you went to a supermarket, you would not find extra-chunky spaghetti sauce. And Prego turned to Howard, and they said, "You're telling me that one-third of Americans crave extra-chunky spaghetti sauce and yet no one is servicing their needs?" And he said yes! And Prego then went back, and completely reformulated their spaghetti sauce, and came out with a line of extra-chunky that immediately and completely took over the spaghetti sauce business in this country. And over the next 10 years, they made 600 million dollars off their line of extra-chunky sauces.[17]

The entire food industry took notice of Moskowitz's analysis. It's why we have "fourteen different kinds of mustards and seventy-one different kinds of olive oil," according to Gladwell. Ragu even hired Moskowitz and today we have 36 varieties of Ragu spaghetti sauce. Gladwell told the Moskowitz story in 10 minutes. He spent the remaining seven minutes offering the lessons the story teaches us. For example, people don't know what they want and, if they do, they have a hard time articulating what they truly desire.

> Assumption number one in the food industry used to be that the way to find out what people want to eat—what will

make people happy—is to ask them. And for years and years and years and years, Ragu and Prego would have focus groups, and they would sit all you people down, and they would say, "What do you want in a spaghetti sauce?" And for all those years—20, 30 years—through all those focus group sessions, no one ever said they wanted extra-chunky. Even though at least a third of them, deep in their hearts, actually did.

Gladwell ended his presentation with what he called the most beautiful lesson of all: "In embracing the diversity of human beings, we will find a surer way to true happiness."

Gladwell succeeds because he combines a "hero" story (which you'll learn more about later in this chapter) about a particular individual with a successful brand story. Your audience wants someone or something to cheer for. They want to be inspired. Give them a hero. Captivate their imagination with stories about yourself, other people, or successful brands.

TEDnote

WHAT STORY CAN YOU INCLUDE? Think about a story (either personal, about someone else, or related to a brand) that you can include in your communications or in your next presentation. If you already do this, then you are one step closer to being a TED-worthy communicator. In a business presentation, telling stories is the virtual equivalent of taking people on a field trip, helping them to experience the content at a much more profound level.

LEAD WITH STORIES AND SUCCEED IN BUSINESS

A well-told story gives leaders a strong advantage in today's increasingly competitive marketplace. A powerful narrative can persuade customers, employees, investors, and stakeholders that your company, product, or idea can help them achieve the success they desire.

We are all natural storytellers, but somehow we lose this part of ourselves when we enter the corporate world. It's especially true when we give PowerPoint presentations. We fall into presentation mode and forget that the most effective way of delivering information is through the emotional connection of story. Stories make concepts and ideas real and tangible. "For too long the business world has ignored or belittled the power of oral narrative, preferring soulless PowerPoint slides, facts, figures, and data,"[18] says Peter Guber, president of Mandalay Entertainment. Guber, who produced such films as *Batman* and *The Color Purple*, wrote an entire book on the power of storytelling titled *Tell to Win*. He adds, "But as the noise level of modern life has become a cacophony, the ability to tell a purposeful story that can truly be heard is increasingly in demand."

Batman Producer Closes His Eyes for Magic

I've spoken to Guber about the power of story in presentations. As Guber looked back on his successful entertainment career, he realized that much of his success was attributed to his ability to persuade customers, employees, shareholders, media, and partners through storytelling. Guber said he lost big business deals because he threw potential investors a barrage of data, stats, and forecasts while neglecting to engage with them emotionally. "To succeed, you have to persuade others to support your vision, dream, or cause. Whether you want to motivate your executives, organize your shareholders, shape your media, engage your customers, win over your investors, or land a job, you have to deliver a clarion call that will get your listeners' attention, emotionalize your goal as theirs, and move them to act in your favor. You have to reach their hearts as well as their minds—and this is just what storytelling does."[19]

In the early 1990s an incident in Guber's office made him

realize that a story—compellingly told—can persuade even the most hardened business executive like himself. At the time, Guber was the CEO of Sony Pictures. Magic Johnson and his business partner, Ken Lombard, visited Guber in his office, and the first thing Lombard said was, "Close your eyes. We're going to tell you a story about a foreign country."[20] Guber thought it a little "unorthodox," but he shut his eyes and went along with it. Lombard continued, "This is a land with a strong customer base, great location, and qualified investors. You know how to build theaters in Europe, Asia, and South America. You know how to invest in foreign countries that have different languages, different cultures, different problems. What you do, Peter, is you find a partner in the country who speaks the language, knows the culture, and handles local problems. Right?" Guber nodded in agreement as his eyes remained shut. "Well, what if I told you a promised land exists that already speaks English, craves movies, has plenty of available real estate, and no competition? This promised land is about six miles from here."

Lombard and Johnson were pitching Guber on building movie theaters in underserved urban communities. Lombard and Johnson cast themselves as the heroes of the narrative, the characters who would help Guber navigate the waters to reach the promised land. In the first four weeks of opening, the first Magic Johnson Theater was one of the top five highest-grossing theaters in the Sony chain.

Guber reminded me that storytelling should be part of every discussion intended to persuade a listener to back your idea—whether it's a formal presentation or a casual conversation. Guber says that as he looks back at his 40 decades in business, his ability to persuade customers, employees, shareholders, and partners through storytelling has been his single biggest competitive advantage.

The Power of Words

Avoid overused buzzwords and clichés. Marketers love to use words such as *leading, solutions,* and *ecosystem.* These words are empty, meaningless, and used so often they've lost whatever punch they may once have had.

Overused metaphors can also be boring. According to a study featured in *The New York Times,* "The way the brain handles metaphors has also received extensive study; some scientists have contended that figures of speech like 'a rough day' are so familiar that they are treated simply as words and no more."[21] Brain scans are revealing that when people hear a detailed description, "an evocative metaphor or an emotional exchange between characters," different areas of the brain are stimulated. Just hearing "the smell of lavender" activates the part of the brain involved in smell. "When subjects in their laboratory read a metaphor involving texture, the sensory cortex, responsible for perceiving texture through touch, became active. Metaphors like 'The singer had a velvet voice' and 'He had leathery hands' roused the sensory cortex." When you tell a story, by all means use metaphors, analogies, and vivid language, but eliminate clichés, buzzwords, and jargon. Your audience will tune out phrases they've heard a million times.

Meet David and Susan

When Toshiba Medical Systems introduced a revolutionary new CT scan, I met with a group of executives to help them shape the story for its global launch. The three-dimensional views of the heart and brain that the machine displayed were indeed impressive, but how could we give an equally impressive presentation without drowning the audience in mind-numbing data? We told a story.

At the press conference we introduced David and Susan, two people who really didn't exist but who did for the purposes of the launch. The presentation demonstrated how this new piece of medical equipment could dramatically cut down the time for doctors to make an accurate diagnosis, thereby saving the lives of the two characters. We gave "David" and "Susan" names, faces, and offered detailed information about their lives. We wanted the audience to see themselves or their loved ones in the faces presented on the screen. Physicians attending the conference later told the speakers that the "David and Susan" part of the presentation was their favorite sequence. It delivered information and made an emotional connection at the same time. That's what a powerful story can do.

You don't have to be launching a revolutionary product like the iPhone or a $2 million piece of medical equipment to tell a good story. During a job interview, tell a personal story about your success managing a team or executing a difficult project. In a new business pitch, share a story about how your product helped a client increase sales despite the economic downturn. During a product launch, tell a personal story behind the product's inception. You might be surprised at how many people remember the stories you tell.

GIVE ME ONE CHARACTER I CAN ROOT FOR

The twentieth-century American writer Kurt Vonnegut was considered a masterful storyteller. A video clip surfaced on the Internet that showed Vonnegut explaining the shape of popular stories. Successful stories—those that connect emotionally with most people—have simple shapes. To illustrate, he drew two lines on a graph (see figure 2.3). On the y axis he wrote I for "Ill Fortune" and the letter G for "Good Fortune." On the x axis he wrote the letter B for "Beginning" and the letter E for "End."

He called the first story shape "Man in a Hole." "Somebody

A Story with a 2,700 Percent Return

Significantobjects.com is a Web site dedicated to the power of story. Significant Objects was a social and anthropological experience devised by Rob Walker and Joshua Glenn. The two researchers started with a hypothesis: a writer can invent a story about an object, investing the object with subjective significance that raises its objective value. The researchers curated objects from thrift stores and garage sales. The objects would cost no more than a buck or two. The second phase of the experiment saw a writer create a short, fictional story about the object. In the third step, the object was auctioned on eBay.

The researchers purchased $128.74 worth of objects. The thrift-store "junk" sold for a total of $3,612.51. The men had discovered that narrative could invest ordinary objects with extraordinary significance. A story had raised the average products' prices by 2,700 percent. For example, a fake banana cost 25 cents and sold on eBay for $76 after a story was added. A tiny miniature turkey dinner was acquired for free (the owner just wanted it off the shelf) and sold for $30 after Jenny Offill wrote a creative story about it. According to the Significant Objects site, "Stories are such a powerful driver of emotional value that their effect on any given object's subjective value can actually be measured objectively."[22]

gets into trouble; gets out of it again. People love that story. They never get sick of it!"[23] The second story shape was called "Boy Gets Girl." The story starts with an average person on an average day and something good happening to that person. Of course, the person comes close to losing the good fortune and gets it back again to end the story happily. "People love that," Vonnegut said.

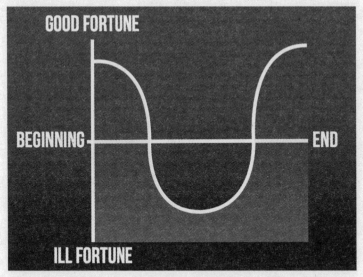

2.3: Re-creation of Kurt Vonnegut's story chart. Created by Empowered Presentations @empoweredpres.

He then said the last story shape was the most popular in Western civilization. "Every time it's retold, someone makes another million dollars. You're welcome to do it," Vonnegut said with a smile.

If you want to grip your audience, the story needs to start at the bottom of the G–I access, with terrible misfortune. "Let's start with a little girl. Her mother has died. Her father has remarried a vile-tempered ugly woman with two nasty daughters. You've heard it?" The audience roars with laughter as they see that Vonnegut is outlining the Cinderella story arc. "There's a party at the palace that night and she can't go." After the fairy godmother helps her get ready for the party and she meets a prince, the protagonist stumbles again, slightly below the G–I line but not all the way to the bottom again. As the story continues, the shoe fits, she marries the prince, and "achieves off-scale happiness."

Vonnegut's writing advice: "give the reader at least one char-acter he or she can root for."

I had Vonnegut's storytelling table in mind when I worked with an executive for Chase, a major U.S. bank, to help him pre-pare the content for a keynote presentation he was asked to give for the United Way. He had personally benefited from United Way programs, but the story he had intended to tell was about his com-pany's commitment to the organization, how much employees had contributed, etc. His early slides were also laden with charts and figures. Good information, but not very emotional.

"Let's forget the slides for a moment. Tell me about your per-sonal connection to United Way," I said. What he said next caught me by surprise.

"I was two years old when my father abandoned the entire family. I was four years old when my mom remarried and that's when I learned the definition of abuse. My first vivid memory was my mother lying in a pile of glass and my stepfather standing over her threatening to cut her throat if she didn't do exactly what he said. I remember thinking, where is my father and why is he al-lowing this man to do this to us?"

The executive went on to tell me how he grew into a very angry young man. At the age of 25 he enrolled in a United Way agency and credited the program for teaching him how to take control of his attitude and putting him on the right path. It also taught him how to become a great father. "I'm proud of the man I've become. I'm proud of what they taught me," he said.

After the goose bumps subsided I encouraged the executive to throw out his existing PowerPoint and open with stories and photographs. That's exactly what he did, showing a black-and-white picture of his biological father holding him and his brother, pictures of his mother, followed by current photographs of him and his family, "the man he had become." This executive received a standing ovation from his audience, brought many to tears, and, after he repeated the presentation for an internal audience of employees, elicited the largest employee contributions of any division within his bank.

The United Way presentation I just described is an extreme example—I'm not asking you to reveal all the skeletons in your family closet. I am urging you, however, to embrace a personal story that has meaning to you and to your topic, own it, and share it.

TEDnote

> **INTRODUCE HEROES AND VILLAINS. Whether it's a movie or a novel, every great story has a hero and a villain. A strong business presentation has the same cast of characters. A spokesperson reveals a challenge (villain) facing a business or industry. The protagonist (brand hero) rises to meet the challenge. Finally, the townspeople (customers) are freed from the villain, the struggle is over, and everyone lives happily ever after. In some cases the villain can be an actual person or competitor, but tread carefully in these cases. Above all, make sure the hero—your product, your brand, or your idea—comes in to save the day.**

When TED invites people to speak at its annual conference, it sends out a stone tablet with the 10 TED Commandments written on it. The fourth commandment reads, Thou Shalt Tell a Story. The novelist Isabele Allende didn't need to be told. She makes a living writing stories about passion.

In Allende's 2007 TED talk, she revealed the recipe for great characters. "Nice people with common sense do not make interesting characters. They only make good former spouses,"[24] Allende said to a roomful of laughter. "Passion lives here," she continued. "Heart is what drives us and determines our fate. That is what I need for my characters in my books: a passionate heart. I need mavericks, dissidents, adventurers, outsiders and rebels, who ask questions, bend the rules and take risks. People like all of you in this room."

Secret #2: Master the Art of Storytelling

Great speakers are indeed mavericks, adventurers, and rule-bending rebels who take risks. They tell stories to express their passion for the subject and to connect with their audiences. Ideas are the currency of the twenty-first century and stories facilitate the exchange of that currency. Stories illustrate, illuminate, and inspire.

3

Have a Conversation

Don't fake it till you make it. Fake it till you become it.

—AMY CUDDY, PROFESSOR, HARVARD BUSINESS SCHOOL

IT TAKES PRACTICE TO APPEAR natural—just ask Amanda Palmer, who stole the show at TED 2013. Palmer's presentation, "The Art of Asking," received more than one million views within days of being posted on TED.com. The week after her presentation Palmer wrote a lengthy post on her blog, thanking the many people who had helped her to craft, rehearse, and deliver the talk of her life. It really did take a village to build a TED talk. The post also confirms that giving a presentation that truly moves people takes hard work.

Secret #3: Have a Conversation

Practice relentlessly and internalize your content so that you can deliver the presentation as comfortably as having a conversation with a close friend.

Why it works: True persuasion occurs only after you have built an emotional rapport with your listeners and have gained their trust. If your voice, gestures, and body language are incongruent with your words, your listeners will distrust your message. It's the equivalent of having a Ferrari (a magnificent story) without knowing how to drive (delivery).

THE ART OF ASKING . . . AND PRACTICING

Amanda Palmer delivered the most-talked-about presentation at TED 2013. Palmer is the first to admit that her punk rock/indie/cabaret music isn't for everyone, but regardless of whether or not you'd like her music, we can all learn something from her approach to public speaking.

Palmer is a performance artist and musician. You'd think she would be comfortable giving a short presentation. The fact that she *is* a performer explains why she spent countless hours over a period of four months to get it just right. "I slaved over the talk, writing and writing and re-writing and timing and re-timing and tweaking and trying to fit the perfect sets of information into 12 short minutes,"[1] Palmer explained on her blog.

In Palmer's 30-page blog post on the making of her TED presentation, she thanked 105 people for their input and credits them for her success. Palmer's first mentor was "Science" musician Thomas Dolby, who helps TED with their music programming. "Be totally authentic," he suggested.

Authenticity doesn't happen naturally. That's right: *authenticity doesn't happen naturally*. How can that be? After all, if you are authentic then wouldn't it make sense just to speak from your heart, with no practice at all? Not necessarily. An authentic presentation requires hours of work—digging deeper into your soul than you ever have, choosing the right words that best represent the way you *feel* about your topic, delivering those words for maximum impact, and making sure that your nonverbal communication—your gestures, facial expressions, and body language—are consistent with your message.

If you don't practice having a conversation, you'll be thinking about a million other things instead of being focused on your story and making an emotional connection with your listener. You'll be thinking, "Did I build an animation on this slide? What's the next one? Why isn't the clicker working? What story did I plan to tell now?" Your expressions and body language will reflect your uncertainty. Have you ever studied dancing? A person is taught to count steps at first. They even talk to themselves. Only after hours and hours of practice do they look effortless. The same rule applies to a presentation. It took Palmer months of hard work to make it look easy.

After meeting with Dolby, Palmer continued her journey to presentation excellence. Here are three steps Palmer took to craft and deliver the presentation of her life.

1. Help with Planning

Palmer has maintained a popular blog for years. She literally "crowd-sourced" her topic by asking readers for suggestions. Ask for help from the people who know you best—be it on a blog, Twitter, or among family, friends, or colleagues. All too often you're simply too close to the content. You might be immersed in the details when the audience might need to see the big picture first. You might assume that the audience knows exactly what you're talking about when they could really use a simpler explanation. Research like this is pivotal to making a connection to your audience.

2. Early Feedback

Palmer read her talk out loud, and the first people who heard it were bored. She was losing them. Her old theater director and mentor from high school gave her "brutal feedback" on the early draft. Palmer reached out to TED speaker and blogger Seth Godin, who said, "Stay vulnerable."

Asking for and receiving early feedback was just the beginning. Dozens of friends, experts, bloggers, and speakers read the content of her presentation or brainstormed ideas on how Palmer should bring her topic to life. Palmer even approached a girl sitting alone at a bar and asked, "Can I tell you a story?"

The greatest business presentations I've ever seen have required hundreds of hours of work crafting the narrative and the story line behind the product or company. One 20-minute product launch at Apple consumed 250 hours total time, including the work of presentation designers, technical specialists, and marketing professionals, as well as the executives who delivered the final presentation.

TEDnote

> **PRACTICE IN FRONT OF PEOPLE, RECORD IT, AND WATCH IT BACK.** Ask friends and colleagues to watch your presentation and to give open, honest feedback. Use a recording device, too. Set up a smartphone on a tripod or buy a dedicated video camera. However you choose to do it, record yourself. It doesn't have to be professional-broadcast quality. Unless you decide to show it to someone else, nobody's going to see it except you. You might be surprised at what you catch—vocal fillers like "ums" and "ahs"; distracting hand motions like scratching your nose or flipping your hair back; lack of eye contact, etc. Pay careful attention to the pace of your speech and ask others for their opinions. Is it too fast? Too slow? The video camera is the single best tool to improve your public speaking ability.

3. Rehearse, Rehearse, and Rehearse

On her blog Palmer posted a photograph of about two dozen people at a potluck-style dinner in someone's living room, watching her perform the TED talk. Among the people she invited: friends, musicians, engineers, a yoga teacher, a venture capitalist, a photographer, a psychology professor. This was brilliant. Creativity thrives in diverse views.

Palmer took every opportunity to practice in front of people. A few days after the potluck, she delivered the same presentation to a group of students at a fine-arts school in Boston. The teacher had invited Palmer to speak to the class on a topic unrelated to TED. She asked the instructor if she could deliver her TED talk instead, and the teacher excitedly accepted. Palmer asked the students to turn off their cameras and gave a "still not-quite-finished talk." Palmer refined the presentation based on the students' input and continued to perform it for any small group she could cobble together.

Three days ahead of the talk, Palmer sketched the outline of the presentation on a long, long piece of paper and scrolled it across the floor. This was a great memory tool, allowing Palmer to "see" the flow of the entire presentation. On the plane trip to California, Palmer continued to rehearse out loud, warning the person sitting next to her that she wasn't schizophrenic, just practicing.

Still, Palmer wasn't finished.

Once she arrived in Long Beach she had a friend listen to her presentation over Skype. She also performed the presentation twice for the TED team, once on Skype and once onstage for the dress rehearsal.

Palmer's talk was titled "The Art of Asking." It could have been titled "The Art of Connecting" because that's what Palmer did. A winning presentation like Palmer's doesn't happen without hours and hours of practice and a huge amount of input. "If I'd done this alone it probably would not have been a good talk. All these people made it a brilliant talk," said Palmer.

When I work with spokespeople who want to improve their body language and delivery, I preach the importance of what I call

Steve Jobs and the 10,000-Hour Rule

It's a well-known theory that it takes 10,000 hours of practice to master a particular skill—playing a piano, shooting baskets, hitting a tennis ball, etc. I strongly believe it applies to the skill of public speaking, too. A lot of people tell me they'll never be as polished as Steve Jobs or other great business speakers because they're simply "not good at it." Well, neither was Steve Jobs at one point. He worked at it.

A video of Steve Jobs's first television interview, in the mid-1970s, appeared on YouTube. It showed him in the chair before the interview began. He was visibly nervous before the interview and asked for directions to the bathroom because he thought he'd be sick. "I'm not kidding," he said emphatically. In his early presentations, including the 1984 launch of Macintosh, Jobs was pretty stiff, holding on to the lectern and reading from prepared notes. He got better every year. In fact, every decade saw a significant improvement in his style and delivery. Jobs built a reputation for practicing relentlessly for a presentation—many, many hours over many, many weeks. Eventually Jobs was considered among the most charismatic business leaders on the world stage. What many people fail to realize is that Jobs made it look effortless because he worked at it!

the three Ps (Passion, Practice, Presence) so that they can learn to deliver their presentations in a genuine, conversational way. The first step requires the spokesperson to identify what she is passionate about and how it connects to her message. The next step is to practice, practice, practice. Only until these first two needs have been met will true presence come to the surface. Palmer is passionate about the topic because it's core to her identity, she practiced for hours, and, as a result, she commanded the stage.

Nobody is born with a PowerPoint clicker in his hands. People are generally not born with the innate ability to distill the essence of a story in a short amount of time, visualize it, bring it to life, and speak comfortably about it without a lot of practice. Yet I can't tell you how many times I hear, "Carmine, public speaking doesn't come naturally to me like it does to other people." I've got news for you—it doesn't come naturally to those others, either. Put in the time. Your ideas are worth the effort.

If your goal is to deliver a memorable presentation that will leave your audience in awe, then you have to practice. During your practice sessions you must pay attention to how you sound (verbal delivery) and how you look (body language). Let's examine both components of a winning package.

HOW TO SAY IT SO PEOPLE LISTEN

The four elements of verbal delivery are: rate, volume, pitch, and pauses.

> RATE: Speed at which you speak
>
> VOLUME: Loudness or softness
>
> PITCH: High or low inflections
>
> PAUSES: Short pauses to punch key words

When you read printed text, it would be natural to use a highlighter to emphasize an important word or phrase. The verbal equivalent of a highlighter is to raise or lower the volume of your voice, change the speed at which you deliver the words, and/or set aside the key word or phrase with a pause before or after voicing it. Each of these four elements is important and I'll give you examples of each one in this chapter, but if you don't have the rate of speech right, nothing else matters.

The Ideal Pace of Public Speaking

Studies show that 150 to 160 words per minute is the ideal rate of speech for audio books. It seems to be the rate at which most listeners can comfortably hear, absorb, and recall the information.[2] Having read my own text for audio books, I can tell you that the ideal pace of dictation is slightly slower than the rate of speech in normal conversation.

When I was asked to read the audio version of my book *The Presentation Secrets of Steve Jobs*, I sat in a sound production studio in Berkeley for four days, carefully reading every sentence of the book in between frequent sips of warm tea and honey. The publisher had assigned me a professional voice-over coach to help with the dictation. According to the vocal coach, my biggest problem was that I was speaking too fast.

"But I'm speaking the way I always talk in casual conversations," I said.

"This isn't a 'casual conversation,'" the vocal coach said. "Audio books should be read at a slightly slower pace because people are listening to it, often in their cars. They don't have the added sensory input of seeing your lips move and your facial expressions."

People who make money as voice-over artists and who read books professionally say that audio books should be read at a slightly slower rate of speech than face-to-face conversation. So it stands to reason that if an audio book is read at 150 words per minute, then the ideal rate of speech for an in-person presentation would be *slightly faster* because of the added sensory inputs of hand gestures, eye contact, and facial expressions.

I tested this theory by examining the vocal pacing of Bryan Stevenson, the civil rights attorney you met earlier in this book.

As you'll recall, Stevenson is a speaker who has successfully argued cases in front of the U.S. Supreme Court. After reviewing hundreds of TED presentations as well as thousands of others presentations in my career as a journalist and communications coach, I'm convinced that Stevenson has the most comfortable pacing of any public speaker I've seen. He's not reading to you; he's having a conversation with you.

When I asked Stevenson about his speaking style, he told me that he likes to sound like he's talking to a friend over dinner in a restaurant. If my theory was correct—that a great presenter speaks slightly faster than the ideal audio-book narration of 150 words per minute—then Stevenson should reflect it. Sure enough, in his now famous TED talk, Stevenson speaks at the *slightly faster* pace of 190 words a minute.

I wanted to test the theory further. If Stevenson reflects the Goldilocks zone of public presentations—not too fast and not too slow—a super-high-energy motivational speaker should speak much, much faster than Stevenson. I turned to motivational guru Tony Robbins, who gave a TED talk in 2006. In that talk Robbins spoke 240 words per minute. That's fast. For comparison, an auctioneer speaks at 250 words per minute. That speed works very effectively for Robbins, who leaps on stage, waves his arms wildly, jumps up and down, and is there to pump up his audience. The audience expects ultra-high energy from Robbins's delivery in both nonverbal body language and verbal pace.

If the theory holds, a person on the opposite end of Robbins on the vocal-pacing spectrum should speak much, much more slowly than even an audio book. To test the theory, I analyzed the rate of speech of Henry Kissinger, secretary of state in the Richard Nixon administration. Kissinger was brilliant, but was hardly considered a charismatic public speaker. He even mocked his own reputation when he said, "Power is the ultimate aphrodisiac."

Kissinger spoke very, very s-l-o-w-l-y and in a monotone that, if you weren't glued to his every word, might lull you to sleep. In his public interviews—the most casual and conversational of his appearances—Kissinger spoke at the rate of only 90 words per minute!

If the ideal rate of speech for a face-to-face pitch or conversation is 190 words per minute then it would reasonable to assume that some of the most popular TED speakers communicate 3,400 words in 18 minutes, or very close to that number. Recall popular TED presenter Sir Ken Robinson. He delivered his talk in 3,200 words. Dr. Jill Bolte Taylor delivers about 2,700 words, not too far off (part of the reason her words fall under 3,000 is that she builds in long pauses for dramatic impact that fill in time). Finally, what about Bryan Stevenson, the man who I believe has the most naturally conversational delivery I've seen on the TED stage? Stevenson's popular talk, "We Need to Talk about an Injustice," contains 4,000 words. On closer inspection, however, I discovered that he bent the rules slightly and talked for 21 minutes. The total number of words in his first 18 minutes: 3,373.

I'm not suggesting that you start counting the number of words in your presentations. If you'd like to try it once, that's fine. It's more important that you pay attention to how you speak in everyday conversation and how it changes during your presentation. Most people slow down their rate of speech when they give a speech or a presentation, making their verbal delivery sound unnatural. Don't deliver a presentation. Have a conversation instead.

TEDnote

SPEAK IN A CONVERSATIONAL TONE. Watch Bryan Stevenson's TED talk. Listen to how he tells his three stories. He sounds like he's shooting the breeze with you. It's natural, conversational, and very authentic. When you practice your presentation, you'll be inclined to slow the rate of your speech as you advance slides

or try to remember the points you want to make. Once you've internalized the content, match the pace of your verbal delivery with your natural conversation style.

Lisa Kristine Punches Key Words

For two years Lisa Kristine has been visiting the far parts of the world to photograph one of the most atrocious crimes against humanity—slavery. Kristine is a photographer and she lets her photos tell the story. During her TEDx talk Kristine directed the audience's focus to her slides, but she decorated the photographs on those slides with her vocal intensity (we'll revisit this skill of hers again in chapter 8).

In the following section of her TEDx presentation, she slowed the pace of the delivery, enunciated every word clearly, and punched key words (accented with an underline):

"Today's slavery is about <u>commerce</u>, so the <u>goods</u> that enslaved people <u>produce</u> have <u>value</u>, but the <u>people</u> producing them are <u>disposable</u>. Slavery exists <u>everywhere</u>, nearly, in the world, [pause] and yet it is <u>illegal</u> everywhere in the world."[3]

Kristine is passionate about her topic. She talks about the moment she learned about slavery, during a conference when she met with someone working to eradicate slavery around the world. She didn't use many gestures but closed her eyes as she said, "After we finished talking, I felt so horrible and honestly ashamed at my own lack of knowledge of this atrocity in my own lifetime, and I thought, if I don't know, how many other people don't know? It started burning a hole in my stomach."

Dr. Jill Acts Out a Story

How you say something leaves as deep an impression on the listener as what you say, yet many of us neglect this all-important skill.

At TEDx Youth Indianapolis Dr. Jill brought her prop—a human brain—onstage (we'll hear more about this unusual prop in chapter 5) to talk to an audience of teenagers and young adults about why they feel out of control during puberty and their teen years. Once they understood their "neurocircuitry," they would be better equipped to handle the inevitable mood swings and inexplicable feelings and emotions. Dr. Jill's presentation is one of the best science talks I've ever seen. If all educators made science as interesting as Dr. Jill does, I'm sure more kids would be excited about pursuing careers in science and math!

Dr. Jill opened her presentation speaking at a Goldilocks pace of 165 words per minute—not too fast and not too slow. She is an accomplished and perceptive speaker. She knows that her verbal delivery must match the content of her narrative. Speaking at the same pace for the entire presentation would surely have bored her audience, no matter how compelling the content. Her goal was to inform *and* entertain.

Dr. Jill reached the point in her presentation when she discussed the changes to the human brain during puberty, the time when teenagers "literally lose half their minds." What does losing your mind sound like? What would it look like? As Dr. Jill's gestures got more erratic and expansive, her voice grew louder and her pace of delivery picked up substantially. She was speaking at the pace of 220 words per minute when she said:

> First, major physical growth spurt. When we go through a major physical growth spurt, our entire body changes. Our amygdala is on a little bit of alert—a little bit of alert. It's very interesting, but it's a little bit of alert. What's going on? What's going on? And then on top of that our hormonal systems are going to start flowing through our body and with that are going to come all kinds of mood swings and all kinds of interesting behaviors and then on top of that there's going to be what we call a pruning back, a pruning back of fifty percent of the synaptic connections inside our brains. We literally lose half our minds![4]

Great speakers act out a story. They must embody their words. While Dr. Jill rehearses her presentation, she chooses the words that best communicate her key messages and also practices the most effective way of delivering those words. Teenagers aren't "crazy," according to Dr. Jill. Instead, there are actual biological reasons for their spontaneous and aggressive behavior. Dr. Jill's advice to teens and parents: Survive until you're 25, when your adult brain is formed. It's an important message and she hopes that millions of teenagers and students will view her presentation now online at YouTube ("The Neuroanatomical Transformation of the Teenage Brain"). Dr. Jill knows that she cannot reach the people who need to hear the message if she delivers it poorly.

Dr. Jill's presentations seem natural, authentic, animated, and conversational. Conversational delivery takes practice. She rehearsed her presentation not once, twice, or even 20 times. She rehearsed it 200 times! Here's how Dr. Jill created her popular presentation.

Dr. Jill's Indianapolis presentation was conceived in Cancun. She was in a creative state of mind as she walked the beach with a notepad. She wrote down everything that came to mind, free-flowing words and ideas, and read what she had written out loud to feel how the words and sounds worked together. She didn't edit. She simply wrote down everything that she thought her audience (teens and parents) needed to know about the subject.

When Dr. Jill arrived back at the hotel room, she typed out the notes she had written in longhand. Back home after her vacation, she had 25 single-spaced pages. Her next step involved condensing the material into five major points (key messages). Dr. Jill's final step was to figure out how to deliver the key messages to be visual, interesting, and entertaining. We'll talk about the visual display of information in chapter 8, but notice that Dr. Jill weighs the entertainment component of her presentation as equally as she does the others.

The problem with most technical or scientific discussions is that the presenters fail to make their content visual, interesting, and entertaining. The people who do all three stand out, get noticed, and inspire positive changes in behavior. Now think about the last component—entertainment. Entertainers use their voices, facial expressions, gestures, and bodies to make us feel emotions. A great presentation is no different.

DEBUNKING BODY LANGUAGE MYTHS

Vocal delivery and nonverbal communication both matter—and they matter a lot. But how much, exactly, do they matter? One urban myth that has been accepted as gospel by body-language "experts" is that 7 percent of a person's message is conveyed through words and 93 percent is conveyed nonverbally (38 percent vocal tone; 55 percent body language). Perhaps you've heard this statistic before. If you have, disregard it. It's wrong.

Several years ago I spoke to the UCLA professor behind the statistics, Albert Mehrabian. Mehrabian, now retired, conducted very limited studies in the 1960s in the area of interpersonal communication. He simply found that when people expressed a message of emotional content, that message could be misconstrued if the speaker's tone and body language were not congruent or consistent with the message. It certainly makes sense, but Mehrabian says the data have been completely taken out of context. In fact he "cringes" every time he hears the grossly misleading statistic.

That said, I'm quite confident that vocal delivery and body language do make up a majority of a message's impact. I don't use Mehrabian's research to back my statement because, as he said, it doesn't apply. Instead, I'll cite more thorough and proven research from the area of behavior analysis—the same data professional interrogators use to determine whether one is lying or telling the truth.

Telling the Truth about Lying

Morgan Wright is an 18-year veteran of law enforcement. He has trained CIA, FBI, and NSA agents in behavior analysis, interviewing, and interrogation techniques.

"Body language makes a world of difference. It helps identify the difference between deception and truthfulness,"[5] Wright told me. According to Wright, the NSA (National Security Agency) conducted a study using 300 criminal cases whose outcomes were known. In one experiment, interviewers were asked to identify whether the suspect was telling the truth only by listening to the audio recording of the interrogation. In the second group, interviewers saw the video of the suspect being questioned but could not hear the audio. The third group saw and heard the interview. The fourth group had access to the video, audio, and case file.

The group that had access only to the audio portion of the interview had a 55 percent success rate. That means verbal behavior (what the suspect said and the tone in which he delivered the information) was only 55 percent accurate in determining whether a suspect was lying or telling the truth. The group who couldn't hear the audio and had only the suspect's body language on video did better—they were accurate 65 percent of the time. Those who had the advantage of hearing and seeing the suspect had an 85 percent success rate, while those who had the background (case file) along with the video and audio correctly assessed truthful versus deceptive behavior in 93 percent of the cases, which is more accurate than a polygraph test.

"When I watch someone give a presentation, I evaluate them the same way as I did during interrogations," Wright said. "When you're delivering information that you don't believe in or are lying about, you manifest the same behaviors as suspects in criminal or espionage cases who are lying to officers or agents."

Wright's advice: believe in what you're saying (chapter 1). "If you don't believe what you're saying, your movements will be awkward and not natural. No amount of training—unless you're a trained espionage agent or psychopath—will allow you to break that incongruence between your words and actions. If you don't believe in the message, you cannot force your body to act as though you believe in the message."

According to Wright, truthful and confident people have command presence. They have the look of authority, and "the look" begins with what people wear and how they carry themselves. The FBI conducted a study on prisoners who had shot or attacked police officers. Before deciding to "engage," the prisoners evaluated how easy it would be to take down the officers by the way they were dressed (sloppy or sharp) and how the officers carried themselves (slouching or straight). "As an officer you can invite trouble if you slouch, avoid eye contact, use vague, imprecise language, and are generally sloppy in your attire."

Of course, there's a big difference between delivering a presentation and approaching a suspect. In the latter, poor vocal tone and body language could get you killed. But it reinforces the point that people are making judgments about you all the time— based largely on the way you walk, talk, and look.

Great Leaders Have an Air of Confidence

In a group presentation, the person with the best "command presence" is usually the leader. He or she understands the material best, shows it, and has the confidence to take charge. They are typically dressed a little better than everyone else. Their shoes are polished and their clothes pressed. They make stronger eye contact and have a firm handshake. They speak concisely and precisely. They don't get flustered. They remain calm. They use "open" gestures, palms up or open and hands apart. Their voices project because they're speaking from their diaphragms. They walk, talk, and look like inspiring leaders.

Several years ago I had the opportunity to meet Commander Matt Eversmann, who teaches leadership at Johns Hopkins University. He led troops into battle in Mogadishu, Somalia in

1993. The battle was turned into a book and movie of the same name, *Black Hawk Down*. One thing that struck me immediately was that Eversmann had presence, loads of it.

"What role does body language play in the development of a leader?" I asked him.

"Great leaders have an air of confidence," he replied. "Subordinates need to look up to somebody who is still standing strong, like an oak, regardless of events around them. You need to convey a feeling that you will always be in control despite the circumstances, even if you don't have an immediate solution . . . someone who doesn't lose focus, doesn't cower, doesn't waffle. The air of confidence must come out."

Do you have that air of confidence on the corporate battlefield? Great communicators do. A leader who fails to instill confidence among his subordinates—during hundreds of everyday actions—will lose the loyalty of his "troops" when it really counts.

You might never see a TED stage, but you're selling yourself all the time. If you're an entrepreneur pitching investors or a software vendor pitching yourself in a trade-show booth, you're giving a presentation. If you're a job candidate pitching yourself to a recruiter or a CEO pitching a new product to customers, you're giving a presentation. A TED talk can be the presentation a lifetime for many people, but your daily business presentations are often just as important for your career or company. Successful TED presenters have strong body language and so should you.

TALK, WALK, AND LOOK LIKE A LEADER

Colin Powell is a very thoughtful leader. His thinking process is rigorous and structured, much like his background as an army general and U.S. secretary of state from 2001 to 2005. When Powell is on television sitting across the desk from an interviewer, he usually starts with his hands folded in front of him on the desk. He doesn't stay that way for long. Within seconds, he is using gestures that complement his message. Researchers have found that rigorous thinkers cannot easily stop using gestures, even when they try to keep their hands folded. Using gestures actually frees up their mental capacities, and complex thinkers use complex gestures.

Powell uses gestures frequently in television interviews and presentations. In October 2012, Powell delivered a heartfelt TED presentation on the topic of kids and why they need structure for a good start in life.

Powell began his presentation as he does his television interviews, with both hands clasped together. Again, it didn't last long. Within 10 seconds his hands came apart and didn't touch each other for another 17 minutes. Table 3.1 shows you an example of the natural, continuous variety of gestures he used in just a short portion of his presentation.

COLIN POWELL'S WORDS WITH CORRESPONDING GESTURES

WORDS	GESTURES
Every child ought to have a good start in life.[6]	Both hands spread shoulder-length apart, palms open toward the audience
I was privileged to have that kind of good start.	Makes circular moment with right hand, palm pointing toward his chest
I was not a great student. I was a public school kid in New York City, and I didn't do well at all. I have my entire New York City Board of Education transcript from kindergarten through college.	Arms extend farther apart past length of body, palms facing each other, using hands to highlight words *kindergarten* and *college*
I wanted it when I was writing my first book. I wanted to see if my memory was correct, and, my God, it was. (Laughter). Straight C everywhere.	Left arm relaxes by side. Right hand held up at chest level and continues gestures

WORDS	GESTURES
And I finally bounced through high school, got into the City College of New York with a 78.3 average, which I shouldn't have been allowed in with, and then I started out in engineering, and that only lasted six months. (Laughter)	Left hand goes up again and mirrors right hand gestures, but both hands still spread apart
And then I went into geology, "rocks for jocks." This is easy. And then I found ROTC. I found something that I did well and something that I loved doing.	Left arm relaxes by side and right hand continues gestures, first three fingers together pointing toward his body
And I found a group of youngsters like me who felt the same way.	Right hand extends and clasps into a fist
And so my whole life then was dedicated to ROTC and the military. And I say to young kids everywhere, as you're growing up and as this structure is being developed inside of you, always be looking for that which you do well and that which you love doing, and when you find those two things together, man, you got it. That's what's going on. And that's what I found. I tell young people everywhere, it ain't where you start in life, it's what you do with life that determines where you end up in life.	Leans forward, raises voice and gets more intense, raises both clenched fists
And you are blessed to be living in a country that, no matter where you start, you have opportunities so long as you believe in yourself.	Points toward himself
You believe in the society and the country.	Extends right hand, chest high, palm facing outward
And you believe that you can self-improve and educate yourself as you go along.	Right hand makes circular waving motion while left hand remains clenched in fist chest high
And that's the key to success.	Left hand held chest high in a fist; right arm extended, palm open

Table 3.1. Colin Powell's words with corresponding gestures during his TED 2012 presentation.

Powell has command presence. He walks, talks, and looks like a leader. He also trains people—soldiers and young adults—to do the same. When Powell talks to a group of students and asks them questions, he will ask the student to walk up to the front of the class, stand at attention like a soldier—arms straight at his sides, eyes up, look straight ahead, and speak loudly. The kids have fun with it, but something inside them changes. They feel different, more confident, ready to take on a challenge. The way you carry yourself actually changes the way you feel when you're delivering a presentation.

> "I have been a professional speaker for most of my adult life. From my first day in my first unit as an army officer, I had to speak to and teach troops. Over time I learned how to reach them, how to make the subject interesting, and how to persuade them that they had an interest in learning what I was teaching. Since they bored easily, a bag of attention-grabbing techniques was essential. In 1966, I was assigned to be an instructor at the Infantry School at Fort Benning . . . you were taught eye contact, how not to cough, stammer, put your hands in your pocket, pick your nose, or scratch your itches. You were taught to stride across the stage, use a pointer, slides, and hand gestures, and how to raise and lower your voice to keep the students awake."[7]
> —Colin Powell, from his book *It Worked for Me*

GESTURES MAKE A STRONG ARGUMENT EVEN STRONGER

Recall Ernesto Sirolli, the passionate economic-development expert you learned about in chapter 1, who told a TEDx audience about the learning experience he had in Zambia teaching the local natives how to grow tomatoes. Table 3.2 recaps part of his presentation we

3.1: **Ernesto Sirolli,** speaking at TEDxEQChCh 2012. Courtesy of Neil Macbeth for TEDxEQChCh.

addressed in chapter 1 in relation to passion, but it now shows you the gestures he used to complement his words. He's an Italian who, like me, has no problem using his hands to make his point, and he does so in an impactful and genuine way in his presentation.

Sirolli's strong case was made stronger by the gestures he used to reinforce every sentence. Sirolli's gestures are so animated, it's

ERNESTO SIROLLI'S WORDS WITH CORRESPONDING GESTURES

WORDS	GESTURES
We had these magnificent tomatoes. In Italy, a tomato would grow to this size. In Zambia, to this size.[8]	Starts with both hands together in the form of a small circle and expands the circle with hands apart
We could not believe it. We were telling the Zambians, "Look how easy agriculture is." When the tomatoes were nice and ripe and red, overnight, some 200 hippos came out from the river and they ate everything. (Laughter)	Both hands extended away from the body, brought forward as Sirolli describes hippos walking into the field. Without saying a word, he continued to use facial expressions (mouth and eyes wide open) to express shock and surprise.
And we said to the Zambians, "My God, the hippos!"	Brings both hands to his head
And the Zambians said, "Yes, that's why we have no agriculture here."	Nods his head

Table 3.2. Ernesto Sirolli's words with corresponding gestures during his TEDxEQChCh 2012 presentation.

impossible to adequately describe them in text. Visit TED.com and search "Ernesto Sirolli" to see him for yourself. Every gesture helps to paint the pictures he's creating verbally. He doesn't even use slides. He doesn't need to. His gestures and animation decorate his words for him. His presence is commanding and dynamic.

The world's most charismatic business professionals have great body language—a commanding presence that reflects confidence, competence, and charisma. *Command presence* is a military term used to describe someone who presents himself or herself as a person with authority, someone who is to be respected and followed. How much would people sacrifice to follow you? Would they leave a high-paying job, good benefits, and a pension? If so, you have command presence.

If you want to make a positive impression in your next meeting, sales pitch, or job interview, pay attention to what your body is saying. Walk, talk, and look like a leader whom people want to follow.

THE GIST ON GESTURES

Are gestures necessary? The short answer is—yes. Studies have shown that complex thinkers use complex gestures and that gestures actually give the audience confidence in the speaker.

Dr. David McNeil says it's all in the hands. The University of Chicago researcher is one of the foremost authorities in the area of hand gestures. McNeil has empirical evidence proving that gestures, thinking, and language are connected. I spoke to McNeil and I can confidently say that the most popular TED speakers reinforce his conclusion: disciplined, rigorous, intelligent, and confident speakers use hand gestures as a window to their thought processes.

Soon after I spoke to McNeil, I had the opportunity to watch Cisco CEO John Chambers in person. He's an astonishing and charismatic presenter who works the room like a preacher, walking offstage and into the audience. He uses his voice masterfully— speeding up or slowing down the pace, raising and lowering his voice, punching key words and phrases, etc. Chambers is considered one of the most intelligent and visionary executives in high-tech and is said to have a prodigious memory. As McNeil observed, complex thinkers have complex gestures, and Chambers, being a complex thinker, uses large, expansive hand gestures to punctuate nearly every sentence.

Based on my conversation with McNeil and my experience working with global leaders on their communication skills, here are four tips you can use today to improve the way you use your hands:

- **Use gestures.** Don't be afraid to use your hands in the first place. The simplest fix for a stiff presentation is to pull your hands out of your pockets and use them. Don't keep your hands bound when you present. They want to be free.

- **Use gestures sparingly.** Now that I've told you to use gestures, be careful not to go overboard. Your gestures should be natural. If you try to imitate someone else, you'll look like a *Saturday Night Live* caricature of a bad politician. Avoid canned gestures. Don't think about what gestures to use. Your story will guide them.

- **Use gestures at key moments.** Save your most expansive gestures for key moments in the presentation. Reinforce your key messages with purposeful gestures . . . as long as it feels genuine to your personality and style.

- **Keep your gestures within the power sphere.** Picture your power sphere as a circle that runs from the top of your eyes, out to the tips of your outstretched hands, down to your belly button, and back up to your eyes again. Try to keep your gestures (and eye gaze) in this zone. Hands that hang below your navel lack energy and "confidence." Using complex gestures above the waist will give the audience a sense of confidence about you as a leader, help you communicate your thoughts more effortlessly, and enhance your overall presence.

Former Michigan governor Jennifer Granholm makes expansive, bold gestures, and keeps those gestures within her power sphere. Granholm pioneered clean-energy policies in her state and kicked off the TED 2013 with a talk on how states can and should use alternative energy sources. Table 3.3 shows an example of the gestures that complemented her words.

Not once did her Granholm's hands—either one—leave the power sphere. It also didn't hurt that she held her back straight, kept her head high, made solid eye contact, and wore solid colors that popped out from the dark background (black slacks, white

JENNIFER GRANHOLM'S WORDS WITH CORRESPONDING GESTURES

WORDS	GESTURES
I was introduced as the former Governor of Michigan, but actually I'm a scientist. All right, a political scientist. It doesn't really count, but my laboratory was the laboratory of democracy that is Michigan, and, like any good scientist, I was experimenting with policy about what would achieve the greatest good for the greatest number.[9]	Leans forward, both hands apart, palms open
But there were three problems, three enigmas that I could not solve.	Right hand and elbow at a 90-degree angle holding the clicker; left hand raised with three fingers
And I want to share with you those problems, but most importantly, I think I figured out a proposal for a solution.	Leans forward, raises index finger on left hand, makes eye contact with each part of the room

Table 3.3. Jennifer Granholm's words with corresponding gestures during her TED 2013 presentation.

blouse, green jacket). Granholm's posture and gestures added to her authority.

Granholm's body language is an example of a style that social scientists have found to be persuasive. It's called "eager nonverbal." In fact, a mismatch or incongruence between your nonverbal communication and your words can significantly detract from the effectiveness of your pitch.

In a groundbreaking study published in the *Journal of Experimental Social Psychology*, Bob Fennis and Marielle Stel performed studies in urban supermarkets. They trained actors to approach shoppers and try to persuade them to buy a box of Christmas

3.2: Jennifer Granholm speaking at TED 2013. Courtesy of James Duncan Davidson/TED (http://duncandavidson.com).

candy. They discovered that when the sales strategy was to make a product more attractive (reducing the cost, covering its benefits, etc.), the "eager nonverbal" style proved most effective. The eager nonverbal style includes three elements: very animated, broad, open movements; hand movements openly projected outward; and forward-leaning body positions.

The analysis showed that a much larger percentage of shoppers (71 percent) agreed to buy a box of candy when exposed to a sales representative who displayed an "eager nonverbal" style than one who had a more reserved style characterized by a backward-leaning position, slower and smaller body movements, and slower speech. The researchers conclude, "If your strategy is aimed primarily at increasing the perceived attractiveness of your request or offer, an eager nonverbal style is more likely to be effective."[10]

Jennifer Granholm fits the theory perfectly. Everything about her posture, gestures, and body language can be classified as eager nonverbal. Her goal is to sell her ideas—her plan—to other states. Her proposal is to pitch a "clean energy jobs race to the top." She's selling something more important than chocolates, of course, but as Fennis and Stel discovered in their research, her body language is the best fit for her desired goal—to make her proposal more appealing and ultimately actionable.

Sit up. It will help you feel more self-confident. A 2009 study published in *The European Journal of Social Psychology* found that posture makes a difference in how people evaluate themselves. Volunteers who filled out a mock job application were told to either sit straight or slouch. Those who sat straight as they filled out the form reviewed themselves far more favorably than the slouchers. When you practice your presentation, stand tall. It'll give you confidence for the real thing!

THREE EASY FIXES FOR COMMON BODY LANGUAGE PROBLEMS

Few of the leaders I work with initially think about how they talk, walk, and look until they see themselves on video. Once they do, most realize they need a lot more work to look natural and conversational. Fortunately the problems are easy to identify and fix.

Here are three common problems I see among leaders who give presentations. Correcting these issues will help you develop command presence, whether you're interviewing for a job, pitching your idea, delivering a sales presentation, occupying the corner office, or running a small business.

Fidgeting, Tapping, and Jingling

These are annoying habits that many of us exhibit during our presentations and conversations. Fidgeting makes you look unsure, nervous, and unprepared. Mannerisms such as tapping your fingers on the table or playing with your pen serve no purpose. Recently

I watched an author who had written a book on leadership discuss his project. He jingled the coins in his pocket during his entire talk. It drove me nuts, and everyone else, too. He didn't sell many books that day, and he certainly didn't score points for leadership.

The quick fix: Move with purpose. Use an inexpensive video camera or your smartphone to record yourself delivering the first five minutes of your presentation, then play it back. Watch yourself and write down all the mannerisms that serve no useful purpose, such as rubbing your nose, tapping your fingers, and jingling coins. Simply seeing yourself in action makes you more conscious of how you come across, making you better equipped to eliminate useless movements and gestures.

I once worked with a leading technology executive who had to inform a major investor of a product delay. The investor was Oracle CEO Larry Ellison, who has a reputation as one of the toughest bosses in the business world. The tech executive and his team had the issue under control and had learned valuable lessons from the delay. However, his body language said otherwise. He fidgeted constantly as he presented—tapping his toe, touching his face, and drumming his fingers on a table next to him. His mannerisms communicated a lack of competence and control. Once he saw himself on video, he caught most of these annoying habits on his own and eliminated them. He gave a confident presentation, Ellison was happy, and the project was completely successful.

Standing Rigidly in Place

Great presenters have animated body movements; they do not stay in one spot or look motionless. Standing absolutely still makes you appear rigid, boring, and disengaged.

The quick fix: Walk, move, and work the room. Most business professionals who come to me for presentation coaching think they need to stand like statues . . . or behind the lectern. But movement is not only acceptable, it's welcome. Conversations are fluid, not stiff. Some of the greatest business speakers walk among the audience instead of standing in front of them.

Here's a simple trick: When you record your presentation, walk out of the frame once in a while. I tell clients that if they don't leave the camera frame several times during a five-minute presentation, they're too rigid.

Hands in Pockets

Most people keep their hands in their pockets when they're standing in front of a group. It makes them appear uninterested or bored, uncommitted, and sometimes nervous.

The quick fix: This one's too easy—take your hands out of your pockets! I've seen great business leaders who never once put both hands in their pockets during a presentation. One hand is acceptable as long as the free hand is gesturing. Remember to keep those gestures within the power sphere.

Fake It Till You Make It

Amy Cuddy is a social psychologist at the Harvard Business School. Her research into body language has landed her in *TIME* magazine, CNN, and on the TED stage. Cuddy believes body language shapes who we are. She says that how we use our bodies— our nonverbal cues—can change people's perceptions of us. Cuddy goes further, however, to argue that simply changing your body position affects how you feel about yourself and, by default, how others see you. Even if you don't feel confident, act like it and your chances of success greatly improve.

We all know that our minds change our bodies. A person who is insecure will close up, bringing his hands and arms in, shrink in his seat, cast his eyes down. Cuddy believes the opposite is true as well—"our bodies change our minds and our minds can change our behavior, and our behavior can change our outcomes."[11]

Cuddy suggests that "power posing" increases testosterone

3.3: Amy Cuddy, speaking at TEDGlobal 2012. Courtesy of James Duncan Davidson/TED (http://duncandavidson.com).

and lowers cortisol levels in the brain, which will make you feel more confident and commanding. She says it's a "tiny tweak" that can lead to big changes.

The power pose works like this—stretch out your arms as far as they'll go and hold that pose for two minutes. You can do it in an elevator, at a desk, or behind the stage, preferably where nobody will see you!

When Cuddy administers the test to students, she finds that "low-power people" experience a 15 percent increase in hormones that configure the brain to be more assertive, confident, and comfortable. "So it seems that our nonverbals do govern how we think and feel about ourselves . . . our bodies change our minds."

It's natural for people to be nervous and it's perfectly okay. We're social beings, and since the beginning of time it's been important than we fit in socially. When our ancestors lived in caves, getting kicked out of a cave wasn't exactly a desirable outcome. Our "nerves" are the result of our biological need to be accepted. But for many people nervous energy becomes stifling. Who hasn't felt her throat closing, palms getting sweaty, and heart racing? We've all been there. I can't tell you how many leaders I work with who get very nervous before public presentations—and these are people at the top of their professions, often worth hundreds of millions of dollars. The secret is not to eliminate nerves but to manage them.

Amy Cuddy offers a solution for nervous speakers—fake it till you make it. Cuddy was identified as a gifted child and her intelligence gave her an identity in her early, formative years. When she was 19 years old Cuddy was thrown from a car and sustained a head injury. She was taken out of college and told she would not be returning. "I really struggled with this, and I have to say, having your identity taken from you, your core identity, and for me it was being smart, having that taken from you, there's nothing that leaves you feeling more powerless than that. So I felt entirely powerless."

Cuddy worked hard, reentered college, and graduated four years later than the majority of her peers. She continued her education at Princeton thanks to an adviser who had a lot of faith in Cuddy's ability. Cuddy didn't believe it herself, though. She felt like an imposter. The night before her first-year talk, Cuddy called her adviser and said she was quitting the graduate program. "You are not quitting, because I took a gamble on you," her adviser responded. "You're going to stay, and this is what you're going to do. You are going to fake it. You're going to do every talk that you ever get asked to do. You're just going to do it and do it and do it, even if you're terrified and just paralyzed and having an out-of-body experience, until you have this moment where you say, 'Oh my gosh, I'm doing it. Like, I have become this. I am actually doing this.'" And that's what Cuddy did: she faked it until she believed it. "And so I want to say to you, don't fake it till you make it. Fake it till you become it."

How Tony Robbins Gets into a Peak Presentation State

Motivational speaker Tony Robbins has enough energy to keep 4,000 people engaged for 50 hours over four days. Featured in an Oprah Winfrey special, Robbins demonstrated his pre-speaking ritual, which involves incantations, affirmations, and movement—lots and lots of movement. This makes sense since one of Robbins's core teachings is that energized movement can change your state of mind. Robbins gets himself in the zone for about 10 minutes prior to taking the stage. He jumps up and down, spins around, pumps his fists, stands with his arms outstretched, and even bounces on a trampoline.

It's not enough to rehearse the words. Before you're "on," some physical preparation will boost your energy level and make a huge impact on the way your audience perceives you. Of course it's not necessary to go to the extreme that Robbins does—and you would look a bit foolish jumping on a trampoline before your next sales pitch—but it's important to adopt some sort of physical pre-presentation ritual since movement and energy are so intimately connected.

YOUR STRENGTH AS A SPEAKER COMES FROM WITHIN

Professional cross-country skier Janine Shepherd was involved in an accident that ended her career. A truck hit her as she was on a training ride. Shepherd broke her neck and back in six places. She broke five ribs and suffered a severe head injury. At TED 2012 she told the audience that a broken body isn't a broken person.

Due to the severity of her injuries, Shepherd used her body and stage props creatively to have a conversation with the audience. She placed five chairs on the stage, each chair giving her an opportunity to sit, acting as a metaphor for each chapter of her life after the accident:

> **First chair (part one: the accident)**
>
> **Second chair (part two: ten days in the hospital)**
>
> **Third chair (part three: move from intensive care to acute spinal ward)**
>
> **Fourth chair (part four: "after six months it was time to go home"[12]). When she "remembered my friend" who was still in the acute spinal unit, she turned and talked to the chair next to her.**
>
> **Fifth chair (part five: Shepherd learns to fly. She sat in chair as she said, "They lifted me into the cockpit and sat me down.")**

Shepherd stood up as she delivered the remaining few minutes, talking about her new career as an aerobatic flying instructor. "My real strength never came from my body . . . who I am is unchanged. The pilot light inside of me was still alive."

Secret #3: Have a Conversation

Shepherd has a point. While she uses her body effectively to tell her story, her "strength" comes from the inside. Your delivery and gestures, mastered through hours and hours of practice, will *enhance* your overall message, but without passion and practice, your presence will be severely diminished. Your strength as a speaker comes from the inside.

PART II

Novel

Novelty recognition is a hard-wired survival tool all humans share. Our brains are trained to look for something brilliant and new, something that stands out, something that looks delicious.

—DR. A. K. PRADEEP, AUTHOR, *THE BUYING BRAIN*

4

Teach Me Something New

Everything I'm going to present to you was not in my textbooks when I went to school.

—*TITANIC* EXPLORER ROBERT BALLARD, TED 2008

DEEP-SEA EXPLORER ROBERT BALLARD TOOK a TED audience on a 17-minute trip to explore the 72 percent of the planet that's under the ocean because, as he said, "It's really naïve to think that the Easter Bunny put all the resources on the continents."[1]. Ballard loves the rush of exploration, especially pursuing mysteries that push human limits. He also loves challenges and told me that he enjoyed TED because he was going up against the best in story-telling.

Ballard is one of the bravest explorers of our time. In 1985, about 1,000 miles east of Boston, Ballard, a naval intelligence officer at the time, discovered the wreck of RMS *Titanic* two and a half miles below the surface of the Atlantic. The *Titanic* discovery is Ballard's most famous expedition, but he's conducted more than 120 undersea explorations to learn something new about the substance that makes up most of our world. Ballard told me that his mission in any presentation—TED or in the classroom—is to inform, educate, and inspire. "When you walk into a classroom you have two jobs: one is to teach and the other is to recruit everyone in that classroom to join the pursuit of truth,"[2] Ballard says.

In his presentation, he challenged the audience with this question: Why are we ignoring the oceans? Ballard said that NASA's budget for one year would fund the National Oceanic and Atmospheric Administration's (NOAA) budget for 1,600 years—just one of many intriguing insights, facts, and observations Ballard revealed. Among others:

- **Everything we're going to talk about represents a one-tenth of one percent glimpse, because that's all we've seen.**

- **Fifty percent of the United States of America lies beneath the sea.**

- **The greatest mountain range on Earth lies under the ocean.**

- **Most of our planet is in eternal darkness.**

- **We discovered a profusion of life in a world that it should not exist in.**

- **It (the deep sea) contains more history than all the museums on land combined.**

Near the conclusion of his presentation, Ballard showed a photograph of a young girl, jaw dropped, with a wide-eyed expression of awe. "This is what we want," Ballard said. "This is a young lady, not watching a football game, not watching a basketball game. Watching exploration live from thousands of miles away, and it's just dawning on her what she's seeing. And when you get a jaw-drop, you can inform. You can put so much information into that mind, it's in full receiving mode." Ballard received a standing ovation. His 2008 TED presentation intrigues, informs, and inspires because it makes people look at the world differently—not from above, but from below.

Secret #4: Teach Me Something New

Reveal information that's completely new to your audience, packaged differently, or offers a fresh and novel way to solve an old problem.

Why it works: The human brain loves novelty. An unfamiliar, unusual, or unexpected element in a presentation intrigues the audience, jolts them out of their preconceived notions, and quickly gives them a new way of looking at the world.

JAMES CAMERON'S "INSATIABLE" SENSE OF CURIOSITY

If it hadn't been for Ballard's discovery of the *Titanic*, one of the most successful films of all time may never have been made. "Curiosity is the most important thing you own,"[3] Cameron told a TED audience in February 2010. "Imagination is a force that can actually manifest a reality."

Cameron revealed things his audience didn't expect from the director of such blockbusters as *Terminator*, *Titanic*, and *Avatar*. He talked a little about moviemaking and a lot about creativity, exploration, innovation, and leadership.

Exploring the oceans ignited Cameron's imagination from the age of 15, when he became certified as a diver. He explained that when he made *Titanic*, he pitched it to the studios as "Romeo and Juliet on a ship." Cameron, however, had an ulterior motive:

What I wanted to do was I wanted to dive to the real wreck of *Titanic*. And that's why I made the movie. And that's the truth. Now, the studio didn't know that. But I convinced them. I said, "We're going to dive to the wreck. We're going to film it for real. We'll be using it in the opening of the film. It will be really important. It will be a great marketing hook." And I talked them into funding an expedition. Sounds crazy. But this goes back to that theme about your imagination creating a reality. Because we actually created a reality where six months later, I find myself in a Russian submersible two and a half miles down in the north Atlantic, looking at the real *Titanic* through a view port. Not a movie, not HD—for real.[4]

I'm a fan of Cameron's movies, especially *Titanic*. Yes, I still shed a tear when Rose throws the Hope Diamond overboard and the theme song starts to play. I'm a sucker for those movies. Although I know a lot about the plot of the movie, Cameron taught me something new wrapped in an interesting anecdote that carried a profound lesson for anyone seeking to explore the full range of his or her potential. By doing so, he inspired his audience and gave them a reason to listen to the rest of his presentation. The director "hooked" his audience, just as he did the film studio.

People are natural explorers. Like Cameron, most of us have an insatiable desire to seek, to learn, to discover. As it turns out, it's the way we're wired.

According to some surveys, people fear public speaking more than dying. I asked Robert Ballard what made him more anxious, diving 2.5 miles under the ocean in a tiny, claustrophobic submersible or giving an 18-minute presentation. He said nearly dying several times in the deep sea was much worse! Keep that in mind the next time you get nervous in front of an audience. As Jerry Seinfeld once said, you'd rather be the person giving the eulogy instead of the one in the casket.

LEARNING IS A BUZZ

Musician Peter Gabriel attended a TED conference in 2006 and told a filmmaker, "Exposure to new ideas and interesting ideas was the main buzz for me." He wasn't kidding. Learning is addictive because it's joyful. It's also necessary for human evolution.

When you introduce a new or novel way of solving an old problem, you are tapping into millions of years of adaptation. If primitive man hadn't been curious, we would have been extinct a long time ago. According to John Medina, a developmental molecular biologist at the University of Washington School of Medicine, 99.99 percent of all species that have ever lived are extinct today. The human brain adapted to its harsh environments, allowing it to survive. "There are two ways to beat the cruelty of the environment: You can become stronger or you can become smarter. We chose the latter,"[5] Medina says.

Medina says we are natural explorers who have an unquenchable need to know and to learn. "Babies are born with a deep desire to understand the world around them and an incessant curiosity that compels them to aggressively explore it. This need for exploration is so powerfully stitched into their experience that some scientists describe it as a drive, just as hunger and thirst and sex are drives."[6] According to Medina, we don't outgrow our "thirst for knowledge" as we grow into adulthood.

Speakers like Ballard and Cameron quench our thirst with a glass of knowledge from the depths of the sea. Your audience craves knowledge, even if they have only a mild interest in the topic. As long as you relate your topic to the audience by teaching them something new they can use in their daily lives, you'll hook them, too.

In my communication work with Intel, the world's largest manufacturer of computer microprocessors, I challenge them to connect their technology to our daily lives. For example, Intel introduced a technology called "Turbo Boost" that, by definition, "enables the processor to run above its base operating frequency via dynamic control of the CPU's clock rate." Got it? The previous definition probably means nothing to you and, most likely, would not inspire you to run out to buy a new laptop or computer with an Intel chip inside. What if I said, "Intel's exclusive Turbo Boost technology makes note of what you're doing on your computer (playing games, watching videos) and adjusts the performance to give you a boost when you need it and to scale it back when you don't, which extends the battery life of your notebook." The second description teaches you something new by demonstrating how the product improves your life, and that's why it worked. Every time an Intel spokesperson used the latter description—connecting the technology to our daily lives—he or she was quoted in the press. Rarely, if ever, did a reporter or blogger use the technical definition.

YOUR BRAIN'S NATURAL "SAVE BUTTON"

Martha Burns is an adjunct professor at Northwestern who believes neuroscience is helping educators to become better teachers. Her insights also explain why we get a buzz out of learning. Learning something new activates the same reward areas of the brain as do drugs and gambling. "A big part of the answer to why some of your students hold onto the information you teach and others do not has to do with a little chemical in the brain that has to be present for a child (or an adult) to retain information. That chemical is called 'dopamine.'"[7]

Dopamine is a powerful chemical. A new relationship can trigger a dose of it (and it subsides after a while, which is why counselors recommend finding ways to keep the spice alive after several years of marriage). Advancing to the next level of a video game can trigger dopamine, as can hearing the clanging of coins in a slot machine, or even a hit of cocaine.

Drugs and gambling are artificial triggers and lead to serious consequences. Isn't there a less-harmful means of achieving that mental high? There sure is. According to Burns, dopamine is also released when people learn something new and exciting—a much healthier way to feel good! "For many of your students and many of us as adults, learning about new things is an adventure and very rewarding, and dopamine levels increase in the brain to help us retain that new information,"[8] Burns writes. "I like to refer to dopamine as the 'save button' in the brain. When dopamine is present during an event or experience, we remember it; when it is absent, nothing seems to stick."

The next logical question is, "How do I increase dopamine?" According to Burns, the answer is remarkably simple and straight-forward: make the information new and exciting. For example, Burns says the best teachers are always thinking of new ways of delivering information. "That is why you love it when your school has *new* text book adoptions—the novelty allows you to teach the information in a new way—which generates enthusiasm on your part and the students . . . Increase *novelty* in a classroom and you increase the dopamine levels of your students . . . Dopamine can be addictive—our goal as teachers is to get our students addicted to learning."[9]

Dopamine is addictive. Now I know why I'm on a high when I hear stirring words of inspiration or encouragement. For several years I accompanied my brother and several friends to a full day of lectures in the town of Bakersfield, California. The Bakersfield Business Conference was held once a year. The tickets were ex-pensive, the trip was long, but the speakers made every dollar and every minute well worth it.

The Bakersfield conference was held in TED fashion with each speaker allowed no more than 20 minutes. The speakers came from the fields of politics, business, and the arts. Some were famous (e.g., Ronald Reagan, Mikhail Gorbachev, Rudy Giuliani, Steve

Wynn, Wayne Gretzky) and others were less familiar. But they were all chosen for their ability to teach the audience something new and novel—fresh ways of looking at old problems. As I made the long, five-hour drive home at the end of each conference, I felt like I could take on the world. I was addicted to learning something new. Learning is one addiction I don't mind admitting to. In fact, I celebrate it.

A STATISTICIAN RESHAPES YOUR WORLDVIEW

Hans Rosling is a rock star among TEDsters. His presentation at TED 2006 stole the show and made him an online "viral" sensation. Rosling's 18-minute video has been viewed more than five million times. Musician Peter Gabriel calls it one of his favorites—the most "surprising," TED talk. Actor Ben Affleck agrees, saying, "Hans is the most creative and entertaining statistician on earth!" Former CEO of AOL/Time Warner Steve Case likes it, too, ranking it in his top three most "unforgettable" talks. When TED asked Bill Gates to curate his favorite talks, he said there were too many to pick. His clear favorite, however, was Rosling's. Rosling succeeds because, as the title of his presentation suggests, he delivers statistics that "reshape your worldview." He delivers information in ways that nobody has ever seen before.

Rosling is a professor of health in Stockholm, Sweden, where he tracks global health and poverty trends. In the hands of most researchers, such data would be, well, boring. Rosling uses software that he codeveloped to bring statistics to life—Gapminder. According to Gapminder's own site, the software "unveils the beauty of statistics by turning boring numbers into enjoyable animations that make sense of the world."

Three minutes into Rosling's presentation, he brings up a visual slide with what appears to be a chart showing random clusters of bubbles—some are small, others much larger than the rest.

Rosling explains that when he asked his students to define the "western world" and the "third world," they answered, "The western world has longer life span and small families. The third world is shorter life and larger families."[10] Rosling theatrically debunked the myth.

On the X-axis of the chart, Rosling put fertility rates (the number of children per woman with data on every country going back to 1962). On the Y-axis he displayed life expectancy at birth (30 years on the bottom of the axis, 70 at the top). In 1962, there was a very clear cluster of large bubbles near the top left, larger industrialized countries with smaller families and higher life expectancy. The bottom right had a fair number of large bubbles as well, representing developing countries with larger families and shorter lives.

What happened next was astonishing, novel, and fun to watch. Rosling put the animation in motion to show the dynamic changes

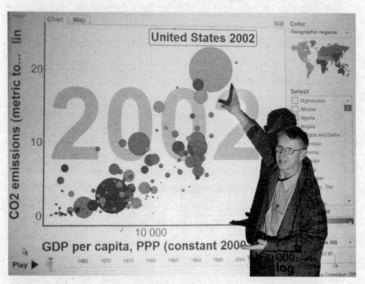

4.1: Hans Rosling, cofounder and chairman of the Gapminder foundation, presenting Trendalyzer data. Courtesy of Stefan Nilsson.

to the world from 1962 to 2003, the last year in which data were available. As the bubbles shifted and bounced rapidly around the screen, Rosling narrated the changes like a sportscaster calling a hockey game:

> Here we go. Can you see there? It's China there, moving against better health there, improving there. All the green Latin American countries are moving towards smaller families. Your yellow ones here are the Arabic countries, and they get larger families, but they—no, longer life, but not larger families. The Africans are the green down here. They still remain here. This is India. Indonesia's moving on pretty fast. (Laughter) And in the '80s here, you have Bangladesh still among the African countries there. But now, Bangladesh—it's a miracle that happens in the '80s: the imams start to promote family planning. They move up into that corner. And in '90s, we have the terrible HIV epidemic that takes down the life expectancy of the African countries and all the rest of them move up into the corner, where we have long lives and small family, and we have a completely new world.[11]

Rosling had revealed a completely new world and a completely new way of looking at global population trends. His audience was laughing, cheering, and, ultimately, intrigued.

In 2012 *TIME* magazine named Rosling one of the most influential people in the world, thanks, in large part, to the explosive popularity of his TED lecture, which has spread online for millions to see. According to *TIME*, Rosling is "a man who is in the vanguard of a critically important activity: advancing the public understanding of science."[12]

Most scientists deliver statistics with mind-numbingly dull presentations. Rosling is one of the first scientists delivering complex statistics that I've actually wanted to watch over and over for any length of time, let alone 18 minutes. The best ideas will fail to inspire an audience if they're not packaged effectively. Don't ever let anyone get away with calling public speaking a "soft skill." Had Rosling failed to package his content in a fresh way, his hard data would have been worthless.

Sometimes the data you present might not be earthshaking or entirely unfamiliar to the audience, but that doesn't mean you can't deliver it in a fresh way. I was preparing executives at San-Disk for their annual investor day (SanDisk is the world's leading maker of flash memory, the storage required for your digital camera, MP3 player, iPad or tablet, and increasingly in your notebook computers). Investors are among the toughest audience. They want to hear numbers (preferably positive ones), technical information, and growth strategies. They also watch a ton of presentations, the majority of which are dry, confusing, and boring.

In this particular presentation, one senior vice president wanted to start with some data that wasn't entirely new to the roomful of analysts (the growing sales of high-capacity storage cards). In this case he didn't have to deliver entirely new data as much as he had to present it in a refreshing way. Analysts expect dry charts, so this executive decided to go personal and inject some emotion into his talk. He explained that he's a digital-photography enthusiast and has a collection of 80,000 digital photos at home, nearly all of them captured on SanDisk cards. He showed pictures of his high-school-age girls playing sports and explained how he wouldn't trust those memories to anything but SanDisk cards. He also enjoys taking panoramic landscape photographs and displayed several of the photos he's taken. He told the analysts that panoramic photos require 10 times more storage capacity than a traditional photo, "10 times more opportunity for SanDisk." By their very nature, financial presentations must include charts, graphs, and tables, but that doesn't mean you shouldn't present the information in a way that jars your audience out of their preconceived notions of how the material will be presented.

The executive I just featured used very personal stories to bring the data alive and connected the stories back to the theme of his presentation. Each of the eight people who spoke that day structured their presentations in the same way—either revealing something entirely new that the investors didn't know or familiar information repackaged in an unfamiliar way. When asked to rate the quality of the presentations on a five-point scale from "poor" to "excellent," nearly 100 percent of the respondents said the presentations were "very good" or "excellent," making the event among the best corporate update the investors had seen all year.

AN INTROVERT STEPS OUT OF HER SHELL

Introvert Susan Cain stepped out of her shell to teach millions of TED viewers something new about the power of solitude. TED celebrates the world's top minds who give the presentation of their lives, yet TED speaker Susan Cain argues there's "zero correlation between being the best talker and having the best ideas."[13] With that one statement, Cain forced many in the audience that day to question their perception that outgoing, social, and talkative people have a corner on ideas. "Some of our transformative leaders in history have been introverts," Cain said.

In a society that encourages brainstorming, group dynamics, "crowd-sourcing," and other collaborative systems, Cain makes a persuasive argument that solitude is a crucial ingredient for creativity to flourish. "The more freedom that we give introverts to be themselves, the more likely that they are to come up with their own unique solutions to these problems."

Cain's book, *Quiet*, became a bestseller and her TED talk has been viewed more than four million times. "Introverts, the world needs you and it needs the things you carry. So I wish you the best of all possible journeys and the courage to speak softly."

Cain is a successful public speaker because she forces us to look at the world differently. In my journalism career and later, as an executive communication coach, I lost count of how many times I heard, "My topic is boring," or, "What I do is not that interesting," or, "They don't pay attention to my presentation because they've heard it before." Maybe your audience has heard some of the information before, but they don't know what you know and they might have seen a version of the data or information that just didn't click. You'll grab their attention if you can teach them just one thing they didn't know before.

Steve Case pioneered the modern Internet when he cofounded AOL. He's a very smart guy. He's also very wealthy, ranking 258 on the Forbes list of richest people in America. When asked for his favorite TED talks, Case said Cain's presentation was "unforgettable" and on his personal top-10 list. As chairman and CEO of the investment firm Revolution, Case is open to fresh insights that will help him make better investment decisions. "Revolution invests in people and ideas that change the world. It takes talent and passion, not just capital, to build great companies."[14] And Cain gave Case a new way of looking at the world.

You might be delivering a presentation to a wealthy venture capitalist or someone whom you perceive to be smarter than you in a particular field. Make no mistake—the smarter they are, the wealthier they are, the more likely they are to be persuaded if you give them a new lens through which to see the world.

I recall speaking to one of the early Google investors at the famous investment firm Sequoia Capital. He told me that when the Google guys, Sergey Brin and Larry Page, walked into the office they offered a one-sentence pitch that changed this investor's perspective. "Google provides access to the world's information in one click." The preceding sentence could very well be the most lucrative 10 words in corporate history. Google was not the world's first search engine, but it was a better system because it ranked sites based on relevance and not just on search terms. Investors had seen a number of entrepreneurs pitch their search technologies and at least one was exploring a similar strategy, but the "Google guys" pitched their company more effectively and won the early funding that helped launch the brand.

EXPLORE OUTSIDE YOUR FIELD

You'll become a more interesting person if you're interested in learning and sharing ideas from fields that are much different from your own. Great innovators connect ideas from different fields. When I wrote *The Apple Experience* about the Apple Retail Store, I learned that Apple executives visited the Ritz-Carlton to learn more about customer service. In turn, many other brands outside of technology have studied Apple to improve their own customer experience. Great innovators apply ideas from fields other than their own.

I knew an executive with a large public relations company who won a major account with a redevelopment agency tasked with the project of securing federal dollars to help New Orleans recover after Hurricane Katrina. I worked in a different division for the same PR firm. As a former vice president of media training for this firm, I sat through plenty of new-business meetings where the group discusses how to pitch a prospect. Usually these meetings are set in the most uncreative environments imaginable—gray, drab conference rooms, darkened so that everyone can see the dry PowerPoint slides. This one executive, however, knew better than to confine his pitch team to a conference room for two days and hope for creative ideas to emerge. Instead, he and his team toured the Lower Ninth Ward, the hardest-hit area of New Orleans after the hurricane.

The executive's team was so moved by the poverty and suffering they saw, they decided it was best to ditch the PowerPoint and speak from their hearts. Each member of the team spoke with no slides and no notes. Instead, they spoke about what they had seen and why they wanted to play a role in the rebuilding effort. It was almost as if they entered the pitch with mud still on their feet. This team did get the account and, later, one of the decision-makers said they had won the account by the time they had left the room.

Only through seeing your own world through a fresh lens will you be able to give your audience a new way of looking at their world.

TEDnote

BOMBARD THE BRAIN WITH NEW EXPERIENCES. Building novel concepts into your presentation does require some creativity and a new way of looking at the world. One technique to jump-start your creativity is to embrace new experiences. The brain takes shortcuts. Its mission, after all, is to conserve energy. Neuroscientists have found that only through bombarding the brain with new experiences do we force our minds to look at the world through a new lens. That means you need to get out of the office once in while. Experience new events, people, and places. Most important, incorporate those new experiences into your presentations.

SUCCESSFUL PRESENTATIONS REVEAL IDEAS YOU'D NEVER CONSIDERED

When *Fast Company* asked famed interviewer Charlie Rose his opinion on what makes a great conversation, he said, "They take you on a ride, on a journey. They grab you, and you hear the sense of rhythm, and it goes and builds. Ultimately, it may even take you to ideas you'd never considered, to places that allow you to reinvent yourself or your business."[15] Great conversations or presentations *take you to ideas you'd never considered*.

Today's social-media climate is a cacophony of ideas, mostly ones that are clichéd, hackneyed, trite, and overused. How many times have you heard an athlete or a CEO say, "There is no *I* in team." How many times have you heard a consultant suggest, "Great leaders listen." How many times have you heard marriage counselors recommend better communication as the secret to a long and happy marriage? There's truth to all these observations, but when you've heard admonitions packaged and delivered the same way time and time again, they lose their punch. They lose their ability to get you to think differently. They lose their ability to inspire. When the marriage counselor John Gray wrote *Men Are from Mars, Women Are from Venus,* it made you think. It was intriguing. It contained some old information and some new, packaged in a way that made the content fresh and novel. It also saved a lot of marriages, but it wouldn't have stood a chance if it hadn't been remarkable.

ARE YOU REMARKABLE?

Seth Godin is a popular blogger and marketer who has made a career out of delivering smart ideas differently. He told the TED audience in February 2003 that in a society with too many choices and too little time, our natural inclination is to ignore most of it.

> My parable here is you're driving down the road and you see a cow, and you keep driving because you've seen cows before. Cows are invisible. Cows are boring. Who's going to stop and pull over and say—oh, look, a cow. Nobody. But if the cow was purple, you'd notice it for a while. I mean, if all cows were purple you'd get bored with those, too. The thing

that's going to decide what gets talked about, what gets done, what gets changed, what gets purchased, what gets built, is: is it remarkable? And "remarkable" is a really cool word because we think it just means neat, but it also means—worth making a remark about.[16]

Seth Godin went on to publish a book titled *Purple Cow* in the same year as his TED talk. Godin's point—one that he has mastered himself—is that delivering the same tired information in the same boring way as everyone else will fail to get you noticed. You'll have a brown cow instead of a purple one. Put a little different spin on your content, give it a "hook" as we call it in journalism, and your listeners will be far more receptive to your message.

The brain is just "a lazy piece of meat," according to neuroscientist Gregory Berns. In order to force the brain to see things differently, you must find new and novel ways to help the brain *perceive* information differently. "The brain must be provided with something that it has never before processed to force it out of predictable perceptions."[17]

This thirst for knowledge, the craving to force the brain out of "predictable perceptions," is why Edi Rama captivated a TEDx audience with his solution to curb corruption and reduce crime in his native Albania. For about a decade, Rama was the mayor of Tirana, the capital of the tiny country.

Tirana was once considered one of the most corrupt cities in the world. It was the city of mud, garbage, derelict buildings, and gray . . . lots and lots of gray. It was a depressing and demoralizing place. In 2000, Rama implemented a series of reforms that included demolishing old buildings and, most noticeably, painting the outside of Tirana's buildings in bright colors. He treated the exterior of the city's buildings as his canvas and, as he'd been a painter before he became a politician, he knew a little about art.

"Within weeks of being elected to City Hall in 2000, Rama began hiring painters to coat Tirana's gray, drab façades with dazzling colors, reminiscent of Marseilles or Mexico City. Today parts of Tirana, a city of about 650,000 people, resemble a Mondrian painting, the blues, yellows and pinks a shattering break from Albania's 45-year grim isolation under a communist dictatorship."[18]

As gray gave way to color, crime dropped and parks sprang up. People felt safer and had more pride in their city. Rama walked down a newly colored street one day and came across a shopkeeper tearing down the old shutters from his window and putting up a glass façade.

"Why did you throw away the shutters?" I asked him.

"Well, because the street is safer now," he answered.

"Safer? Why? They have posted more policemen here?"

"Come on, man! What policemen? You can see it for yourself. There are colors, streetlights, new pavement with no potholes, trees. So it's beautiful; it's safe."

Rama's passion for art, along with his natural curiosity, allowed him to solve a problem most people thought could never be solved. Rama did exactly what Gregory Berns recommends—he perceived the information differently.

Audiences of any type, speaking any language, love to hear about new and novel ways to solve problems. After all, we're wired for it!

Some speakers take a defeatist attitude. They don't think they have anything new to teach people. Sure they do. We all do. We all have unique stories to tell. You might not have the same experiences as the speakers in this chapter, but you have stories just as interesting and valuable in your journey of discovery. Pay attention to the stories of your life. If they teach you something new and valuable, there's a good chance other people will want to hear about it.

Sex Sells, Even at TED

TEDsters have a ravenous appetite for knowledge in a variety of categories. Sex is no exception. Some speakers have raised intriguing answers—or at the least promise of an answer—to intimate topics.

In February 2009, science journalist Mary Roach revealed "The 10 Things You Didn't Know about Orgasm" and received more than three million views.

Helen Fisher attracted 2.5 million views with her presentation "Why We Love, Why We Cheat." At TEDMED in April 2012, Diane Kelly revealed what people don't know about the male sex organ. Jenny McCarthy talked about what we don't know about marriage, and Amy Lockwood educated a TED audience on what we don't know about distributing condoms to reduce HIV in Africa. It seems as though when it comes to sex, people are more curious about what they don't know than they are about what they know for sure.

TED GIVES YOUR BRAIN A CONSTANT WORKOUT

Dr. James Flynn, political-studies professor at the University of Otago in New Zealand, believes the world's population is getting smarter, and not just a little smarter, but much, much smarter. His theory is so widely accepted in academic circles, it's been named the "Flynn Effect." Flynn himself describes it this way: "If you compare people today of eighteen years of age with people who were eighteen years old ten, twenty, thirty, forty, fifty years ago, the present eighteen-year-olds will get much higher scores on IQ tests."[19]

Flynn discovered that IQ scores rose for each generation, not just in a few places but in all countries in which IQ data were available. Discussions of the Flynn Effect don't necessarily focus on the finding but on the *reasons* behind it. The most logical and accepted answer seems to be greater access to education. People in most countries are spending more time learning, in formal educational settings and online, through sites like TED.com. According to an article in *The New York Times*, "Flynn argues that IQ is rising because in industrialized societies we give our brains a constant mental workout that builds up what we might call our brain sinews."[20]

TED's success may rely partly on our growing IQs and the fact that people crave a mental workout. TED.com videos have been viewed more than one billion times. That's an extraordinary number of views if you consider the fact that the 18-minute videos are, essentially, presentations. Think about most of the business presentations you see—are they inspiring? Interesting? Intriguing? It's not likely. The speakers simply haven't learned to *Talk Like TED*. They haven't learned that the brain loves novelty or how to deliver it.

"What TED celebrates is the gift of the human imagination."
—Sir Ken Robinson, TED 2006

THE TWITTER-FRIENDLY HEADLINE

In July 2009, the bestselling author of *Drive*, Dan Pink, unraveled the puzzle of motivation in a TED presentation that has been viewed over five million times. When I asked Pink to describe his talk, he did it in one sentence: "The set of motivators we rely on doesn't work nearly as well as we think." The preceding sentence is comprised of 74 characters, easily conforming to the restrictions of a Twitter post, which has a maximum character count of 140.

If you can't explain your big idea in 140 characters or less, keep working on your message. The discipline brings clarity to your presentation and helps your audience recall the one big idea you're trying to teach them.

Before he became an author and a public speaker, Pink spent his career as a speechwriter, thinking about words and crafting words for political leaders. "Before a presentation I ask myself, 'What's the one thing I want people to take away?' After someone listens to your presentation the real test is when they leave and someone asks, 'What did that person talk about?' I want to be good enough that they have a clear answer to that question."[21] The answer, says Pink, is not an accumulation of little things, but the one big idea. "Executives and experts tend to get lost in the weeds and aren't always able to see things with a beginner's mind and from the audience's perspective."

It's not as easy to get lost in the weeds in 140 characters.

The first step to giving a TED-worthy presentation is to ask yourself, *What is the one thing I want my audience to know?* Make sure it easily fits within a Twitter post, what I call a "Twitter-friendly headline."

Remarkably, after reviewing the topics of every one of the more than 1,500 publicly available TED presentations on TED .com, I couldn't find one—not one—that was over 140 characters. And one of the longest titles, "Three predictions on the future of Iran, and the math to back it up" (67 characters), contains a rhetorical element that makes it easy to remember—the rule of three (see chapter 7).

Here are some sample topics from the most-viewed presentations on TED.com. Notice how each promises to teach you something new.

- **"Schools Kill Creativity" (Sir Ken Robinson)**

- **"How Great Leaders Inspire Action" (Simon Sinek)**

- **"Your Elusive, Creative Genius" (Elizabeth Gilbert)**

- **"The Surprising Science of Happiness" (Dan Gilbert)**

- **"The Power of Introverts" (Susan Cain)**

- **"8 Secrets of Success" (Richard St. John)**

- **"How to Live Before You Die" (Steve Jobs)**

The Twitter headline works for two reasons: (1) it's a great discipline, forcing you to identify and clarify the one key message you want your audience to remember and (2) it makes it easier for your audience to process the content.

Cognitive research has demonstrated that our brains need to see the big picture before details. John Medina once explained it to me this way: "Carmine, when primitive man ran into a tiger, he did not ask, 'How many teeth does the tiger have?' He asked, 'Will it eat me?'"[22] Your audience needs to see the big picture before learning the details. If you can't explain your product or idea in 140 characters, keep working at it until you can.

"Remarkable ideas come from every area of knowledge,"[23] according to TED curator Chris Anderson. "Every so often it makes sense to emerge from the deep trenches we spend our working lives digging, to step out and see the big picture and how the trenches interconnect. It's very inspiring." You might have one of these remarkable ideas, but it's imperative that you show your audience the big picture, "how the trenches interconnect."

TEDnote

CREATE A TWITTER-FRIENDLY HEADLINE. As you craft your next presentation, ask yourself, "What is the one thing I want my audience to know about my company, product, service, or idea?" Remember to make your headline specific and clear. Oftentimes my clients create what's really a tagline instead of a headline,

but it still doesn't tell me the one thing I need to know. From a well-crafted headline I should be able to identify what the product, service, or cause is as well as what makes it different or unique. Make sure your headline fits within the 140-character limit of a Twitter post. It's not only a good exercise; it's essential for marketing. Twitter is such a powerful platform for marketers that it's critical to create a 'tweetable' description that can be easily remembered and shared across social networks.

WE'RE EXPLORATION ADDICTS

Ben Saunders "drags heavy things around cold places," according to his Twitter profile. He was the youngest man to ski solo to the North Pole. Saunders is an adventurer, an arctic explorer. For 10 weeks he dragged 400 pounds of food, supplies, and a computer for blogging. It wasn't unusual for the temperature to sink to 50 degrees below zero. At times, Saunders was the only human within five million square miles.

Why did he do it? There was little to gain. No maps to be drawn, no gold or coal to source, no food to be found. Exploration fed his addiction. "I think polar expeditions are perhaps not that far removed from having a crack habit,"[24] Saunders told a TED audience in London. "In my experience, there is something addictive about tasting life at the very edge of what's humanly possible."

Keep in mind that your audience is made up of people who are naturally wired to explore. According to Saunders, people don't want to just watch and wonder. They want "to experience, to engage, to endeavor . . . that's where the real meat of life is to be found."

Saunders suggests that inspiration and growth come from "stepping away from what's comfortable . . . In life, we all have tempests to ride and poles to walk to, and I think metaphorically speaking, at least, we could all benefit from getting outside the house a little more often, if only we could sum up the courage."

TED.com videos allow you metaphorically to "step out of the house" and take these journeys of exploration with the world's top minds. Open the door. Take a look outside. You'll discover a world of magnificent presentations that will help you improve your public speaking skills and give you the tools to be a more successful person in any of your life's roles.

Secret #4: Teach Me Something New

Reveal information that's completely new to your audience, is packaged differently, or offers a fresh and novel way to solve an old problem.

TEDx speaker and designer Oliver Uberti once said, "Every superhero has an origin story. So do you. Don't follow someone else's. Create your own masterpiece." I find that most communicators are far more creative than they give themselves credit for. When they're encouraged to unleash their creativity and to take an innovative approach to presenting their ideas, they rise to the challenge.

5

Deliver Jaw-Dropping Moments

Thou shalt not simply trot out thy usual shtick.

—TED COMMANDMENT

NBC NEWS ANCHOR BRIAN WILLIAMS covers war, politics, and the economy. He doesn't cover presentations. Why should he? There are millions of PowerPoints delivered every day, so presentations, even those given by CEOs and other famous leaders, do not qualify as "breaking news." Williams made an exception for billionaire Bill Gates, who spoke at TED in February 2009.

Gates wants to solve big problems related to global poverty and childhood deaths. He can't do it alone. He needs to engage audiences. Remember, the brain does not pay attention to boring things. Gates knows this, so he came up with a unique hook to grab his audience's attention. It caught Williams by surprise, too. According to Brian Williams that night:

> Bill Gates, the billionaire founder of Microsoft, wanted to make a point when he appeared at a conference of some of

the biggest leaders of the tech industry. While on stage, he opened up a glass jar and said, "Malaria is spread by mosquitoes. I brought some here. I'll let them roam around. There is no reason only poor people should be infected." We're told the audience just sat there stunned, as any of us would be. Moments later he let them off the hook, letting the audience know the mosquitoes he brought were malaria free, but he did it to prove a point and point taken. Gates and his wife Melinda have dedicated their lives and their fortune to a lot of different charitable causes . . . including the eradication of malaria in poor countries in Africa and Asia where there are up to 500 million new cases every year.[1]

I know this might come as a shock, but television news reports often get things wrong. They did in the Williams piece. Gates did not say that there's no reason why only poor people should be infected. He said, "Malaria is, of course, transmitted by mosquitoes. I brought some here, just so you could experience this. We'll let those roam around the auditorium a little bit. There's no reason only poor people should have the experience."[2] Also, the audience did not sit in "stunned silence." They roared with laughter, cheered, and applauded. Gates effectively demonstrated:

Secret #5: Deliver Jaw-Dropping Moments

The jaw-dropping moment in a presentation is when the presenter delivers a shocking, impressive, or surprising moment that is so moving and memorable, it grabs the listener's attention and is remembered long after the presentation is over.

Why it works: Jaw-dropping moments create what neuroscientists call an emotionally charged event, a heightened state of

5.1: Bill Gates releasing mosquitos during his TED 2009 presentation. Courtesy of James Duncan Davidson/TED (http://duncandavidson.com).

emotion that makes it more likely your audience will remember your message and act on it.

GATES WASN'T FLIPPANT AT ALL. A few sentences earlier, Gates was talking about how many children's lives are saved due to better medicines and vaccines. "Each one of those lives matters a lot," he said. He delivered an empathetic presentation, saying that millions of people die from malaria every year. Gates used humor and a shocking moment to drive home his main point.

One popular technology blogger wrote the headline, "GATES UNLEASHES SWARM OF MOSQUITOES ON CROWD." Well, it wasn't exactly a "swarm" of mosquitoes (the small jar contained only a few). Regardless, the presentation went viral.

A Google search returns 500,000 links to the event. The original video on the TED.com site has attracted 2.5 million views, and that doesn't include the other Web sites that link to it.

Entrepreneur and Path CEO Dave Morin was the first to announce it on Twitter: "Bill Gates just released mosquitoes into the audience at TED and said: 'Not only poor people should experience this.'" eBay founder Pierre Omidyar tweeted: "That's it, I'm not sitting up front any more." A memorable moment gets shared, spreading the message much farther than in its immediate audience, often around the globe.

Gates spoke for 18 minutes. The mosquito shtick took up less than 5 percent of his total speaking time, yet today the mosquito moment is the part of the presentation people remember the most. Most water-cooler moments last as long as it takes to grab a drink of water before heading back to your office. Gates's water-cooler moment still gets noticed, discussed, and shared five years later.

In journalism we call the mosquito shtick "the hook." It's the wow moment, the showstopper, a rhetorical device that grabs your attention and persuades you to read or to share the story ("You've got to see Bill Gates releasing mosquitoes," you might tell a friend as you e-mail the link).

I'm not suggesting that you bring a jar of mosquitoes to your next presentation, but I am suggesting that you think about your content and identify the most important points you need to make. Then find a novel and memorable way to communicate those messages. Sometimes you need to surprise your audience in order to get them to care.

What's the first thing you should do when creating a Power-Point presentation? If you're like many people you'll say, "Open PowerPoint." Wrong answer. You should plan the story first. Just as a movie director storyboards the scenes before he begins shooting, you should create the story before you open the tool. You'll have plenty of time to design pretty slides once the story is complete, but if the story is boring, you've lost your audience before you've spoken a word.

I like to tap in to several senses when planning the story—seeing, touching, feeling. Stand up and go to a whiteboard, pick up a pen or a yellow legal pad, use a drawing application on a tablet, or even think while taking a walk—anything that engages several areas of your brain. Above all, regardless of the software you use (PowerPoint, Keynote, Prezi, etc.), don't open the software as your first step. Your presentation will be uninteresting and uninspired if you do.

PowerPoint gets a bad rap, but it's not a bad tool. It can—and is—often used to create stunning presentations. But if you don't have the story in the first place, your gorgeous slides won't matter. Every memorable story, film, or presentation has one scene or one event that everyone remembers because it's so impactful. It's such a well-known psychological device, researchers have at term for it.

UNLEASH AN EMOTIONALLY CHARGED EVENT

When Gates unleashed his "swarm" of mosquitoes, he hooked his audience precisely because it was shocking, unexpected, and different. It was what brain researchers call an "emotionally charged event." As with every technique in this book, it works because your brain is wired for it.

"An emotionally charged event (usually called an ECS, short for emotional competent stimulus) is the best-processed kind of external stimulus ever measured,"[3] says molecular scientist John Medina. "Emotionally charged events persist longer in our memories and are recalled with greater accuracy than neutral memories."

Medina says it all has to do with the amygdala, which is located in the prefrontal cortex. "The amygdala is chock-full of the neurotransmitter dopamine, and it uses dopamine the way an office assistant uses Post-it notes. When the brain detects an emotionally

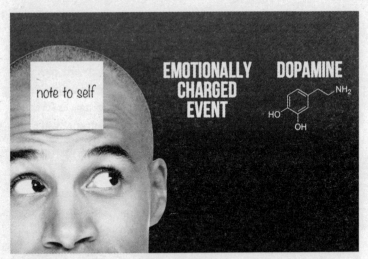

5.2: Illustration of Dopamine's influence on the brain. Created by Empowered Presentations @empoweredpres.

charged event, the amygdala releases dopamine into the system. Because dopamine greatly aids memory and information processing, you could say the Post-it note reads 'Remember This!' Getting the brain to put a chemical Post-it note on a given piece of information means that information is going to be more robustly processed."[4]

You're more likely to remember events that arouse your emotions than events that elicit a neutral response. Some scientists refer to such events as "flashbulb memories." As it turns out, there's a reason why you remember where you were on September 11, 2001 but you forget where you put your keys this morning. And understanding the difference can help you create more memorable, "jaw-dropping" presentations.

REMEMBERING 9/11 AND FORGETTING YOUR KEYS

When you experience an emotionally charged event (shock, surprise, fear, sadness, joy, wonder), it impacts how vividly you remember that particular event. You can probably remember not only *where* you were on September 11, 2001, when terrorists hijacked planes and flew them into the World Trade Center, but you also vividly recall *what* you were doing, and *whom* you were with, the expressions on their faces, what they may have said, and other small items in your environment that you otherwise wouldn't pay attention to. People remember vivid events; they forget mundane ones.

The University of Toronto psychology professor Rebecca Todd discovered that how vividly a person experiences an event influences how easily he or she can recall the event or the information later. Todd published her research in the *Journal of Neuroscience*. "We've discovered that we see things that are emotionally arousing with greater clarity than those that are more mundane,"[5] says Todd. "Whether they're positive—for example, a first kiss, the birth of a child, winning an award—or negative, such as traumatic events, breakups, or a painful and humiliating childhood moment that we all carry with us, the effect is the same. What's more, we found that how vividly we perceive something in the first place predicts how vividly we will remember it later on. We call this 'emotionally enhanced vividness' and it is like the flash of a flashbulb that illuminates an event as it's captured for memory."

Todd and her colleagues found that the brain region responsible for tagging memories, the amygdala, was most active when experiencing a "vivid" event. The researchers showed participants photographs that were "emotionally arousing and negative" such as scenes of sharks bearing their teeth, "emotionally arousing and positive" such as mild erotica, and "neutral scenes" such as people standing on an escalator. The researchers then performed two different studies to measure how much detail the participants retained. One study was done 45 minutes after they viewed the photographs and a follow-up study was performed one week later. "Both studies found that pictures that were rated higher in emotionally enhanced vividness were remembered more vividly," says Todd.

"Why did the audience remember Bill Gates releasing the mosquitoes?" I asked Todd in an interview for this book.

"It's memorable precisely because it's emotionally arousing, whether it is pleasant or unpleasant,"[6] she said.

"In the brain when you're emotionally aroused you produce higher levels of norepinephrine as well as stress hormones. We've known for some time that emotional arousal enhances memory. Our study was the first to show another effect of emotional arousal is that you actually perceive events more vividly at the time they occur, and that, too, increases the likelihood you'll remember it. Bill Gates's mosquitoes must have evoked surprise and fear in the audience members given that they didn't know the mosquitoes didn't carry malaria. Surprise and fear are both high arousal emotions."

Todd discovered that we actually encode important events in a far richer way than ordinary events. "It's as if the event is burned more vividly into our perceptual awareness," she told me. "Part of the reason is that the amygdala, a brain region that is key for tagging the emotional importance of things, talks to the visual cortex—the part of the brain that allows sight—and ramps up its activity so that we are actually perceiving those events more actively."

"Bottom line—what does your research teach people who are delivering presentations or communicating information that needs to be remembered and recalled?" I asked Todd.

"If you connect to an audience's emotional responses then they will perceive the information more vividly, be less distracted, and will be more likely to remember it. Use very concrete and meaningful examples to illustrate abstract points. Use images skillfully, whether they be beautiful, surprising, or disgusting."

The brain was not meant to process abstract concepts. Earlier I told you about my experience preparing executives at Toshiba America Medical Systems to present a new CT brain-scan machine. They told me that the machine was "the first dynamic high-volume CT that utilizes 320 ultra-high-resolution detector rows to image an entire organ in a single gantry rotation." I told them it was too abstract. "Can you make it concrete? Why should I care?" They said, "If you enter the hospital having suffered a stroke or a heart attack, doctors will be able to make a much more accurate diagnosis in far less time and that could save your life. Let's put it this way: our product could mean the difference between going home and living a full life or never recognizing your family again."

The clearest messages require specific, tangible explanations. You can't "wow" your audience if they don't understand you.

THE ICKIEST PRESENTATION

Recall neuroanatomist Dr. Jill, whose TED talk has had more than 10 million views. It was also the ickiest. If you have a weak stomach, you might want to avoid watching Dr. Jill's presentation. If you're brave enough, you'll see a real human brain with a 17-inch spinal cord attached.

Two minutes into Dr. Jill's presentation she said, "If you've ever seen a human brain, it's obvious that the two hemispheres are completely separate from one another. And I have brought for you a real human brain. So this is a real human brain."[7] With that, she turned to an assistant carrying a tray with a brain. Dr. Jill put on gloves, picked up the brain, and let the brain stem and spinal cord flop over the tray. The vocal expressions of disgust were audible from the audience. "This is the front of the brain, the back of brain with the spinal cord hanging down, and this is how it would be positioned inside of my head," Dr. Jill said as she held the organ for everyone to see.

Dr. Jill explained how the sides of the brain are positioned, how they communicate, and what roles they play. Many people in the audience squirmed, shuffled uncomfortably, and pinched their lips in disgust. But if you look carefully at their facial expressions you'll find something remarkable. People were leaning in, literally on the edge of their seats. Some people had their hands over the mouths; others placed their index fingers on the cheek, completely immersed in the presentation. They were deeply involved. Disgusted, perhaps, but emotionally aroused and engaged—really paying attention.

If more teachers gave "icky" presentations—emotionally charged ones—students would retain more of what they learn in high school and college.

Dr. Jill trotted out her real-human-brain prop again in 2013 for a presentation for TEDxYouth. "This is a real human brain. And when I look at this brain I am reminded that we are neurocircuitry . . . we know more about the human brain than we've ever known before and we've learned things in the last ten to twenty years—most of your life span—that have completely shifted the way neuroscientists think about this organ and our relationship with it."[8] By holding the brain as she opens her talk, the audience is riveted and more vividly focused on her words, not just the prop in her hands. Now they are receptive to her fundamental theme and key lesson: teenagers' brains are vulnerable, but teens also have the ability to choose their thoughts, which trigger a positive or negative physiological response. "This is your brain. This is your instrument. This is your tool. And this is your power," she concluded. In 16 minutes, Dr. Jill gave the teens in her audience one of the most profound and memorable presentations they're likely to see in school.

So, back to the original point made earlier in this chapter: why do you remember the details about an event such as 9/11 but tend to misplace your keys? Why do we remember Dr. Jill's demonstration or Gates's mosquitoes but we forget 99 percent of PowerPoint presentations that we see? The brain is wired to recall emotionally vivid events and to ignore the ordinary, the mundane. If you want to stand out in a sea of mediocre presentations, you must take emotional charge of your audience.

> "The brain remembers the emotional components of an experience better than any other aspect."
> —John Medina, molecular biologist and author of *Brain Rules*

THE UNDISPUTED KING OF WOW

Steve Jobs was the king of the emotionally charged event, the "wow moment." In every presentation, he informed, educated, and entertained. Jobs transformed a presentation into a spectacle worthy of a Broadway production. His presentations had heroes, villains, props, characters, and that one memorable showstopper when you knew that the price of admission was well worth it.

Years before PowerPoint or Keynote software were even invented, and even years before TED exploded on the scene, Steve Jobs was doing TED-like presentations that kept the audience on the edge of their seats.

In 1984, more than 2,500 employees, analysts, and media filled the Flint Center at De Anza College for a product launch that would revolutionize everything about the way we use computers—Macintosh. The 16-minute product launch also stands the test of time as one of most dramatic presentations ever delivered by a corporate titan.

First, Jobs described the power and the features of the new computer, along with pictures. "All of this power fits into the box that is one-third the size and weight of an IBM PC,"[9] he said. Most presenters would have wrapped up, telling the audience when the product would go on sale and what its price point would be. Instead Jobs wowed the crowd with one extra, unexpected surprise.

"You've just seen pictures of Macintosh. Now I'd like to show you Macintosh in person. All of the images you are about to see on the large screen are being generated by what's in that bag." Jobs walked over to a small table in the middle of the stage. A black canvas bag was the only item in the middle of the table. Slowly, and without saying a word for nearly one minute, Jobs lifted the Macintosh from the bag, placed it on the table, reached into his pocket, pulled out a floppy disk, carefully inserted the disk into the computer, and walked away. The lights dimmed, the *Chariots of Fire* theme began to play, and a series of images filled the screen, fonts and art that had never been seen on a personal computer.

The audience cheered, hollered, and applauded. If Jobs had ended there, it would have been one of the most memorable presentations of its time. But Steve Jobs didn't become Steve Jobs by being understated. He had one more wow moment to pull on the audience. Jobs said he would let "Macintosh speak for itself for the first time ever." On cue, Macintosh spoke in a digitized voice: "Hello, I am Macintosh. It sure is great to get out of that bag. Unaccustomed as I am to public speaking, I'd like to share with you a maxim I thought of the first time I met an IBM mainframe: Never trust a computer you can't lift."

The video from the event has been viewed well over three million times on YouTube. It was a profound moment—unexpected and unique—an emotionally charged event that left an indelible stamp on the audience in the room that day and on millions who have watched it since.

The 1984 Macintosh presentation was far from being the only dramatic presentation Steve Jobs ever gave. Fortunately for presenters everywhere, he continued to refine his style and deliver wow moments with every major product announcement, most of them captured forever on YouTube. Here are just a few examples of how Steve Jobs built wow moments into his presentations. They should give you some ideas, too.

"We See Genius"

In 1997 Steve Jobs returned to Apple after a 12-year absence. With about two minutes left in his first public presentation since his return, Jobs slowed the rate of his speech, lowered his voice, and said, "I think you always had to be a little different to buy an Apple computer . . . I think the people that do buy them are the creative spirits in the world. They are the people that are not out just to get a job done; they are out to change the world and they are out to change the world using whatever great tools they can get. And we make tools for those kind of people . . . A lot of times, people think they're crazy. But in that craziness, we see genius. And those are the people we're making tools for."[10]

A showstopper can be as simple as speaking to the audience from your heart—no slides, no props, no video, just you. If you'll recall from chapter 1, it's often as easy as filling in the rest of this sentence: What makes my heart sing is . . ."

1,000 Songs in Your Pocket

In 2001 Apple introduced the iPod. The MP3 music player was not the first portable player on the market (remember the Sony Walkman)? The MP3 did transfer music faster from a computer, but that wasn't the wow moment. Jobs had decided to focus on the size of the device as his showstopper.

"What's so special about iPod?"[11] he asked the audience. "It's ultra-portable. iPod is the size of a deck of cards. That's tiny. It's also lighter than most of the cell phones you have in your pocket. But we didn't stop there . . . this amazing little device holds 1,000 songs and goes right in my pocket. I happen to have one, as a matter of fact." Jobs reached into the pocket of his jeans and pulled out the first device that could store that much music and fit into your pocket.

Jobs was a genius at using statistics as showstoppers. Apple executives continue to do the same, introducing statistics in such a novel way that the stats themselves become memorable. Introducing the iPad Mini for the first time, Apple vice president of marketing Phil Schiller said the tablet is "7.2 mm thin. That's about a quarter thinner than a fourth generation iPad." Schiller knew the statistics alone wouldn't be memorable so he chose a novel way of representing the data. "To put it into context, it's as thin as a pencil," he said as a pencil appeared next to the iPad Mini on Schiller's slide. "It weighs just .68 pounds. That's over 50 percent lighter than the previous iPad. In context, it's as light as a pad of paper. We were going to say a book, but books are much heavier!" I've talked to bloggers who covered the event—most don't remember the exact specs of the tablet but they all remember the pencil and the pad of paper. Schiller's novel approach to numbers created an emotionally charged event.

Three Products in One

In 2007, Steve Jobs introduced the iPhone. Remember, an emotionally charged event can include the element of surprise. Steve Jobs did just that. He told the audience that Apple would introduce three new products. "The first one is a wide-screen iPod with touch controls. The second is a revolutionary mobile phone. And the third is a breakthrough Internet communications device."[12] He repeated the three products again. Then he said, "An iPod, a phone, and an Internet communicator. An iPod, a phone, are you getting it? These are not three separate devices. This is one device. And we are calling it iPhone."

The audience erupted with laughter, cheers, and applause. This is one of my favorite examples of an emotionally charged event because it proves that you don't have to be extravagant or to have elaborate props to elicit a memorable moment. Sometimes, all it takes is a surprising, creative twist on the message.

CREATE A HOLY SMOKES MOMENT

I call the "emotionally charged event"—or what some refer to as the wow moment—the "holy smokes moment." It's the one moment in a presentation when you drive your point home, your listener's jaw drops, and she says to herself, "Holy smokes, I get it now!" It's the first thing they remember about your presentation and the first thing they say to someone else who didn't see it but wants to know about your presentation. A holy smokes moment need not be fancy. It might be something as simple as a short, personal story. Here are five ways to create a holy smokes moment in your very next presentation (each of these has appeared in TED presentations).

Props and Demos

Mark Shaw created Ultra-Ever Dry, an invention with one astonishing feature—it repels liquids and stays dry. At TED 2013, he demonstrated his superhydrophobic nanotechnology coating that he said acts as a shield against most liquids.

Shaw took a bucket of red paint and threw it on a whiteboard. As the paint dripped down and off the board, letters began to be appear—the giant capital letters were coated with Ultra-Ever Dry. Slowly the audience saw a *T* followed by an *E* and finally the *D* to spell TED. The audience cheered and rose to their feet. Shaw had created a memorable demo that uniquely connected with the conference and its audience. It would certainly be a demo they would always remember.

When I worked with a group of nuclear scientists at one of America's top labs run by the U.S. Department of Energy, I learned two things about nuclear science. First, nothing is more complicated than nuclear technology. So, don't ever make the excuse that your content is too complex or technical to be explained simply. Second, America's nuclear labs are involved in a lot more than protecting the stability of our nuclear resources. They provide important research and data in the areas of global climate change, nuclear nonproliferation, clean energy, and counterterrorism.

This particular group in the organization had the task of developing presentation material that scientists would take to Congress to ask for funding projects. One of the projects involved next-generation weaponry. One example was a bomb that could be remotely guided into a room filled with bad guys, wipe out the room, and leave the neighboring rooms and adjacent homes or buildings unscathed.

I realize it's controversial, but the technology can save lives by taking out the bad guys—the terrorists—and saving the innocent.

The scientists decided to build an emotionally charged event into their presentation. They marked the meeting room in which the presentation would be delivered with two rows of tape on the floor. During the presentation, they would point to the floor. "Everyone standing within xx feet would be eliminated [they never told me how many feet]. Those of you beyond the second row of tape would survive without a scratch." I wasn't in the room when the presentations were delivered, but I'm sure the lawmakers in that room experienced a jaw-dropping moment.

Suffice it to say they received their funding.

TEDnote

DOES YOUR PRESENTATION NEED A PROP? Let me share an example of why it might. I work with a lot of agribusiness clients, and I know more about sustainability and protecting against food-borne illnesses than most people due to my extensive work with growers who supply most of the nation's produce. One client was launching a product to help growers track crates of produce back to the source and the technology for this product was housed in a green box that contained all the necessary tools to execute the "trace back." While preparing them for a major presentation that would roll out this product to the larger agricultural community, I realized that something was missing. I asked the group, "Are you going to incorporate the actual box into the presentation somehow?" They responded, "No. We didn't think about that. We just intended to show PowerPoint slides."

Far too often presenters "don't think about it." It's highly

possible that your presentation could benefit from using a prop of some sort to emphasize a key message. Sometimes it takes an outsider to help you figure it out, so don't hesitate to show your content to a friend or colleague for his or her input. The minds working together may come up with the perfect idea.

Unexpected and Shocking Statistics

Nearly every popular TED presentation contains data, statistics, or numbers to reinforce the theme of the talk. Every presentation intended to influence a decision should do the same. However, some of the best TED speakers are known to deliver statistics that are more than a bit shocking. Among them:

- "This country is very different today than it was 40 years ago. In 1972, there were 300,000 people in jails and prisons. Today, there are 2.3 million. The United States now has the highest rate of incarceration in the world."   —Bryan Stevenson

- "Why are we ignoring the oceans? If you compare NASA's annual budget to explore the heavens, that one-year budget would fund NOAA's budget to explore the oceans for 1,600 years."   —Robert Ballard

- "One in a hundred regular people is a psychopath. So there's 1,500 people in this room. Fifteen of you are psychopaths."   —Jon Ronson

I work with many executives to help them craft their stories. Delivering statistics in new and novel ways can often result in jaw-dropping moments. I recall a meeting with an executive who represented the strawberry industry in California—the same executive I discussed in chapter 1. Most Californians do not realize that strawberries are an important crop to their state, even those people who live in the counties where strawberries are grown.

A full 90 percent of all strawberries consumed in the United States are grown in California. Importantly, strawberries enrich the communities where they are grown. In my conversation with the spokesperson, I learned that strawberries make up only .5 percent of California's farmland yet create 10 percent of all agricultural jobs in the state. I learned that the payroll taxes paid in one California county alone were equivalent to the combined salaries of all elementary-school teachers in the county and that the average strawberry farmworker made more than the average retail-store employee. These statistics were intended to explain the importance of the industry to the California economy, but the raw numbers themselves would have lost their punch without context. The stats were not new to the executive, but they were to the majority of people he had to influence (consumers, press, retail buyers, partners).

TEDnote

STATS CAN ROCK. Persuasion occurs when you reach a person's heart and head—logic and emotion. You'll need evidence, data, and statistics to back up your argument. Make numbers meaningful, memorable, and jaw-dropping by placing them in a context that the audience can relate to. A statistic doesn't have to be boring. My advice: never leave data dangling. Context matters. If your presentation has a number or data point that is groundbreaking or paramount, think about how you might package it and make it appealing to the listener. Enlist the help of someone else on your team. Sometimes it takes a brainstorm to package statistics in the best, most memorable way.

Pictures, Images, and Videos

Raghava KK is an artist who uses brain waves to manipulate his art in real time. As he spoke to his TED audience, Raghava was wearing a biofeedback headset that recorded his brain activity.

The headset was connected to the computer on which he was displaying the images.

The audience saw a photo of an old woman's face that Raghava affectionately called "Mona Lisa 2.0." The borders of the slide revealed his brain wave activity. In the live demo, Raghava said that not only could the audience see his mental state (attentive, meditative, focused), but he could actually project his mental state onto the woman's face. "When I am calm she is calm. When I am stressed she is stressed,"[13] he said. Sure enough, when his brain waves or mental state changed, so did the woman's smile. Her frown grew more intense before turning up into a smile.

Visuals have punch. An evocative slide, a funny or insightful video clip, a thrilling demonstration—all are novel elements that could really move the needle with your audience.

Memorable Headlines

Stewart Brand is a futurist who presented a bold prediction to the TED 2013 audience in Long Beach. Biotech is accelerating four times faster than digital technology, he said. In Brand's opinion, that means we can bring extinct animals back to life. "We will get woolly mammoths back," he said. *We will get woolly mammoths back.* In media training, we call that a sound bite—a short, provocative, repeatable phrase that is likely to be retweeted, posted on Facebook, and repeated in the news cycle. At this point in my career, I know a sound bite when I hear it. Sure enough, Brand's prediction blew up on social media networks, including Twitter thanks to a retweet from the National Geographic Channel.

When I started training executives to appear in the media, the sound bite was critical to getting the story across in newspapers and television news. Today, social media make the sound bite even more important. The key to being a great spokesperson is also to craft a succinct message that conveys your big idea. When people share quotes via Twitter, Facebook, LinkedIn, and other social networks, it's even more important that you feed those platforms with catchy, repeatable quotes.

The sound bite is so important that TED has a site and a Twitter handle dedicated to the best quotes from its speakers (@TEDQuote). Here are some of most popular ones:

- **"If you're not prepared to be wrong, you'll never come up with anything original."** —Sir Ken Robinson

- **"There's zero correlation between being the best talker and having the best ideas."** —Susan Cain

- **"Don't fake it till you make it. Fake it till you become it."** —Amy Cuddy

- **"Behind most Afghan girls who succeed is a father who recognizes that her success is his success."** —Shabana Basij-Rasikh

- **"Numbers are the musical notes with which the symphony of the universe is written."** —Adam Spencer

If you'd like to see more quotes, you can visit TED.com/quotes and read more than 2,000 quotes from speakers. You can search all the quotes, the top quotes, or browse by category. Repeatable quotes are so important in spreading the message that TED actually attempts to find the most memorable quotes of the talk on which to hook viewers.

Hook people. Craft and deliver repeatable quotes. Your ideas deserve to be remembered.

Personal Stories

I dedicated a whole chapter to storytelling earlier, but it's impossible not to discuss stories here again because personal stories often become the jaw-dropping moment in a presentation. Freeman Hrabowski tells stories to attract publicity for his cause. Hrabowski is the chancellor for the University of Maryland, Baltimore. He has been featured on *60 Minutes* and was named one of *TIME* magazine's most influential people for his work to inspire more minority and low-income students into graduate school for science and engineering.

In February 2013 Hrabowski mesmerized a TED audience with stories—success stories showcasing his students as well as stories of his personal transformation. He began with a story about a transformational experience in his life at the age of 12.

> One week in church, I didn't really want to be there, I heard this man say, "If we can get children to participate in this peaceful demonstration here in Birmingham, we can show America that even children know the difference between right and wrong and that children really do want to get the best possible education." I looked up and said, "Who is that man?" They told me it was Dr. Martin Luther King. I said to my parents, "I want to go." And they said "absolutely not." We had a rough go of it. Somehow I said, "You guys are like hypocrites. You make me go to this, make me listen, the man wants me to go and now you say no." They thought about it all night. They literally cried and prayed and thought, "Will we let our twelve-year-old participate in this march? He'll probably have to go to jail." They decided to let me . . . while I was there in jail, Dr. King came in and said, "What you children do this day will have an impact on children who have not been born."[14]

Great communicators are good storytellers. Stories create impact moments. Not only do they make an emotional impact, as we learned in chapter 2, well-told stories that reinforce your theme will draw in your audience.

I always challenge executives to let their guard down, to break down the barrier between themselves and the audience, and to teach us something about themselves that will help their audiences see them in a different light. The stories they tell are often very emotional. I worked with one woman who had a leading role at one of the world's largest and most admired technology companies, Intel. She grew up poor in an African-American home of six children. That little girl fell in love with science and math and became an engineer. The story didn't end there, however. All of her five siblings became successful engineers as well. By the time this Intel engineer finished her story, her colleagues in the room were left in tears and truly inspired by this "new" information. The story wasn't new to her, but it was to the rest of us.

ENDING ON A HIGH NOTE

While I was writing this book, I took a break and accompanied my wife to a concert by the pop musician Pink. I like some of Pink's songs and expected an okay performance, in other words, the usual shtick. But, like a great TED presentation, Pink didn't trot out the usual pop-music show.

Near the end of the concert, Pink, dressed in a gold bodysuit, jumped into a harness that propelled her high in the air like Tinker Bell and carried her across the entire length of the sold-out 17,000-person arena. Perches were stationed around the arena, where Pink would land for a few moments, closer to fans, then get pulled away to zip across the stadium while belting out one of her anthems. A reviewer for the *Hollywood Reporter* called it the showstopper. "It was beginning to seem like just another pop show with song-and-dance routines, but she pulled out all the stops with the encore of *So What* . . . The stunt was so mind-blowing that most of the crowd attempted to capture it on their camera phones, while others watched in amazement."

Pink's "mind-blowing" moment in the show was designed to leave the artist—and audience—on a high note. Everyone needs a showstopper: musicians, actors, and performers of all types, including presenters and public speakers. The showstopper seals the deal and permanently brands the message in our minds.

As we've discussed, a showstopper might be something as simple as a short personal story. I was in a conference room with the business-development officer of one of the world's leading oil-and-energy companies. His staff and I had created a narrative for his presentation at the annual global meeting of internal employees. He had solid information about the past year's results and a positive message about the future. We structured the story so that it was concise, clear, and memorable. But it was missing a jaw-dropping moment.

I turned to the executive and said, "Why are you really passionate about this company? Set aside your talking points and your PowerPoint. Just tell me, from your heart."

What happened next offered an astonishing lesson in developing an emotionally charged event. The executive paused, thought about it, reached into his pocket, and pulled his business card from his wallet. "Carmine, this card gets me an audience with prime ministers and presidents. It opens the door. But it's our commitment to protecting their most precious resources that keeps the door open." As he spoke, the executive's eyes began welling up with tears, and his voice broke. He continued, "When Russia awarded us with an exploration contract for the Baltic Sea [a contract worth $32 billion], the Russian president said to me, 'We've given you access to Russia's most prized asset because we trust you to protect it.' Our partners trust us because our people do business with integrity. I've never been more proud to work for any organization in my life."

We all looked at one another across the table, a little uncomfortable because the executive was clearly moved and so were we.

After a short pause I quietly said, "Have you ever said that in a public presentation?"

"No, I haven't."

"Well, you will now," I said.

The executive delivered his presentation to thousands of employees and concluded it by taking the card out of his wallet and repeating the same thing he had told us in the conference room. I didn't think he would get emotional again when he delivered it publicly, but he did. The employees saw a different side to their leader. They gave him a standing ovation, some employees could be seen wiping tears from their eyes, and at least one person approached the executive and said, "I've never been more proud to work for this organization."

Several weeks later we reviewed the surveys employees had been asked to fill out. They gave this particular executive the highest marks of any leader in the company's long history. Now he designs a showstopper in every presentation. It's usually a story, a video, a demonstration, a surprise guest, or simply a personal anecdote. All tactics get results.

Secret #5: Deliver Jaw-Dropping Moments

Every performer has at least one jaw-dropping moment—an emotionally charged event that your audience members will be talking about the next day. Every presentation needs one. Get one and use it. Your presentation content will make a better impact if it can be stamped onto the minds of your listeners.

6

Lighten Up

Over the past century a sense of humor has become a highly prized personality characteristic.

—ROD A. MARTIN, PSYCHOLOGIST

THE MOST POPULAR TED TALK ever is an unlikely winner: Sir Ken Robinson on why schools kill creativity. I mentioned earlier that his presentation is the most popular TED talk ever, but how could his 18-minute talk about education reform possibly attract more than 15 million views? People who are far more famous than Robinson have given speeches uploaded to YouTube—Conan O'Brien, Stephen Colbert, J. K. Rowling, and Oprah Winfrey— yet none of their videos comes close to matching Robinson's popularity.

Robinson's video went viral because our brains cannot ignore novelty. The brain also loves humor. Combine humor and novelty and you've got presentation gold. Robinson used a novel approach to discuss an old problem. The problem: how to teach our kids better. The novelty: humor.

"If you're at a dinner party, and you say you work in education—actually, you're not often at dinner parties, frankly, if you work in education,"[1] Robinson said as he opened his talk. The laughter started immediately and didn't let up as Robinson followed up his observation about working in education with another funny insight: "But if you are [asked to a party], and somebody says, 'What do you do?' and you say you work in education, you can see the blood run from their face. They're like, 'Oh my God, why me? My one night out all week.'"

Secret #6: Lighten Up

Don't take yourself (or your topic) too seriously. The brain loves humor. Give your audience something to smile about.

Why it works: Humor lowers defenses, making your audience more receptive to your message. It also makes you seem more likable, and people are more willing to do business with or support someone they like.

SIR KEN ROBINSON ARTFULLY WOVE anecdotes, stories, and humor into a narrative that drove home his main theme: America's educational system rewards test takers and stifles creativity, risk taking, and innovation. Here are some other examples of how Robinson made his audience think and laugh at the same time.

- "I heard a great story recently—I love telling it—of a little girl who was in a drawing lesson. She was six and she was at the back, drawing, and the teacher said this little girl hardly ever paid attention, and in this drawing lesson she did. The teacher was fascinated and she went over to her and she said, 'What are you drawing?' And the girl said, 'I'm drawing a picture of God.' And the teacher said, 'But nobody knows what God looks like.' And the girl said, 'They will in a minute.'"

- "I lived in Stratford-on-Avon until about five years ago. In fact, we moved from Stratford to Los Angeles. So you can imagine what a seamless transition that was. (Laughter) Actually, we lived in a place called Snitterfield, just outside Stratford, which is where Shakespeare's father was born. Are you struck by a new thought? I was. You don't think of Shakespeare having a father, do you? Do you? Because you don't think of Shakespeare being a child, do you? Shakespeare being seven? I never thought of it. I mean, he was seven at some point. He was in somebody's English class, wasn't he? How annoying would that be? Being sent to bed by his dad, you know, to Shakespeare, "Go to bed now and put the pencil down. And stop speaking like that. It's confusing everybody.""

- "Anyway, we moved from Stratford to Los Angeles, and I just want to say a word about the transition, actually. My son didn't want to come. I've got two kids. He's 21 now; my daughter's 16. He didn't want to come to Los Angeles. He loved it, but he had a girlfriend in England. This was the love of his life, Sarah. He'd known her for a month. Mind you, they'd had their fourth anniversary, because it's a long time when you're 16. Anyway, he was really upset on the plane, and he said, "I'll never find another girl like Sarah." And we were rather pleased about that, frankly, because she was the main reason we were leaving the country."

- "I like university professors, but you know, we shouldn't hold them up as the high-water mark of all human achievement. They're just a form of life. But they're rather curious, and I say this out of affection for them. There's something curious about professors in my experience—not all of them, but typically—they live in their heads. They live up there, and slightly to one side. They're disembodied, you know, in a kind of literal way. They look upon their body as a form of transport for their heads, don't they? (Laughter) It's a way of getting their head to meetings."

Robinson received a prolonged standing ovation. He inspired a live audience of 1,200 people that included billionaires, philanthropists, scientists, thinkers, and influencers. He inspired millions of others online.

I study inspiring communicators: who they are, how they do it, and how the rest of us can be inspiring, too. If Robinson had relied simply on content, few people would have paid attention to his presentation, because facts and literal content—by themselves—are unemotional. As we know from chapter 5, statistics are boring unless they are wrapped in an emotionally appealing package. When a skilled communicator brings statistics alive, data has the power to move us, inspire us, and call us to action.

Humor plays a key role in the playbooks of the world's most inspiring public speakers. Humor worked for Robinson. It will work for you, too, but you must learn to incorporate humor creatively and naturally. Repeating tired or, worse, crass or dirty jokes won't get you far. In fact it might turn off your audience. The most popular TED speakers do not tell jokes! Unless you're a professional comedian, jokes are not authentic. Think about it. When you meet a customer for the first time do you open the conversation with the latest joke you read on the Internet? No? Then why would you feel compelled to start a business presentation with one? A humorous observation, however, is perfectly appropriate and very effective. In this chapter you'll learn five humorous alternatives to telling a joke.

A joke poorly told or, worse, a well-delivered but tactless joke can diminish your reputation with your audience very quickly. I once held a workshop for a group of sales reps at a large, global travel company. Each sales agent gave a short presentation to the rest of the group. The person—a male—who delivered one

continued

of the most nicely designed presentations ended his pitch with a tactless joke about women.

Sexist jokes are not acceptable in any professional business presentation, and, given that the majority of his audience were successful saleswomen, it really bombed. As we went around the room to critique the presentation, nearly everyone complained about the joke. It distracted his audience from the very strong story he had told about the product. A comedian like Chris Rock can get away with jokes about the sexes, he gets paid handsomely to do it, and his audiences expect it. Your audiences don't expect you to be Chris Rock, so don't try to be.

THE BRAIN LOVES HUMOR

Dr. A. K. Pradeep is the founder of NeuroFocus, a Berkeley-based research company that uses neurological research to determine why consumers watch and buy what they do. "At their emotional core, the brains of modern humans are remarkably alike,"[2] he writes in *The Buying Brain*. Humor, it seems, is one of those tools the brain is hardwired to react to and is key to making a message new and novel.

When I met with Pradeep at his research facility, I learned that his experiments validate the existing research that brief, clear, and interesting conversations are more likely to resonate with listeners and are much more likely to be remembered and acted upon. How do you make messages interesting? According to Pradeep, use humor to make it novel. "The brain loves it," he says.

The University of Western Ontario psychology professor Rod A. Martin says people use humor to "reinforce their own status in a group hierarchy. For example, you are more likely to crack jokes and amuse others in a group in which you are the leader or have a position of dominance than in a group in which you have lower status and less power than others."[3]

In *The Psychology of Humor*, Martin argues that humor is used as an "ingratiation tactic," making it easier to be accepted in a group. This explains why so many famous comedians have experienced difficult childhoods or have gone through a period when they felt like outcasts. They used humor to ingratiate themselves to the group, and they used it so often that they refined it to the point where they could make a living at it. According to Martin:

> When we meet other people for the first time, we tend to quickly form impressions and make judgments about their personality characteristics such as their friendliness, trustworthiness, motives, and so on. Indeed, the ability to form relatively accurate impressions of others rapidly and efficiently may have been important for survival in our evolutionary history. One source of information that contributes to our initial impressions of others is the way they express humor. Humor is a form of interpersonal communication, and a good sense of humor is therefore an important social skill that we typically admire in others.[4]

Laughter also plays an important role in strengthening group cohesion, according to Martin. Humor, and laughter, is an example of what Martin calls affect-induction: "a method of communication, designed to capture the attention of others, to convey important emotional information, and to activate similar emotions in others . . . Laughter not only conveys cognitive information to others but it also serves the function of inducing and accentuating positive emotions in others, in order to influence their behavior and promote a more favorable attitude toward the one who is laughing."[5]

According to Martin, studies show that when we meet people who have a good sense of humor, we are more likely to attribute other desirable traits to their personalities. Studies have shown that humorous people are seen as friendly, extroverted, considerate, pleasant, interesting, imaginative, intelligent, perceptive, and emotionally stable.

When popular online dating sites in the United States ask their members what quality they find the most desirable trait in a mate, more than 80 percent answer "a sense of humor." When it comes to finding a mate, survey after survey shows that humor is more important than educational level, career success, or physical attraction. Unless you're pitching yourself into a round of speed-dating, you're probably not looking for a mate when you give a presentation, but you are seeking the attention and respect of your audience. Your audience is turned on by humor. Arouse them. Their devotion will help you be far more successful.

LAUGHING ALL THE WAY TO THE BANK

Having a sense of humor is important on the TED stage, for personal relationships, and in any business setting. In a study published in the *Harvard Business Review* ("Laughing All the Way to the Bank"), Fabio Sala compiled more than four decades of humor research and found, "Humor, used skillfully, greases the management wheels. It reduces hostility, deflects criticism, relieves tension, improves morale, and helps communicate difficult messages."[6]

Sala conducted his own research. He chose 20 executives from a food-and-beverage company, half of whom had been rated as average performers by their colleagues while the other half were characterized as outstanding performers. All the executives took part in a two-hour interview on the topic of leadership performance. Two observers categorized the content of the interviews and noted humorous references. Humor that included put-downs of others was coded as negative, while humor used to point out funny things or absurdities was coded as positive.

According to Sala, "The executives who had been ranked as outstanding used humor more than twice as often as average executives, a mean of 17.8 times per hour compared with 7.5 times per hour . . . When I looked at the executives' compensation for the year, I found that the size of their bonuses correlated positively with their use of humor during the interviews. In other words, the funnier the executives were, the bigger the bonuses."

Sala points out that merely "being funny" wasn't the key ingredient; rather, it reflected the important success component of emotional intelligence. "In my studies, outstanding executives used all types of humor more than average executives did, though they favored positive or neutral humor. But the point is not that more humor is always good or that positive humor is always better than negative, disparaging humor. In business, as in life, the key to the effective use of humor is how it's deployed. Don't try to be funny. But do pay closer attention to how you use humor, how others respond to your humor, and the messages you send. It's all in the telling."

If it's all in telling, how do you say something funny in a presentation? The first step sounds counterintuitive, but I assure you it's critical: *don't try to be funny*. Avoid telling jokes. The moment you start telling the joke about the blonde or the one about the rabbi and the priest, you're dead. Jokes work only for professional comedians at the top of their game.

You're not Jerry Seinfeld. When Seinfeld is working on a new act, he says, two-thirds of his jokes are garbage and largely bomb with his audience. Seinfeld works on jokes for years before he gets it just right.

In a video for the *New York Times* Web site, Seinfeld deconstructed the anatomy of a joke in great detail. He said he's been working on a "Pop-Tart joke" for two years. "It's a long time to spend on something that means absolutely nothing; but that's what I do and that's what people want me to do,"[7] he said. Then he deconstructed the joke he had been working on: "I like the first line to be funny right away. 'When I was a kid and they invented the Pop-Tart, the back of my head blew right off.' That got [the joke] started—a specific part of my head blew right off, not just my head . . ." For the next five minutes Seinfeld dissected each component—every sentence—of the rest of the joke. If a sentence is too long, he'll shave letters off words and count syllables to get it just right.

The video of Jerry Seinfeld is a fascinating insight into a brilliant comedian's mind. It taught me two things: (1) comedy is hard work and (2) the humor we use in presentations and how we deliver that humor should be carefully crafted and considered.

How can you be funny without telling jokes? I'd be rich if I got paid every time a client told me, "I'm not funny." You don't have to be funny to be humorous. You just have to be willing to do your homework to make your presentation entertaining. Here are five ways to add just the right amount of humor to your speech or presentation without spending two years developing a joke.

1. Anecdotes, Observations, and Personal Stories

Most TED presenters who elicit laughs from the audience tend to relate anecdotal information about themselves or people they know, observations about the world, or personal stories. If something happened to you and you found the humor in it, there's a good chance others will, too. Most of Sir Ken Robinson's humor was in the form of anecdotes and stories about himself, his son, his wife, etc.

This is the type of humor that works best in most business presentations. Anecdotes and observations are short stories or examples that are intended not to elicit a huge laugh but rather to put a smile on people's faces and endear the speaker to his or her audience. For example, at TED 2013, Dan Pallotta, the founder of the AIDS rides, made this observation about his role: "I also happen to be gay. Being gay and fathering triplets is by far the most socially innovative, socially entrepreneurial thing I have ever done."[8]

Dr. Jill Bolte Taylor generated a big laugh when she made a joke about herself recounting the moment when she was actually experiencing a stroke. Recall her earlier statement: "I realized, 'Oh my gosh! I'm having a stroke! I'm having a stroke!' The next thing my brain says to me is, 'Wow! This is so cool! How many brain scientists have the opportunity to study their own brain from the inside out?'"[9] With a comedian's perfect timing, Dr. Jill followed it up with this sentence: "Then it crosses my mind, 'But I'm a very busy woman! I don't have time for a stroke!'"

Starting a presentation with observational humor is the way to go. Don't go for the big laugh right out of the gate. You might get the big laugh later, but if you work too hard to draw it out as soon as you step onto stage or launch your presentation, you might bomb, and while there's no good time to bomb, you may never recover if it happens too early.

TEDnote

> **REMEMBER WHAT WORKED. Think back to anecdotes, stories, observations, or insights that have made you or your colleagues smile in the past. If they worked there and are appropriate to your presentation, weave them into your narrative and practice telling it.**

2. Analogies and Metaphors

An analogy is a comparison that points out the similarities between two different things. It's an excellent rhetorical technique that helps to explain complex topics. In my work with Intel, we use the classic technology analogy that a semiconductor (computer chip) is "like the brain of your computer." When Intel launched its first dual-core chip, we said simply, "It's like having two brains in one computer." I recall working with the head of storage computing at the same company, who said, "By 2020 the world will have 40 zetabytes of data. That's 57 times more data than every grain of sand in the world. Carmine, where the heck are we going to store all of that information?!"

By comparing data and sand, the storage expert put the enormous statistic into perspective and had fun delivering it. I advised her to start her presentations that way. She did so and they were very well received by her internal and external audiences. You see, you can't tell someone to "be funny" or to tell a joke. If you ask them to do something onstage that they don't typically do in everyday conversation, you're setting them up for failure. Often, making a simple analogy can bring a smile to your listener.

Many popular TED presenters provoke laughter by using analogies. For example:

- "Chris Anderson asked me if I could put the last 25 years of antipoverty campaigning into 10 minutes for TED. That's an Englishman asking an Irishman to be succinct."   —Bono

- "If you hear an expert talking about the Internet and saying it does this or it will do that, you should treat it with the same skepticism that you might treat the comments of an economist about the economy or a weatherman about the weather."

    —Danny Hillis, inventor, TED 2013

- "Trying to run Congress without human relationships is like trying to run a car without motor oil. Should we be surprised when the whole thing freezes up?"

    —Jonathan Haidt, social psychologist, TED 2012

- "If Americans want to live the American dream, they should go to Denmark."

    —Richard Wilkinson, professor at the
    University of Nottingham, TEDGlobal 2011

3. Quotes

An easy way to get a laugh without being a comedian or telling a joke is to quote somebody else who said something funny. The quotes can be from famous people, anonymous people, or family and friends. TED speakers do this all the time. For example, Carmen Agra Deedy quoted her mother, who said, "I gave shame up with pantyhose—they're both too binding." Some speakers quote others and add one pithy observation to highlight the humor in the statement. "In 2006, the head of the American Mortgage Bankers Association said, 'As we can clearly see, no seismic occurrence is about to overwhelm the U.S. economy.' Now there is a man on top of his job," said Rory Bremner (Two years later, the subprime-mortgage crisis led to the financial collapse of several major financial institutions, heralding the worst economic downturn in the United States since the Great Depression).

At TED 2013, Columbia University linguist John McWhorter taught the audience something new by providing a novel lens through which to view the 22 million text messages sent every day. McWhorter argues that instead of lamenting the abbreviated language that defines teenage texting, we should look at it as a "linguistic miracle" in the evolution of spoken language.

McWhorter showed a series of five slides, each of which had a quote from someone who criticized the way young people were speaking. In this case, the quotes themselves weren't funny, but the way McWhorter used the slides to make his point made his audience laugh.

He started with a quote from an English professor in 1956: "Many do not know the alphabet or multiplication table, cannot write grammatically . . ."[10] The audience didn't laugh, nor did McWhorter expect them to. He advanced to the second slide, which had a 1917 quote from a Connecticut schoolteacher: "Every high school is in despair because its pupils are so ignorant of the merest rudiments." No laughter yet. "You can go further back,"

McWhorter said. On his third slide he showed a quote by Harvard president Charles Eliot in 1871: "Bad spelling, incorrectness as well as inelegance of expression in writing . . . are far from rare among young men of eighteen otherwise well prepared for college studies." The audience started to get it and some began to laugh.

McWhorter continued, showing earlier and earlier quotes until he reached a quote from 63 A.D., a man saddened about the way people were speaking Latin, upset about the language that ultimately became French. After several quotes, the audience understood the premise and they were laughing at both the quotes and themselves for not seeing the evolution of language from McWhorter's perspective. People always complain about the way young people are using the language, but "the world keeps spinning," McWhorter said.

Creatively adding quotes to your presentation breaks up the slides nicely and gives your audience a mental break. Try to avoid quotes that are common and overused. And don't just visit a quote library on the Internet, randomly pulling a quote from a category. Really think about the humor and the quotes you use. Make sure they're relevant. When I give keynote speeches at an association or corporate conference, I often use quotes from association members, founders, or CEOs of the companies I'm speaking to. The quotes draw a laugh and help me connect with my audience. Building in good quotes requires some homework. Grabbing a famous quote would be easier, but not nearly as creative or effective. Do your homework.

TEDnote

DO YOUR HOMEWORK ON QUOTES. Search for third-party quotes that lighten up the mood of your presentation or cut through the complexity of your topic. Don't feel that you need to stick with famous quotes. Go off the beaten path. In many cases, quotes from people you know can be quite funny and engaging.

4. Video

At TEDxYouth in 2011, YouTube trends manager Kevin Allocca had the audience laughing hysterically with three short YouTube videos—a man in ecstasy over seeing a rainbow, a teenager girl singing a catchy, silly song called "Friday," and a really silly animation called "Nyan Cat." Allocca's theme wasn't silly at all. In an insightful presentation, he revealed the three reasons why the videos went viral (the videos had hundreds of millions of views): "tastemasters, communities, and unexpectedness." In between the videos he showed charts and statistics about each video. By themselves the statistics would have been dry, but Allocca added silly videos to draw a laugh from the audience.

Very few people use video clips in presentations, even at TED talks. Video, however, is a very effective way of bringing humor into a presentation: it takes the pressure off you to be funny.

In one of my keynote presentations on the topic of the Apple Store and customer service, I show two videos. In one clip a comedian sees what he can get away with at an Apple Store; he brings in a goat, orders a pizza for delivery in the store, even hires a small band to serenade him and his wife as they dance. In a second clip the audience sees a young woman dancing in an Apple Store as the employees continue about their business on the sales floor. Both clips are meant to highlight the point that Apple Store employees are trained not to "sell stuff" but to "enrich lives" and to make sure people are happy when they're in the store. The videos always draw a good laugh and, best of all, I don't have to play the comedian; I let others do it for me.

5. Photos

When you think back to your favorite college class, there's a good chance the professor you most enjoyed injected a fair amount of humor into his or her presentations. If I had to guess, economics was probably not the class that comes to mind for most people when they're asked about their most humorous professors. They didn't have economist and TED speaker Juan Enriquez as a teacher. If they had, they would have enjoyed going to class.

Enriquez has given four TED talks and takes the complexity out of economics by adding humor, usually in the form of photographs. His subjects are complex, and humor makes the topics easier to grasp because the photos place the topic in a context that everyone can understand.

At TED 2009, Enriquez opened his talk by saying, "There's a great big elephant in the room called the economy. So let's start talking about that. I wanted to give you a current picture of the economy."[11] The "picture" was a slide titled "The Economy." The rest of the slide was black. In the year 2009 America was at the depth of a recession so no further explanation was needed. The black slide said it all and elicited a strong laugh from the audience right out of the gate.

Regarding the economy, Enriquez continued, "There's a couple of really big problems that are still sitting there. One is leverage. And the problem with leverage is it makes the U.S. financial system look like this." Enriquez advanced to a slide showing a photograph of people in a pool. They were laughing as their radio sat on a small table in the middle of the water, its power cord running through the water and plugged into an electrical socket that dangled over the edge of the pool. Again, Enriquez didn't have to explain the slide. The photo acted as a metaphor for the problem of borrowing money against assets. It's all fun and games while the money rolls in, but its consequences could prove deadly. The technical definition of "economic leverage" is: volatility of equity divided by volatility of an unlevered investment in the same assets. Enriquez never gave the definition. That would have gone over their heads and put the audience to sleep. Instead, he creatively chose a photograph that acted as a metaphor for the problems that leverage causes. Enriquez made his audience laugh . . . and think.

Showing another series of photographs, Enriquez says, "The government, meanwhile, has been acting like Santa Claus. We all love Santa Claus, right?" At this point Enriquez shows a stock photo of what appears to be a typical Santa you'd see at a shopping mall. He continues, "But the problem with Santa Claus is, if you look at the mandatory spending of what these folks have been doing and promising folks [entitlements], now that the bill's come due it turns out Santa isn't quite as cute." The next slide shows a heavy man with a white beard sitting on a golf cart . . . naked with his private parts blocked out. The audience roars with laughter. They get the point—we love government money if we get it, but we cringe when the results of government spending are exposed.

Comedians work on jokes with different audiences to see what resonates, and I use photos and stories in the same way. In one section of my keynote presentation about customer service and communication, I use a series of photos from the Ritz-Carlton. The story (narrative) goes like this:

> When employees are empowered to do what's right for the customer, magical things happen. A family stayed at the Ritz-Carlton Amelia Island. When they got home, they realized they had left the little boy's beloved stuffed animal, "Joshi," in the room. The dad called the hotel, the staff found the toy in the room, and offered to mail it. "Can you do me a favor?" said the boy's father. "Can you take a picture of it so I can show my son that Joshi is okay?" The staff did one better. They sent several photographs showing Joshi enjoying the resort. Here's Joshi near the pool; Joshi on the beach; Joshi in a golf cart; and Joshi getting a facial.

If you simply read my story in text form, you might appreciate the customer service, but it won't necessarily make you laugh. I assure you the photos are hilarious. Seeing a stuffed animal lying on a massage bed with cucumbers on its eyes while someone massages its shoulders is funny stuff. The humor helps people remember the photos. More important, the pictures reinforce my key message—empowered employees create memorable moments for their customers.

Remember, in the Ritz-Carlton example, the *photos* get a laugh; I'm not trying to make the audience laugh by forcing a joke on them. It's natural, authentic humor. I'm not trying to be something I'm not. You may have no hope of making it on the comedy circuit, but that shouldn't stop you from delivering a presentation that's informative *and* entertaining.

TEDnote

LIGHTEN UP YOUR PRESENTATION WITH VIDEO AND PHOTOS. Most PowerPoint presentations are dreadful because they have so little—if any—emotional impact. Incorporate a humorous photograph or video clip to lighten the mood.

I use each of these five techniques in my presentations. I was never the guy who told jokes. I love comedy, enjoy watching stand-up comedians, but I rarely remember or tell jokes. Yet, I laugh easily (and often) and find the humor in just about every situation. My wife and I laugh a lot. As I developed as a speaker, I realized that I didn't have to *make* the audience laugh; all I had to do was *reveal* the humor in a particular situation. You don't have to go for a laugh all the time, but you should try to elicit at least a smile.

> "There's this mental delight that's followed by the physical response of laughter, which, not coincidentally, releases endorphins in the brain. And just like that, you've been seduced into a different way of looking at something because the endorphins
>
> *continued*

have brought down your defenses. This is the exact opposite of the way that anger and fear and panic, all of the flight-or-fight responses, operate. Flight-or-fight releases adrenaline, which throws our walls up sky-high. And the comedy comes along, dealing with a lot of the same areas where our defenses are the strongest—race, religion, politics, sexuality—only by approaching them through humor instead of adrenaline, we get endorphins and the alchemy of laughter turns our walls into windows, revealing a fresh and unexpected point of view."[12]

— Chris Bliss, TEDx

LET'S TALK S***

Always try to inject some humor when you are trying to help people wrap their heads around a complex subject, especially if they are new to the topic or have a low level of understanding about it. Humor is also a useful tool to deflect controversy or to relieve your audience from traumatic events. Millions of people tuned in to *Saturday Night Live* after 9/11 to get some relief from the constant barrage of horrifying images that were ubiquitous on television, in newspapers, and on the Internet. When comedian Will Ferrell appeared in one of the first skits with nothing but an American-flag-colored thong that showed his butt cheeks, the world knew it was okay to laugh again—not to forget, but to give our brains a break from the trauma.

Rose George sees the humor in poop. One day the UK-based journalist went to the bathroom and asked herself, "Where does this stuff go?" As a journalist, she was intrigued to find an answer to the question. For the next ten years she dug herself deeper into the world of sanitation, so to speak, writing articles and a book on the topic of how proper sanitation saves lives in third-world countries.

George takes her topic seriously, but she doesn't take herself too seriously and she realizes that her audience needs a mental break from some of the heartbreaking images she displays on the screen. Her combination of humor and seriousness won the hearts and, yes, minds, of the TED 2013 audience.

George is smart enough to know that open defecation isn't a pleasant topic. Her solution is to offer a careful, creative blend of humor and shock. George's first slide showed a photo of a pretty female model standing next to a high-tech toilet at a conference of the world toilet organization, "the other WTO," as she called it.

George says she grew up thinking that "a toilet like that was my right. I was wrong. It's a privilege. Two-and-half billion people worldwide have no adequate toilet."[13] George advanced to the second slide, which shows a little boy "going potty" off the side of the road while people walk by, a way of life in many third-world countries.

George says the problem is that feces carry pathogens that cause many problems, including diarrhea. "Diarrhea is a bit of a joke," George says as she advances to the next slide—a humorous one. "If you search for a stock photo associated with diarrhea from a leading photo agency, this is the picture you come up with." Her audience sees a photo of a woman in a bikini standing outside a toilet with her eyes closed and fists clenched, obviously grimacing as she's trying to hold it. The photo is funny and the audience laughs. Then George hits her audience with this: "Here's another image of diarrhea. This is Maria Salie. She's 9 months old [the audience sees a photo of a man crying as he stands in field]. You can't see her because she's buried under green grass in a little village in Liberia. She died in three days from diarrhea. She wasn't alone that day. Four thousand other children died of diarrhea . . . it's a very potent weapon of mass destruction."

By now you can tell how George's formula works: humor, shock, statistics. Statistics alone would put people to sleep. An overly shocking presentation would turn people off. Too much humor would take away from the serious implications of the topic. George skillfully blends the three into a magic formula for persuasion.

If Rose George can bring humor to her topic, you can certainly do so with your subject. Don't take your topic too seriously, or yourself. The famous theoretical physicist Stephen Hawking was diagnosed with ALS at the age of two. Now in his 70s, Hawking has been confined to a wheelchair for much of his life and since 1985 has had to communicate through a computer.

Despite his circumstances, he has a remarkable and disarming sense of humor. His wit makes audiences feel more comfortable around him. In 2003, Jim Carrey was promoting the film *Dumb and Dumber*. While he was being interviewed on Conan O'Brien's show, Carrey got a phone call from Hawking and the two launched into a comedy skit. "I just wanted to tell you how happy I am that you're excited about the new ekpyroptic universe theory,"[14] Hawking said to Carrey as the two men complimented each other on being a genius. When asked about it later, Hawking said he'd done it because it sounded like fun. He doesn't take himself too seriously.

Hawking brings his humor to public presentations. He knows his listeners' brains will turn to mush if they work too hard to understand his theories. His levity adds a much-needed laugh to the discourse.

In February 2008, Hawking appeared on a TED stage to discuss the big questions: "Where did we come from? How did the universe come into being? Are we alone in the universe? Is there alien life out there? What is the future of the human race?" Pretty heavy stuff. Among the theories he debunks—being visited by aliens.

We don't seem to have been visited by aliens. I am discounting the reports of UFOs. Why would they appear only to cranks and weirdos? If there is a government conspiracy to suppress the reports and keep for itself the scientific knowledge the aliens bring, it seems to have been a singularly ineffective policy so far. Furthermore, despite an extensive search by the SETI project, we haven't heard any alien television quiz shows. This probably indicates that there are no alien civilizations at our stage of development within a radius of a few hundred light years. Issuing an insurance policy against abduction by aliens seems a pretty safe bet.[15]

Secret #6: Lighten Up

Humor involves some risk and most people don't have the courage for it, which is why most business presentations are awfully dry and boring. It takes courage to be vulnerable, to poke some good-natured fun at yourself and your topic. The key is to be authentic. Don't try to be someone you're not. But if something makes you laugh, there's a good chance it will make someone else laugh, too.

If you're still not convinced that humor can help you win over audiences, think of it this way—studies show that humor is good for your health. Laughter lowers blood pressure, strengthens the immune system, improves breathing, increases your energy, and just makes you feel good. If you feel good, you'll deliver a better presentation, and that's something to smile about!

PART III

Memorable

You have to really be courageous about your instincts and your ideas. Otherwise you'll just knuckle under, and things that might have been memorable will be lost.

—FRANCIS FORD COPPOLA

7

Stick to the 18-Minute Rule

I'm both challenged and excited. My excitement is, I get to give something back. My challenge is, the shortest seminar I usually do is fifty hours.

—TONY ROBBINS, TED 2006

THE UNIVERSITY OF WATERLOO ECONOMICS professor Larry Smith gives three-hour lectures. In November 2011 he gave a 15-minute talk for a TEDx audience. He had no idea it would be viewed nearly 1.5 million times. "For me, it was a personal challenge to condense my content into 18 minutes," Smith told me. "I think my students asked me to do it because they thought it would kill me!"[1]

Why do you think the 18-minute rule works so well?" I asked Smith.

"Thinking is hard work. In 18 minutes you can make a powerful argument and attract people's attention."

Yes, thinking *is* hard work, and that's why the 18-minute rule is critical to the transfer of ideas. A TED presentation must not exceed 18 minutes in length. It's a fundamental rule that applies to *all* TED speakers. It doesn't matter if you're Larry Smith, Bill Gates, or Tony Robbins—18 minutes is all you get.

Secret #7: Stick to the 18-Minute Rule

Eighteen minutes is the ideal length of time for a presentation. If you must create one that's longer, build in soft breaks (stories, videos, demonstrations) every 10 minutes.

Why it works: Researchers have discovered that "cognitive backlog," too much information, prevents the successful transmission of ideas. TED curator Chris Anderson explained it best:

> It [18 minutes] is long enough to be serious and short enough to hold people's attention. It turns out that this length also works incredibly well online. It's the length of a coffee break. So, you watch a great talk, and forward the link to two or three people. It can go viral, very easily. The 18-minute length also works much like the way Twitter forces people to be disciplined in what they write. By forcing speakers who are used to going on for 45 minutes to bring it down to 18, you get them to really think about what they want to say. What is the key point they want to communicate? It has a clarifying effect. It brings discipline.[2]

LISTENING IS DRAINING

Dr. Paul King at Texas Christian University has been an influential scholar in the field of communication studies for 30 years. I spoke to King about his research into "state anxiety in listening performance." Most of us believe that anxiety impacts only the person giving the speech or presentation. Dr. King has discovered that audience members feel anxiety, too.

"We studied research participants—college students—who

listened to information knowing that they will be asked questions about it afterwards. As time went on, their state anxiety levels just went up and up and up until after they took the test. Then their anxiety level dropped off,"[3] King said. According to King, the accumulation of information results in "cognitive backlog," which, like piling on weights, makes the mental load heavier and heavier. "As more and more stuff you need to remember piles on, it creates greater and greater pressure and pretty soon you're going to drop it all."

King says that cognitive processing—thinking, speaking, and listening—are physically demanding activities. "I was on the debate team in high school. I also played basketball. I was able to run up and down the court all day long. I reached the finals of my first debate tournament and had a series of three debates. After I finished I could hardly move. I climbed into an old yellow school bus, fell asleep, and didn't wake up until I reached home. That was strange for me. If you're really concentrating, critical listening is a physically exhausting experience. Listening as an audience member is more draining than we give it credit for."

King says that listening is an exhausting activity because the learner is continually adding material to be remembered—retrieved—later. This is what he means by "cognitive backlog." Simply put, the longer the task or the more information that is delivered, the greater the cognitive load. Listening to a five-minute presentation produces a relatively small amount of cognitive backlog; an 18-minute presentation produces a little more, while a 60-minute presentation produces so much backlog that you risk seriously upsetting your audience unless you create a very engaging presentation with "soft breaks"—stories, videos, demonstrations, or other speakers.

The longer the presentation, the more the listener has to organize, comprehend, and remember. The burden increases along with a listener's anxiety. They become increasingly frustrated, even angry. King says the bulk of current research into memory processing suggests that it's better to study content on two or three occasions for a short period of time instead of spending an entire evening cramming. "What I'm suggesting is that once you make a point, if you just beat the point to death you're not really helping people to process it better and to store the content away in long-term memory."

King applies the results to his graduate class on research methods. If given a choice, most graduate students would rather attend a single three-hour class than three 50-minute classes. When King taught his class once a week, he found that the students returned for the next class having lost most of the information they had learned the prior week. King discovered the "better practice" was to schedule the same content on three separate occasions, such as Monday, Wednesday, and Friday. King said that despite objections, when he made the class mandatory across three shorter segments his students scored better and exhibited a better retention of the complex material.

THE BRAIN IS AN ENERGY HOG

Both professors Smith and King allude to the amount of energy it takes to listen and learn. The brain gets tired easily. Remember how exhausted you felt after the first day in a new job or after hours of studying a complicated manual for the first time? High school students call the exhaustion they feel after taking college-entrance exams the "SAT hangover." It takes energy to process new information.

Learning can be draining. The average adult human brain weighs only about three pounds, but it's an energy hog, consuming an inordinate amount of glucose, oxygen, and blood flow. As the brain takes in new information, millions of neurons are firing at once, burning energy and leading to fatigue and exhaustion.

In *Willpower*, author Roy Baumeister explains that we have a finite amount of willpower each day, which becomes depleted as our brains consume more energy. He found that completely un-related activities (resisting chocolate, working on math puzzles, listening to a presentation) drew on the same source of energy. This helps to explain why we're so tired, especially later in the day, after we've been making decisions all morning or trying to sup-press distractions (like the tempting piece of pie for lunch).

The culprit is glucose, or lack of it. Glucose is a simple sugar manufactured in the body from all kinds of foods. It enters the bloodstream and acts as fuel for the muscles, which include your heart, liver, and brain. Glucose enters your brain after being con-verted into neurotransmitters, chemicals your brain cells use to send signals to one another.

Baumeister talks about a series of experiments designed to measure glucose levels in people before and after doing simple tasks, such as watching a video while words were flashed at the bottom of the screen. "Some people were told to ignore the words; others were free to relax and watch however they wanted. Afterward, glucose levels were measured again, and there was a big difference. Levels remained constant in relaxed viewers but dropped signifi-cantly in the people who'd been trying to avoid the words. That seemingly small exercise in self-control was associated with a big drop in the brain's fuel of glucose."[4]

A long, confusing, meandering presentation forces your lis-tener's brain to work hard and to consume energy. Your brain cells need twice as much energy as other cells in your body. Mental activity rapidly depletes glucose. That's why an 18-minute presenta-tion works so well. It leaves your audience with some brainpower and glucose remaining to think about your presentation, share your ideas, and act on them. Talk for too long and your audience will find ways to distract themselves from your content. When is the last time you saw college students so inspired by a three-hour lecture that they raced back to their dorms to study the topic in more depth? It doesn't happen. Instead they head to the nearest pizza joint or beer hall to commiserate about their shared misfortune and to change the subject. Eighteen minutes is thought-provoking. Three hours is mind-numbing.

I've spent considerable time in this chapter explaining the science behind the 18-minute rule. I feel as though I need to. Keeping presentations on the shorter side elicits the strongest reaction from many of the CEOs and business professionals whom I've worked with. I often hear the lament, "But, Carmine, we have too much information to deliver!" Once people understand the science and logic behind the 18-minute rule and the concept of soft breaks, they are much more willing to consider shortening their presentations. Once they do, they find that their creative juices are unleashed. You see, creativity thrives under constraints.

CREATIVITY THRIVES UNDER CONSTRAINTS

Constraints are key to a creative presentation. I'm often asked, "How long should my presentation be?" I believe the Goldilocks zone is a very TED-like 18 to 20 minutes. It's not too short and not too long. It's just the right amount of time in which to persuade your audience. If it's shorter, some members of your audience (especially investors, clients, and customers) might not feel that they received enough information. Any longer, however, and you risk losing the attention of your audience.

I often use John F. Kennedy's inaugural speech as a guide to presentation length. Since Kennedy inspired the nation in a 15-minute inaugural speech, you should be able to pitch your product or idea in the same amount of time. Kennedy instructed speechwriter Ted Sorensen to keep it brief because "I don't want people to think I'm a windbag." The result was one of the shortest inaugural addresses up to that point in history—1,355 words. Kennedy realized that capturing the imagination of his audience required a strong delivery, carefully crafted sentences, and a reasonably short speech (the average length of presidential inaugural speeches is 2,300 words).

Kennedy's inaugural speech is an excellent example of a short, inspiring message. A more instructive example is an influential though lesser-known speech that Kennedy gave at Rice University on September 12, 1962. It was there that Kennedy outlined his vision to explore the moon. When Kennedy challenged America to "go to the moon" by the end of the decade, he galvanized the collective imagination of millions of Americans as well as thousands of its top scientists to put their time and energy into the effort. It was one of the most important speeches in American history. At 17 minutes and 40 seconds, Kennedy's speech would have made the ultimate TED talk.

Some people might argue, "I have too much to say. I can't possibly deliver all the information in 20 minutes." Try to do it anyway. Your presentation will be far more impactful and creative simply by going through the exercise.

In *The Laws of Subtraction*, Matthew May explains the science behind it. According to May, "Creativity thrives under intelligent constraints."[5] May persuasively argues that by establishing a boundary or limit to your presentation, you provide a focus and a framework for creativity to flourish. "Recent studies offer evidence that, contrary to popular belief, the main event of the imagination—creativity—does not require unrestrained freedom; rather, it relies on limits and obstacles."

May believes that the law of subtraction positively impacts nearly every aspect of our lives, not just presentation design and public speaking. What *isn't* there often trumps what is. "When you remove just the right thing in just the right way, something good usually happens," says May.

"Creativity is often misunderstood. People often think of it in terms of artistic work—unbridled, unguided effort that leads to beautiful effect. If you look deeper, however, you'll find that some of the most inspiring art forms—haikus, sonatas, religious paintings—are fraught with constraints."

—Marissa Mayer, Yahoo! CEO

TED talks have been viewed more than one billion times, proving that a "constrained" presentation is often more inspiring, creative, and engaging than longer, meandering presentations that are boring, confusing, and convoluted.

THE HISTORY OF THE WORLD IN 18 MINUTES

A simple explanation of a complex topic gives the audience confidence in the speaker's mastery of the subject. Albert Einstein once said, "If you can't explain it simply, you don't understand it well enough." Einstein would have been proud of David Christian, who, in March 2011, narrated the complete history of the universe for a TED audience and took all of 18 minutes to do it (17 minutes and 40 seconds, to be exact).

Christian told me that he teaches a world-history course that examines the entire history of the universe—from the Big Bang 13 billion years ago to today. The Big History course is offered by The Teaching Company in a series of 48 half-hour lectures. Christian's deep understanding of the subject helped him condense the content into just the right amount of time to grab the audience's attention and inspire them to take better care of our fragile planet. "I've been teaching Big History now for over 20 years, so I have a pretty good feel for the story and that means I can tell it in many different versions,"[6] Christian told me.

E. F. Schumacher, economist and author of *Small Is Beautiful*, once said, "Any intelligent fool can make things bigger, more complex. It takes a touch of genius and a lot of courage to move in the opposite direction." Courage is the key word. It takes courage to keep things simple. It takes courage to put one picture on a PowerPoint slide instead of filling it with tiny text that most people in the audience won't even be able to read. It takes courage to reduce the number of the slides in a presentation. It takes courage to speak for 18 minutes instead of rambling on for much longer. Leonardo da Vinci once said, "Simplicity is the ultimate sophistication." Be sophisticated. Keep your presentations and pitches short and simple.

> "Our life is frittered away by detail. Simplify, simplify."
> —Henry David Thoreau

THE RULE OF THREE

All the science behind the importance of conciseness is interesting, but it doesn't mean much unless you can apply it to improve the impact of your pitch or presentation. How can you condense your knowledge into an 18-minute presentation? Understanding the rule of three will help. The rule of three simply means that people can remember three pieces of information really well; add more items and retention falls off considerably. It's one of the most powerful concepts in writing and communication. I've used the rule of three very successfully with communicators in nearly every industry. It works for me every time, and it works for some of the most popular TED talks.

Neil Pasricha's blog covers a lot of ground. It's dedicated to "1,000 awesome things" such as snow falling on Christmas, your birthday landing on a weekend, someone naming their kid after you, etc. The simple blog idea landed Pasricha a book deal, 25,000 Twitter followers, and a TEDx talk in Toronto that has attracted more than one million views. In this presentation Pasricha did not attempt to cover all 1,000 small things that make life worth living. Instead he focused on three secrets—all starting with the letter *A*—to leading a life that's truly rewarding. He titled the presentation, "The 3 A's of Awesome."

The Three A's of Awesome

In an intensely personal talk Pasricha told a story about his life in 2008. It wasn't going well. His wife sat him down one day and said, "I don't love you anymore."[7] It was the most heartbreaking thing he had ever heard, until a month later, when he got more bad news. "My friend Chris had been battling mental illness for some time . . . he took his own life."

As the "dark clouds" were circling him, Pasricha logged on to a computer and started a tiny Web site to force himself to think about positive things. The exercise put him in a better mood, but he didn't think anything of it because 50,000 blogs are started each day. The blog, 1000awesomethings.com, quickly became popular, however, and one day Pasricha received a call from someone who said, "You've just received the best blog in the world award." "That sounds totally fake," Pasricha said as the audience laughed. It wasn't fake. He accepted a Webby Award for best blog. When he returned to Toronto, ten literary agents were eager to represent him. The book he eventually wrote, *The Book of Awesome*, hit the bestseller list for 20 straight weeks.

The Three A's of Awesome that Pasricha shared with the TEDx audience that day were: attitude, awareness, authenticity. He spoke briefly about each one. On attitude, Pasricha said we are all going to have bumps in the road, but we have two choices on how to face them. "One, you can swirl and twirl and gloom and doom forever, or two, you can grieve and then face the future with newly sober eyes. Having a great attitude is about choosing option number two, and choosing, no matter how difficult it is, no matter what pain hits you, choosing to move forward and move on and take baby steps into the future."

On awareness, Pasricha encouraged his listeners to embrace their inner three-year-old. "That three-year-old boy is still part of you. That three-year-old girl is still part of you. They're in there. And being aware is just about remembering that you saw everything you've seen for the first time once, too."

On authenticity: "It's just about being you and being cool with that. And I think when you're authentic, you end up following your heart, and you put yourself in places and situations and in conversations that you love and that you enjoy. You meet people that you like talking to. You go places you've dreamt about. And you end up following your heart and feeling very fulfilled."

The Magical Number Seven, Plus or Minus Two

Pasricha intuitively understood and leveraged this powerful communication technique: The rule of three. Simply put, the human mind can consume only about three "chunks" of information in short-term, or working, memory. As more and more items are added to a list, the average person retains less and less. Four items are a bit harder to remember than three. Five items are even harder. Once the number of items on a list hits eight, most people have little chance of remembering the entire sequence.

In 1956, Bell Labs reached out to Harvard professor George Miller, who published a classic paper titled "The Magical Number Seven, Plus or Minus Two." Miller found that most people have a hard time remembering more than seven pieces of new information. Now you know why phone numbers are seven digits. Contemporary scientists, however, have put the number of items we can easily recall in short-term closer to three or four chunks of information. Think about it. When someone leaves a phone number on a voice message, you're likely to recall the number by "chunking" the number into two parts—one section made up of three digits, the other comprising the remaining four digits.

The Rule of Three Pervades Our Daily Lives

Every July fourth America celebrates the three inalienable rights voiced in the U.S. Declaration of Independence: life, liberty, and the pursuit of happiness. Life, liberty, and happiness might very well be the three most important words in American history. The words are so eloquent, so impactful, that they warrant their own Wikipedia page. According to Wikipedia, some consider the phrase one of "the most well-crafted, influential sentences in the history of the English language." Those three words inspired other countries, most notably France, to seek its own freedoms from oppression and to delineate the rights of its citizens into groups of three. The French motto "liberty, equality, and fraternity" traces its origin to the French Revolution. The list of countries that were directly inspired by the U.S. Declaration of Independence is so large, I don't think it's a stretch to argue that those three words might very well be the most important three words in human history.

Why did Jefferson choose three rights instead of, say, twelve? Jefferson was a skilled writer and his famous phrase reflects a rhetorical technique that can be traced to ancient Greece—a figure of speech using three words to express one idea.

The rule of three pervades every aspect of our business and social lives. In literature you'll find three little pigs, three musketeers, and three wishes granted to an ambitious Aladdin. Painters are familiar with the three primary colors; they know their three secondary colors, too. In science, Newton discovered three laws and scientists discovered three elements that make up the atom. At the dinner table, you'll find three pieces of cutlery: spoon, knife, fork. The flag of the United States of America has three colors, as do the flags of the United Kingdom, France, Italy, Argentina, the Russian Federation, Nepal, and many others. There are three medals in the Olympics. Three wise men appeared with three gifts for baby Jesus. Jesus himself is part of the holy trinity—the Father, Son, and Holy Spirit. The rule of three helped get U.S. president Barack Obama elected; "Yes we can," voters chanted. Some of the world's most famous brands are ING, UPS, IBM, SAP, CNN, and the BBC. Three is everywhere.

In writing and speaking, three is more satisfying than any other number. It's no accident that threes are all around us. It worked for Jefferson, it worked for the world's greatest writers, and it works for many TED speakers. Dr. Jill, who delivered the second-most-popular presentation in TED history, divided her talk, "My Stroke of Insight," into three parts, each lasting six minutes. By doing so, the presentation was easier for her to remember and deliver, and it made the presentation easier for the audience to follow. Here are some other examples of the rule of three in TED presentations.

TED Talkers Who Talk in Threes

You'll recall Kevin Allocca from chapter 6, the YouTube trends manager who gets paid to watch videos. Actually he studies the viral nature of popular videos. Allocca says 48 hours of video are uploaded to YouTube every minute and only a tiny percentage go viral, generating millions of views in a short period of time.

"So how does it happen? Three things: tastemakers, communities of participation and unexpectedness,"[8] Alloca began. In his 10-minute presentation, Allocca offered marketers valuable information and, by dividing his presentation into three areas, made the material easy to remember.

Allocca isn't the only TED speaker who divides content into three. Don Norman explained three ways design makes you happy. Tom Wujec talked about the three ways the brain creates meaning. V. S. Ramachandran revealed the three clues to understanding your brain. Tim Leberecht discussed the three ways brands lose control of their identity. Ric Elias talked about the three things he learned when his plane crashed. Mikko Hypponen revealed the three types of ways crooks can steal your digital data. Dan Ariely offered three irrational lessons from the Bernie Madoff scandal. There's even a three-minute TED talk— "TED in 3 Minutes"—featuring snack-size nuggets of inspiration from Arianna Huffington, *New York Times* tech columnist David Pogue, and Terry Moore, who gave the first-ever three-minute TED talk and showed the audience a better way to tie their shoes. The "shoe talk" has been viewed more than 1.5 million times. People want to be taught something new and they don't want to wait too long to learn it!

THE THREE-STORY STRUCTURE

In the spirit of the rule of three, many effective TED presenters and TED-worthy presenters use three stories as the outline for their presentations. Here is one example followed by a detailed explanation of how to create an outline of your own.

Three Stories of Eco-Entrepreneurship

Majora Carter says she likes to create an environment where all dreams can thrive. Carter has built a reputation as an expert in green infrastructure and how it can revitalize inner cities like the South Bronx, South Chicago, or New Orleans' Ninth Ward. Carter's 2006 TED talk titled "Greening the Ghetto" was one of the first TED talks to be posted online. Four years later, Carter was invited to give a TEDx Midwest presentation on the topic of eco-entrepreneurship. Since she had only 18 minutes, she decided to tell three stories; stories of three people who didn't know one another but who "had an awful lot in common."[9]

Carter first told the story of Brenda Palms-Farber, who created a business that makes skin-care products from honey. She hired "seemingly unemployable" men and women, many of whom had prison records, to do the beekeeping and harvesting. Her products are sold at Whole Foods. Best of all, less than 4 percent of the people she hires go back to jail.

Carter's second story was about a man in Los Angeles, Andy Lipkis, who convinced the city to replace millions of dollars' worth of asphalt with grass and trees for inner-city schools. Lipkis "linked trees, people, and technology to create a more livable city."

The protagonist in Carter's final story was a coal miner's daughter—not Loretta Lynn, but Judy Bonds—who introduced wind energy as a power source for her hometown in West Virginia. After Carter explained Bonds's plan, she paused and delivered the bad news: "A few months ago, Judy was diagnosed with stage-three lung cancer. And it has since moved to her bones and her brain. And I just find it so bizarre that she's suffering from the same thing that she tried so hard to protect people from. But her dream of Coal River Mountain Wind is her legacy. And she might not get to see that mountaintop. But rather than writing some kind of manifesto or something, she's leaving behind a business plan to make it happen."

Carter tied the three stories together with a central theme: "They all understand how to productively channel dollars through our local economies to meet existing market demands, reduce the social problems that we have now, and prevent new problems in the future."

Three stories. Three examples. Three lessons that reinforce Carter's theme.

Build a Message Map in Three Easy Steps.

I wrote the popular *Forbes* column "How to Pitch Anything in 15 Seconds."[10] I introduced readers to an effective tool called a message map—perfect for a pitch or presentation. The technique helps to keep your content clear and concise, but it doesn't work unless you understand the rule of three.

A message map is the visual display of your idea on one page. It is a powerful tool that should be a part of your communication arsenal. Building a message map can help you pitch anything (a product, service, company, or idea) in as little as 15 seconds or to shape the framework for a longer, 18-minute presentation. Here is the three-step process for using a message map to build a winning pitch. For this exercise you will need a notepad, Word document, PowerPoint slide, or whiteboard.

Step One: Create a Twitter-Friendly Headline

As you'll recall from chapter 4, the headline is the one single overarching message that you want your customers to know at the end of your presentation. Ask yourself, "What is the single most important thing I want my listener to know about my [product, service, brand, idea]?" Draw a circle at the top of the message map (or page) and insert the answer to this question—this is your headline. Remember to make sure your headline fits in a Twitter post (no more than 140 characters). If you cannot explain your product or idea in 140 characters or less, go back to the drawing board.

Step Two: Support the Headline with Three Key Messages

As we discussed earlier in this chapter, the human mind can process only about three pieces of information in short-term memory. When you're designing a presentation outline, include the three supporting messages that support the overall theme. You'll recall that Dr. Jill divided her popular TED talk, "My Stroke of Insight," into three sections that lasted six minutes each: the circuitry of the brain, the day of the stroke, and the insight the experience offered about life, the world, and her place in it.

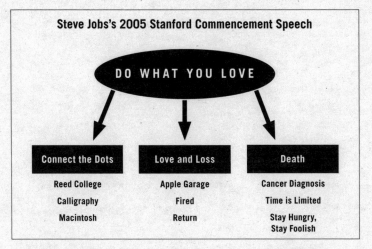

Steve Jobs's 2005 Stanford Commencement Speech

DO WHAT YOU LOVE

Connect the Dots	Love and Loss	Death
Reed College	Apple Garage	Cancer Diagnosis
Calligraphy	Fired	Time is Limited
Macintosh	Return	Stay Hungry, Stay Foolish

7.1: Message Map Example: Steve Jobs's Stanford Commencement Speech 2005. Created by Gallo Communications Group, www.carminegallo.com.

Step Three: Reinforce the Three Messages with Stories, Statistics, and Examples

Add bullet points to each of the three supporting messages. You don't have to write out the entire story. Instead, write a few words that will prompt you to deliver the story. Remember, the entire message map must fit on one page.

TO ILLUSTRATE THE PROCESS, FIGURE 7.1 is what a message map would look like for Steve Jobs's famous commencement speech at Stanford University in 2005. The speech comes in a very TED-friendly 15 minutes. It has one theme, the Twitter-friendly headline: DO WHAT YOU LOVE. It's divided into three parts (connect the dots, love and loss, and death) with three supporting points for each part. The result is a clear view of what the listener needs to know in one glance. Creating a message map for your presentation content is an efficient and effective way to ensure your presentation isn't too long or unorganized.

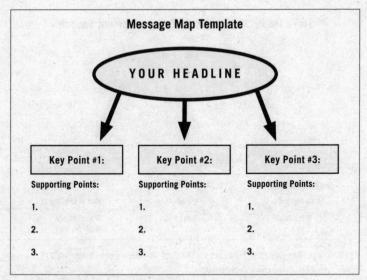

Message Map Template

YOUR HEADLINE

Key Point #1:	Key Point #2:	Key Point #3:
Supporting Points:	Supporting Points:	Supporting Points:
1.	1.	1.
2.	2.	2.
3.	3.	3.

7.2: Message Map Template. Created by Gallo Communications Group, www.carminegallo.com.

TEDnote

BUILD YOUR OWN MESSAGE MAP. Using the blank template in figure 7.2, insert in the bubble at the top the headline I asked you to create in chapter 4. Now, what's your rule of three? Take the product, service, brand, or idea you built your headline around and create three points to support it. If you have more than three key messages, divide the content into three categories. Insert your points in the three bubbles below the headline bubble. Finally, can you create sub-points of three within each category? Supporting points can include stories, examples, anecdotes, or meaningful statistics, as we've discussed in earlier chapters. You can use the message map to pitch any idea, product, service, or company. It's one of the most effective and valuable communication tools you'll ever use.

Secret #7: Stick to the 18-Minute Rule

Long, convoluted, and meandering presentations are dull; a sure-fire way to lose your audience. The 18-minute rule isn't simply a good exercise to learn discipline. It's critical to avoid overloading your audience. Remember, constrained presentations require more creativity. In other words, what *isn't* there makes what *is* there even stronger!

Paint a Mental Picture with Multisensory Experiences

It is better to present an explanation in words and pictures than solely in words.

—DR. RICHARD MAYER, PSYCHOLOGIST, UNIVERSITY OF CALIFORNIA, SANTA BARBARA

WATER ISN'T EMOTIONALLY VIVID UNLESS you don't have it. Then it becomes the only thing you ever think about. Michael Pritchard was inspired to invent a portable water-filtration system after the events of the Indian Ocean tsunami of 2004 and Hurricane Katrina in 2005. In those events, people died or became seriously ill because they lacked safe drinking water. Pritchard invented the portable LIFESAVER filter, which turns filthy water into drinkable water. In 2009 Pritchard delivered a TED presentation about his invention. It's been viewed more than three million times, garnering attention any entrepreneur would envy.

Pritchard opens the presentation with a photograph of a little boy, dressed in rags, scooping up rancid, dirty water from a muddy field. "Now I see you've all been enjoying the water that's been provided for you here at the conference over the past couple of days. And I'm sure you'll feel that it's from a safe source,"[1] he begins telling the audience. "But what if it wasn't? What if it was from a source like this? Then statistics would actually say that half of you would now be suffering with diarrhea." Pritchard had grabbed the attention of the audience right out of the gate (a jaw-dropping moment) with a simple yet evocative photograph and a statistic that made the audience squirm. And he was just getting started.

Three minutes into Pritchard's presentation, he walks up to a fish tank filled to about three-quarters with water he took from the nearby river Thames. It's mostly clear, and only slightly murky. "I got to thinking, you know, if we were in the middle of a flood zone in Bangladesh, the water wouldn't look like this. So I've gone and got some stuff to add into it." And with that Pritchard begins adding more water—water from his pond, sewage runoff, and, in an act that really turned up the emotional vividness of the demonstration, a "gift from a friend of mine's rabbit."

Pritchard scooped up some of the water with his device, gave it a few pumps, and poured clean, safe drinking water into a glass. He drank it, as did curator Chris Anderson, who was seated near the stage. The entire demonstration lasted no more than three minutes.

Pritchard's presentation consisted of photographs, statistics, and demonstrations. It wasn't *one* thing that made his presentation especially memorable—it was all three.

Secret #8: Paint a Mental Picture with Multisensory Experiences

Deliver presentations with components that touch more than one of the senses: sight, sound, touch, taste, and smell.

Why it works: Remember, the brain does not pay attention to boring things. It's nearly impossible to be bored if you're exposed to mesmerizing images, captivating videos, intriguing props, beautiful words, and more than one voice bringing the story to life. Nobody is going to ask you to build multisensory elements into your presentation, but once they experience it, they'll love every minute of it. The brain craves multisensory experiences. Your audience might not be able to explain why they love your presentation; it will be your little secret.

MULTIMEDIA EXPERIENCES ENHANCE LEARNING

Several years ago I had a conversation with Dr. Richard Mayer, a professor of psychology at UC Santa Barbara and the principal proponent of multimedia learning. In a study titled "A Cognitive Theory of Multimedia Learning," Mayer suggests that it's far more effective to explain concepts using multiple methods of sensory inputs—such as auditory, visual, and kinesthetic. Mayer is convinced that one of the most important areas of study in cognitive psychology is the understanding of how multimedia can foster student learning.

In Mayer's experiments, students who were exposed to multisensory environments—text, pictures, animation, and video—always, not sometimes, *always* had much more accurate recall of the information than those students who only heard or read the information. Mayer said the principle should not be surprising. When the brain is allowed to build two mental representations of an explanation—a verbal model and a visual model—the mental connections are not just a little stronger. They are much, much stronger. Add touch and you've got a winner!

The differences between two types of learning (auditory and visual) were even more striking when the "audience," the people learning the information, lacked prior knowledge of the material. Students with high prior knowledge of the content can generate their own mental images while simply listening or reading.[2]

Think about the most important presentations you deliver—they are probably given to people with "low" prior knowledge of the information:

- pitching a new idea, product, company, or campaign

- explaining new rules, processes, or guidelines

- teaching students on the first day of class

- training employees or salespeople on new tools or customer-service initiatives

- selling a product to a customer who's never used or heard of it

- launching a unique, revolutionary product or service

- asking an investor for money to grow your company

In each of these cases, a multisensory experience often leads to the best results. These audiences are made up of human beings who might be skeptical and hard to persuade, but they are not immune to the psychology that drives our behavior. We respond to visual, auditory, and tactile stimulation.

Great public speakers know this and build presentations around one of the senses predominantly, but they incorporate at least one or two others: sight, sound, touch, smell, and taste. Smell and taste are harder to incorporate in a presentation, but Pritchard offered an example of how to stimulate both senses without physically touching the audience (if a person imagines how water smells or tastes, it triggers the same areas of the brain as if the person has actually ingested the water). So, with smell and taste out of the way, let's focus on sight, sound, and touch.

See It
In presentation slides, use pictures instead of text whenever possible. Your audience is far more likely to recall information

when it's delivered in a combination of pictures and text rather than text alone. Because vision trumps all other senses, I devote a large portion of this chapter to the technique of making your presentation visual. Taking your audience on a journey with the pictures you paint is part art and part science. You must think creatively about transferring your ideas to visually engaging images. For 30 years the world's best minds have captivated TED audiences around the world with powerful, captivating, inspiring, and memorable images. That's how they get ideas to spread.

Al Gore's Multimedia Presentation Ignites the Climate Change Movement

Former U.S. vice president Al Gore won the Nobel Peace Prize in 2007 for his work on global warming. Gore was the highlight of the TED conference in Monterey the preceding year, where he displayed some of the same slides he made famous in the Academy Award–winning documentary *An Inconvenient Truth*. When Al Gore won the Nobel Peace Prize, the TED online community asked TEDsters who had seen Gore's presentation at the conference how it had impacted them or changed their lives. Among the responses:

Al Gore's talk at TED opened my eyes to what I needed to do for my grandchildren's generation, and I now consider the impact we have on our earth in every venture we undertake.
—Howard Morgan, venture capitalist

Gore's TED presentation on the climate crisis was at once riveting and inspiring—his passion was so evident—it prompted me to share the talk with our children, and our eldest, Charlie, now 11, has become a one-man global warming marketing machine. Charlie has created his own PowerPoint presentation, which he shares with virtually everyone he meets. — Jeff Levy, CEO

Al Gore's talk at TED 2006 was a turning point in my life. —David S. Rose, angel investor[3]

THESE ARE JUST A FEW of the remarks from people who have been inspired after watching Gore's presentation on the threat of global warming, its causes, and what people can do about it.

Al Gore's slide show, designed with Keynote presentation software, is an astonishing example of how the visual display of information has the power to inspire action. The TED audience assembled in Monterey in February 2006 got a preview of the slides that would appear in the movie a few months later.

The story behind *An Inconvenient Truth* begins two years earlier. On May 27, 2004, during a New York City appearance after the premier of the film *The Day After Tomorrow*, Gore gave an abbreviated, 10-minute version of his presentation at a town-hall meeting about climate change. Producer Laurie David was in the audience. "I had never seen it before, and I was floored,"[4] she said. "As soon as the evening's program concluded, I asked him to let me present his full briefing to leaders and friends in New York and Los Angeles. I would do all the organizing if he would commit to the dates. Gore's presentation was the most powerful and clear explanation of global warming I had ever seen. And it became my mission to get everyone I knew to see it too."

Think about Laurie David's observation—the most powerful and clear explanation she had ever *seen*. If Gore had not used slides to visualize the topic of global warming, he would have stood little chance to inspire David to make a movie based on it.

David was inspired because she experienced a multimedia event that looked more like a movie than a typical presentation.

> I had an opportunity to interview Sir Richard Branson for my Forbes.com column on leadership and communication. I asked Branson if he had ever seen a presentation that blew him away. His answer: Al Gore's global-warming presentation.
>
> > He [Al Gore] presented the irreversible effects of doing business as usual on our fragile planet. We had a constructive discussion about how a businessman in dirty fuels businesses [airlines, trains] can open up clean tech markets and start new ways of doing better business. It led me to pledge 100% of Virgin's transportation profits to clean energy and to encourage more businesses to equally prioritize people, planet, and profits."[5]
> >
> > —Sir Richard Branson, founder, Virgin Group

If Gore had simply read the text with no supporting visuals, few people would have been inspired or intrigued. His ideas would have been lost or, at best, relegated to a very small group of individuals who were exceptionally engaged in the topic. The visual display of complex information made the topic clear and easy to grasp. In table 8.1 you can see how Gore explains the basic science of global warming. The left column shows his words; the right column explains the image on the corresponding slides and the visual animation that made the visuals so impactful.

Gore understands that complex material requires a simple explanation and more pictures to help the audience understand the

AL GORE'S WORDS WITH CORRESPONDING SLIDE DESCRIPTIONS

GORE'S WORDS	GORE'S SLIDES
The most vulnerable part of the earth's ecological system is the atmosphere; vulnerable because it's so thin . . . it's thin enough that we are capable of changing its composition. That brings up the basic science of global warming. The sun's radiation comes in the form of light waves that heat up the earth.[6]	Image of earth, sun, and animated yellow rays emanating from sun
Some of the radiation that is absorbed and warms the earth is then re-radiated back into space in the form of infrared radiation.	Animation showing red lines—representing infrared radiation—leaving earth's atmosphere
Some of the outgoing infrared radiation is trapped by this layer of atmosphere and held inside the atmosphere.	Some red lines get trapped under thin line of atmosphere instead of leaving for space.
That's a good thing because it keeps the temperature of the earth within certain boundaries, relatively constant and livable. The problem is this thin layer of atmosphere is being thickened by all the global warming pollution that's being put up there. What that does is thicken this layer of atmosphere so more of the outgoing infrared is trapped and the atmosphere heats up worldwide.	Photos of factories spewing smoke

Table 8.1. Al Gore's words with corresponding slide descriptions from his Inconveniet Truth presentation.

concepts. Remember *Titanic* explorer Robert Ballard in chapter 4? His 2008 TED presentation contained 57 slides. There were no words on any slide! He showed photographs and artists' renderings of the fascinating undersea worlds he's discovered, but no text. Why? "I'm storytelling, not lecturing," Ballard told me.

Presentation-design expert and author of *Resonate*, Nancy Duarte, created the slides for Al Gore's global-warming presentation. I know Nancy very well and we share an aesthetic for slide design and a philosophy of how presentations can truly transform the world. According to Duarte in a TEDx talk, "A single idea can start a groundswell, be a flashpoint for a movement, and it can actually rewrite our future,"[7] said Duarte. "But an idea is powerless if it stays inside of you . . . if you communicate an idea in a way that resonates, change will happen."

The End of PowerPoint As We Know It

TED represents the end of PowerPoint as we know it. Since we're all sick of "Death by PowerPoint," it's time to kill it permanently. Let me be clear—I'm not advocating the end of PowerPoint as a tool, but the end of traditional PowerPoint design cluttered with text and bullet points. The average PowerPoint slide has 40 words. It's nearly impossible to find one slide in a TED presentation that contains anywhere near 40 words, and these presentations are considered among the best in the world.

Brené Brown is a research professor at the University of Houston Graduate College of Social Work. Her presentation that I introduced earlier, "The Power of Vulnerability," has been viewed more than seven million times. Brown did not get the memo that the average PowerPoint has 40 words, and it's a good thing she didn't. Cluttered slides detract from the message; Brown's slides complemented the narrative. How? She used images to replace words whenever possible. As a result, it took Brown 25 slides before she hit 40 words, the number of words on a single PowerPoint slide in most presentations.

For example, Brown started her presentation with a personal history of her experience as a doctoral student. Her first research professor would tell her, "If you can't measure it, it doesn't exist."

8.1: Brené Brown speaking at TED 2012. Courtesy of James Duncan Davidson/TED (http://duncandavidson.com).

For the next two minutes, as she spoke, Brown's audience saw only that sentence—the quote from her professor—on the screen. She followed the slide with a picture of a baby's fingers in the hand of her mother as she spoke about her study into interpersonal "connections." Brown scored points with the audience by using her slides as a backdrop to her story and not as a replacement for the story she delivered verbally.

Some of the comments on Brown's TED.com page include the following:

Exceptional, power-packed presentation. Leaned into every word.
—Melanie
A powerful message. —Bill
Genuine content. No fillers. —Juliette

These viewers were captivated by Brown's message, content, and story structure. If Brown had forced them to read wordy slides as she spoke, the message would have been lost. Why? Because the brain cannot multitask as well as you may think it can.

Multitasking Is a Myth

"Multitasking, when it comes to paying attention, is a myth,"[8] according to John Medina, a molecular biologist at the University of Washington School of Medicine. Medina acknowledges that the brain does multitask at some level—you can walk and talk at the same time. But when it comes to the brain's ability to *pay attention* to a lecture, conversation, or presentation, it is simply incapable of paying equal attention to multiple items. "To put it bluntly, research shows that *we can't multitask*. We are biologically incapable of processing attention-rich inputs simultaneously."

Think about it. Aren't we adding an impossible load on our audience when we ask them to listen intently to our words and read a lengthy PowerPoint slide at the same time? They can't do both! So how do you engage the audience, make an emotional connection with them, and get them to pay attention without being distracted? Once again, neuroscience gives us the answer: Picture Superiority Effect (PSE).

Pictures Are Superior

Scientists have produced a mountain of evidence showing that concepts presented as pictures instead of words are more likely to be recalled. Put simply, visuals matter—a lot. If you hear information, you are likely to remember about 10 percent of that information three days later. Add a picture, however, and your recall rate will soar to 65 percent. To put that into context, a picture will help you remember six times more information than listening to the words alone.

"Human PSE is truly Olympian,"[9] writes Medina. "Tests performed years ago showed that people could remember more than 2,500 pictures with at least 90 percent accuracy several days post-exposure, even though subjects saw each picture for about 10 seconds. Accuracy rates a year later still hovered around 63 percent . . . sprinkled throughout these experiments were comparisons with other forms of communication, usually text or oral presentations. The usual result was PSE demolishes them both. It still does."

Our brains are wired to process visual information—pictures—very differently than text and sound. Scientists call the effect "multimodal" learning: pictures are processed in several channels instead of one, giving the brain a far deeper and meaningful encoding experience.

The University of Western Ontario psychology professor Allan Paivio was the first to introduce a "dual-coding" theory. According to his theory, visual and verbal information are stored separately in our memory; they can be stored as images, words, or both. Concepts that are learned in picture form are encoded as both visual and verbal. Words are encoded only verbally. In other words, pictures are more richly stamped in our brains and easier to recall. For example, if I ask you to remember the word *dog*, your brain will register it as a verbal code. If I show you a picture of a dog and ask you to remember the word—*dog*— the concept will be recorded visually and verbally, significantly increasing the chance that you will recall the concept. Now, dogs are familiar, and if you're familiar with the concept, it increases your ability to recall it. If, however, you are unfamiliar with the material, much like the presentation of new information as you would hear in a TED presentation, storing the concept as pictures and words is much more effective.

fMRI studies have confirmed Paivio's theory. Today we know that students who learn through pictures and words recall the information more vividly than those students who learned only through text. Researchers also use the term *multimedia principle*: retention is improved through words and pictures rather than through words alone. This has enormous implications on how best to design and deliver presentations that are intended to inspire or persuade people to take action.

Bill Gates Becomes a Fan of Visuals

Since Bill Gates left Microsoft to dedicate his efforts to philanthropy, he has been thinking about how to communicate complex topics simply. Gates tackles topics ranging from cutting carbon emissions to reforming education to helping the poorest two billion people, mostly children, live better lives. These are complex problems with complex solutions. What's not complex are Gates's slides. They are models of clarity and picture superiority.

At TED 2010, Gates gave the very popular presentation "Innovating to Zero!" U2 lead singer Bono said the presentation "gives me hope," and he ranks it among his all-time favorite TED talks. Remember when I said the average PowerPoint slide has 40 words? It took Gates 15 slides to reach 40 words. Instead of words, he showed photos and images. Gates's first slide showed a photograph of poor children in a small African village. "Energy and climate are extremely important to these people. In fact, more important than to anyone else on the planet,"[10] he began. "The climate getting worse means that many years, their crops won't grow. There will be too much rain, not enough rain, things will change in ways that their fragile environment simply can't support. And that leads to starvation, it leads to uncertainty, it leads to unrest. So, the climate changes will be terrible for them."

Gates is remarkable at making complex content easy to grasp. He explained global warming in seven seconds and used a "straightforward" visual formula to do it. According to Gates, "CO_2 gets emitted. That leads to a temperature increase and that temperature increase leads to some very negative effects." Gates's slide displayed a formula over a photo of a sky. Figure 8.2 shows a re-creation of Gates's slide.

8.2: Re-creation of Bill Gates's CO2 formula slide from his TED 2010 presentation. Created by Empowered Presentations @empoweredpres.

The Scrambled Egg Video That Launched a Global Movement

You'll recall that one of Bill Gates's favorite presentations on TED.com is David Christian's "The History of Our World in 18 Minutes." Christian's presentation plays on the senses, especially the visual sense. In the first two and a half minutes of Christian's presentation, there is no text on any of his slides.

Christian walked out onstage and said, "First, a video."[11] The audience then saw a video of what appeared to be an egg being scrambled. It soon became clear that the video was in reverse, showing the egg being unscrambled, the yolk and the white coming back together and heading upward into the eggshell.

Christian told the audience that the video should make them uneasy because it's not natural. The universe doesn't work that way.

A scrambled egg is mush. An egg is a beautiful, sophisticated thing that can create even more sophisticated things, such as chickens. And we know in our heart of hearts that the universe does not travel from mush to complexity. In fact, this gut instinct is reflected in one of the most fundamental laws of physics, the second law of thermodynamics, or the law of entropy. What that says basically is that the general tendency of the universe is to move from order and structure to lack of order, lack of structure—in fact, to mush. And that's why that video feels a bit strange.

Viewers on TED.com call Christian's presentation "engaging," "amazing," and "stunning." The presentation, however, would have been very difficult to follow without the slides, images, and animations. The slides did not replace the narrative; the slides complemented the story.

"Use visuals to enhance words, not duplicate."

—TED Commandment

Bono Gets a Rise out of Data

Leave it to a rock star to introduce a sexual innuendo in a TED presentation. That's exactly what U2 lead singer Bono did when he delivered the data showing the progress that mankind has made in reducing extreme poverty (defined as $1.25 a day). "The number of people living in back-breaking, soul-crushing extreme poverty has declined from 43 percent of the world's population in 1990 to 33 percent by 2000 and 21 percent by 2010,"[12] Bono said as the statistics appeared on the slides behind him. "If you live on less than $1.25 a day, this is not just data. It's everything. This rapid transition is a road out of despair and into hope . . .

8.3: Bono speaking at TED 2013. Courtesy of James Duncan Davidson/TED (http://duncandavidson com).

If current trends continue, the amount of people living on $1.25 a day gets to zero by 2030. For number crunchers, the zero zone is the erogenous zone," Bono said as the audience laughed and applauded.

Bono's slides were professionally designed, which I recommend for anyone who has a mission-critical presentation intended to be delivered to several audiences or important enough to attract new customers or investments.

Watch Bono's performance on TED.com and pay attention to the one technique that is common to all good presentation design: one theme per slide. When most presenters deliver data, they bombard the audience with an avalanche of numbers and charts, all in one view. Every time Bono delivered a statistic, the number—and that number only—appeared on the slide. Bono advanced one slide per data point. When he said that extreme poverty had been halved since the year 2000, the slide simply read: "Extreme Poverty Halved." The technique of making numbers and data visually appealing is effective at getting your listeners to notice and care about the impressive statistics behind your content.

Bono continued with a litany of numbers that show life is getting better for many of the world's poor people:

> Since the year 2000 there are eight million more AIDS patients getting life saving drugs. Malaria. There are eight countries in sub-Saharan Africa that have their death rates cut by 75 percent. For kids under five, child mortality is down by 2.85 million deaths a year. That's a rate of 7,256 children's lives saved each day. Wow. Have you read anything, anywhere, in the last week that is remotely as important as that number?

If you read the paragraph and do nothing more, neuroscience tells us you'll remember about 10 percent of the information if I ask you to recall it three days from now. Add a picture, however, and your retention will go up to 65 percent of the information. That's exactly what Bono did. He verbally communicated the content and used multimedia, mostly in the form of visuals, to reinforce the data.

Bono's multimedia presentation included animated charts, graphs, and photographs. No matter how cleanly presented your charts are, a person's eyes are going to gloss over slides that show chart after chart after chart. So, Bono added stories and photos to break up the slides and to give the eyes a rest. He also brought the data to life by including personal stories of those lives behind the data.

"Seven thousand kids a day [lives saved]. Here's two of them. Michael and Benedicta. They are alive today, thanks in large part to their nurse, Dr. Patricia Asamoah, and the Global Fund." Bono showed two slides as he delivered the preceding two sentences. The first was a close-up picture of two smiling children, Michael and Benedicta. The second showed a photo of Dr. Asamoah in what appeared to be a small village. This is the way you want to deliver data: one statistic (or theme) per slide, followed by photographs or images to give the brain a break from the monotony of the graphs, tables, and charts. Although Bono's stories were stimulating to hear, the real impact of this presentation lies with his skillful use of visuals.

32,000 Barbie Dolls

Photographer Chris Jordan plays with Barbie dolls. In February 2008, Jordan showed the TED audience a photograph he had taken with about 50 Barbie dolls placed in circular patterns. Jordan advanced to a second photograph—a larger view of the first—that showed many thousands of Barbie dolls. If you didn't know they were Barbie dolls, you would think the photo was a beautiful floral painting. The third and final photograph of the series pulled out even farther and revealed a silhouette of a woman's breasts. "As you get all the way back, you see 32,000 Barbie dolls, which represents the number of breast augmentation surgeries that are performed in the U.S. each month. The vast majority of those are on women under the age of 21,"[13] said Jordan. "It's rapidly becoming the most popular high school graduation gift given to young girls who are about to go off to college." Jordan is another master of packaging data in visually appealing ways.

In another sequence Jordan displayed an image of white paper cups stacked on top of one another. Jordan says we use 40 million cups a day to carry hot beverages, mostly coffee. "I couldn't fit 40 million cups on a canvas, but I was able to put 410,000. That's what 410,000 cups looks like," he said, as the audience saw a photograph of what appeared to be white lines. "That's 15 minutes of our cup consumption," he added. The final image in the sequence showed a day's worth of coffee cups. "That's as high as a 42-story building, and I put the Statue of Liberty in there as a scale reference," Jordan said as an image of the statue was shown and appeared dwarfed by the cups in the background.

In another art piece, Jordan wanted to visualize the number of people who die each year from cigarette smoking. The first photograph showed a close-up of cigarette boxes stacked on top of one another. As Jordan pulled back, the next photographs revealed the big picture—he had re-created Vincent van Gogh's 1886 piece, *Skull of a Skeleton with a Burning Cigarette*, with thousands of cigarette packets.

Jordan believes that it's difficult for the average person to make meaning out of enormous statistics, yet these statistics reveal some very troubling issues in our society, issues that can evoke a more visceral response from people when visually and creatively presented.

Very much in the way Bono gets a rise out of data, Jordan believes that by "feeling" big numbers, we can do something about it. "I have this fear that we aren't feeling enough as a culture right now. There's this kind of anesthesia in America at the moment. We've lost our sense of outrage, our anger and our grief about what's going on in our culture right now, what's going on in our country, the atrocities that are being committed in our names around the world. They've gone missing; these feelings have gone missing."

Jordan's presentation is a profound example of transforming dry statistics—some of which we've all heard numerous times—and adding a multimedia element in the form of visuals to bring the data alive. The visuals reinforce each point and help us "feel" the emotion behind the numbers. Maya Angelou once said, "People will forget what you said, people will forget what you did, but people will never forget how you made them feel." Don't think just about what you want people to know; think about how you want them to feel.

How LinkedIn Simplified Its Marketing PowerPoint

Nine months before LinkedIn went public, its vice president of marketing at the time invited me to give a workshop to 130 of his sales and marketing staff. He wasn't happy with his team's existing PowerPoint slides. "It overcomplicated things," he said. The executive encouraged his team to incorporate some of the concepts from my previous books into a new and more compelling slide deck to encourage enterprise-level customers to advertise and recruit on LinkedIn. They tossed out the existing Power-Point entirely and transitioned to TED-like slides with little text, no bullet points, and plenty of photographs and visuals. If a statistic needed to be highlighted, the data point was the only number on the slide, accompanied by a photograph of the LinkedIn site or some other relevant image.

One key idea I stressed with the team was the need to paint a picture for their audience with the images they show and the words they use to describe the slide. For example, the most important slide of the deck had one statistic on it: 70 million. It was accompanied by an artist's rendering of the LinkedIn logo made up of people representing LinkedIn members. The statistic represented the number of LinkedIn members at the time (today the company has more than 200 million members). The narrative we worked on went like this: "Today LinkedIn has 70 million members and we are adding three million more every month. That's the equivalent of adding the population of San Francisco to our network every 30 days."

LinkedIn's marketing and sales professionals loved the new design and went on to use the deck for the next nine months ahead of their stunning IPO (the stock doubled on its first day, making the company worth $9 billion). CEOs and sales and marketing executives for many of the world's most admired brands are tossing out their old PowerPoint presentations and replacing them with ones that take their audiences on a visual journey. The old adage "you wouldn't bring a sword to a gunfight" fits quite nicely here. The old style of PowerPoint is an anachronism on the modern corporate battlefield. Don't let your competitors kill your dreams because you failed to keep up with the times.

TEDnote

> **VISUALIZE CONTENT.** Add images or include background pictures to pie charts, tables, and graphs. I recommend striving for no more than 40 words in the first 10 slides. This will force you to think creatively about telling a memorable and engaging story instead of filling the slide with needless and distracting text. Kill bullet points on most of your slides. The most popular TED presenters deliver slides with no bullet points. Text and bullet points are the least memorable way of transferring information to your audience. You might not be able to achieve this goal with every slide, but it's a good exercise. Once you force yourself to eliminate wordy slides, you'll realize how much more fun you can have with your presentation. The best part—your audience will love it!

Hear It

While vision is our predominant sense, we recall information much better when multiple senses are stimulated at the same time. Our auditory sense is very powerful. How you say something (pitch, rate, volume, intensity, articulation) can touch your listener's soul.

150 Feet down an Illegal Mine Shaft

For more than 25 years Lisa Kristine has traveled the most hidden parts of the world to capture the beauty and expose the hardships of indigenous peoples. Let's revisit her TEDx talk and focus on how she used her words to reach her audience.

The audience sat silent, transfixed, as Kristine took them on a visual journey with photographs as their guide. Her timing was impeccable and dramatic. Instead of showing the photographs as she spoke, she started reciting the story first and then displayed the photo shortly after she began the narrative. This technique forced the audience to listen to her words carefully before seeing the photo of the characters she revealed in her story. In table 8.2 you can read what Kristine said to open her presentation, the nature of the photograph, and when it appeared.

LISA KRISTINE'S WORDS WITH CORRESPONDING PHOTO DESCRIPTIONS

LISA KRISTINE'S WORDS	PHOTO DESCRIPTIONS
I'm 150 feet down an illegal mine shaft in Ghana. The air is thick with heat and dust, and it's hard to breathe. I can feel the brush of sweaty bodies passing me in the darkness, but I can't see much else. I hear voices talking, but mostly the shaft is this cacophony of men coughing, and stone being broken with primitive tools.[14]	Black-and white-photo of shirtless miner holding a primitive-looking tool. Only the miner's silhouette is visible in the blackness, barely lit with a small flashlight affixed to his head.
Like the others, I wear a flickering, cheap flashlight tied to my head with this elastic, tattered band . . .	Black-and-white photo of a miner crawling his way down the shaft
and I can barely make out the slick tree limbs holding up the walls of the three-foot square hole dropping hundreds of feet into the earth.	Extreme close-up of a miner's face in the blackness with only the reflection of his head-mounted flashlight showing his visage
When my hand slips, I suddenly remember a miner I had met days before who had lost his grip and fell countless feet down that shaft. As I stand talking to you today, these men are still deep in that hole, risking their lives without payment or compensation, and often dying.	Photo of Kristine climbing out of mine
I got to climb out of that hole, and I got to go home, but they likely never will, because they're trapped in slavery.	Photo of miners helping Kristine out of mine

Table 8.2. Lisa Kristine's words with corresponding photo descriptions form her TEDx Maui 2012 presentation.

The first two minutes of Kristine's talk is the most gripping opener I've ever seen in a presentation. No text on the slides, just photographs, a compelling narrative, and a carefully crafted delivery. Although her photographs tapped in to her audience's visual sense, it was how she used her voice that sealed the deal. The impact you can make by stimulating your listener's auditory sense can be just as powerful as using visuals.

Painting Pictures with Words

Kristine's presentation was extraordinary because the power of her words matched her showstopping photographs. Read her evocative description of visiting brick kilns in India:

> This strange and awesome sight was like walking into ancient Egypt or Dante's Inferno. Enveloped in temperatures of 130 degrees, men, women, children, entire families in fact, were cloaked in a heavy blanket of dust, while mechanically stacking bricks on their head, up to 18 at a time, and carrying them from the scorching kilns to trucks hundreds of yards away. Deadened by monotony and exhaustion, they work silently, doing this task over and over for 16 or 17 hours a day. There were no breaks for food, no water breaks, and the severe dehydration made urinating pretty much inconsequential. So pervasive was the heat and the dust that my camera became too hot to even touch and ceased working. Every 20 minutes, I'd have to run back to our cruiser to clean out my gear and run it under an air conditioner to revive it, and as I sat there, I thought, my camera is getting far better treatment than these people.

Kristine is doing something Dr. Pascale Michelon calls "creating a visual imprint on a person's mind." Neuroscientists have found that the visual cortex of your brain cannot tell the difference between what's real and what's imagined. If you can think of something vividly—really imagine it—the same brain areas are activated as if you were actually seeing the event. That's why metaphors, analogies, and rich imagery are powerful ways to paint a picture in a mind's eye, in some cases even more effective than an actual image.

"To boost your memory, transform verbal information to visual information as much as possible,"[15] Michelon suggests. "You can do it with visual aids or how you talk, the examples you use to paint pictures in someone's head." Pascale recommends that communicators use concrete examples as much as possible. Simply put, the brain is not designed to grasp abstractions. Even in sales pitches, use concrete examples to put your clients in a situation they can picture with their mind's eye. This is much more effective than using abstract words to describe your sales strategy. "We remember pictures better than words, so when I talk if I help you create visual images, you will remember that information much better than if I just use abstract words," says Pascale.

Painting a Mental Picture with No Pictures at All

The brain can't tell the difference between what it actually sees and what it imagines. Janine Shepherd, the injured cross-country skier you met in chapter 3, painted a picture for her TEDx audience and didn't show a single slide or photograph to do it. As she tells the story, Shepherd was a member of the Australian ski team preparing for the Winter Olympics when she took a bike ride that changed her life. By using evocative and descriptive words, she took her audience along the bike path.

As we made our way up towards the spectacular Blue Mountains west of Sydney, it was the perfect autumn day: sunshine, the smell of eucalyptus and a dream. Life was good. We'd been on our bikes for around five and half hours when we got to the part of the ride that I loved, and that was the hills, because I loved the hills. And I got up off the seat of my bike, and I started pumping my legs, and as I sucked in the cold mountain air, I could feel it burning my lungs, and I looked up to see the sun shining in my face. And then everything went black.[16]

A utility truck had hit Shepherd. She was badly injured, airlifted to a spinal unit in Sydney, and was rendered a partial paraplegic. In the rest of her presentation she talked about the long road to recovery, connecting her narrative to the theme: you are not your body. Determined to prove her doctors wrong, Shepherd found a new dream to pursue—flying. She earned a pilot's license within one year of the accident and eventually became an aerobatics-flying instructor.

Shepherd's presentation has been viewed more than one million times. She has received e-mails from people who were inspired to keep fighting through their own setbacks. One person who e-mailed Shepherd said the video saved her life. The person had been fighting an ailment for 19 years. "It has become so bad that for the past few weeks I am contemplating suicide. But today after seeing and listening to Janine I got a new ray of hope. My journey begins NOW."

One Second Every Day

Cesar Kuriyama saved enough money to quit his advertising job at the age of 30 and spent the next year traveling and pursuing projects that interested him. He also recorded his daily experiences on video—only one second of video every day. He told a TED audience, "Visualization is the way to trigger memory . . . even just this one second allows me to remember everything else I did that day."[17]

Imagine . . . A Songwriter Has a Way with Words

The auditory sense can be stimulated by the rhetorical devices you use to deliver your words. For example, Martin Luther King's "I have a dream" speech is one of the most famous and quoted speeches in contemporary history. King didn't used PowerPoint, Prezi, or Apple Keynote. Instead, he painted images with his words—images that have stuck with us for half a century. King used a public-speaking device called anaphora, repeating the same word or words at the beginning of successive clauses or sentences. "I have a dream . . ." is repeated in eight successive sentences.

In addition to the charts, animation, and photographs in his presentation, U2's Bono used anaphora very effectively to add more stimulation to the senses. Here are two examples:

> **Facts**, like people, want to be free. And when they're free, liberty is right around the corner, even for the poorest of the poor. **Facts** that can challenge cynicism and apathy that leads to inertia. **Facts** that tell us what's working and what's not, so we can fix it. **Facts** that if we hear them and heed them could meet the challenge that Nelson Mandela made in 2005 when he asked us to be that great generation that overcomes that most awful expense to humanity, extreme poverty.

> I'm thinking of Wael Ghonim, he set up one of the Facebook groups behind Tahrir Square in Cairo. He got thrown in jail for it. I have his words tattooed on my brain. 'We are going to win because we don't understand politics. We are going to win because we don't play their dirty games. We are going to win because we don't have a party political agenda. We are going to win because the tears that come from our eyes actually come from our hearts. We are going to win because we dream dreams and we are willing to stand up for those dreams.' Wael is right. We are going to

win if we stand up as one, because the power of the people is so much stronger than the people in power.[18]

It's important to note that when he delivered the last paragraph, Bono didn't show any slides. He wanted the audience to focus on the auditory sense—his words. Tears filled Bono's eyes as he spoke, reflecting his deep emotional attachment to the words. Powerful, well-crafted words have a way of stirring deep emotions in all of us. A slide would have detracted from the moment. Bono received thunderous applause and a standing ovation from the TED audience. It's no wonder. He aroused their senses with his words.

Three People and a Computer Amplify One Man's Voice

In March 2011, film critic Roger Ebert, who lost his voice to cancer and eventually his life in April 2013, "spoke" to a TED audience of more than 1,000 people. "These are my words, but this is not my voice. This is Alex, the best computer voice I've been able to find, which comes as standard equipment on every Macintosh,"[19] the audience heard from a digitized voice as Ebert sat in a chair with a Mac on his lap.

As a film critic with decades of experience in front of the camera, as well as deep knowledge of the craft of moviemaking, Ebert knew how difficult it is to hold an audience's attention and so came prepared with a trick up his sleeve—a multisensory auditory experience.

The audience had been listening to Ebert speak through the digitized voice for about one minute when he said, "I've found that listening to a computer voice for any great length of time can be monotonous. So I've decided to recruit some of my TED friends to read my words aloud for me." Three others shared the stage with Ebert, all sitting in chairs alongside him. They included his wife, Chaz, Dean Ornish, and John Hunter. It's a very moving

18 minutes, especially as it shows the deep love and affection between Ebert and his wife.

The story of how Ebert remade his voice is interesting, but Ebert was absolutely right: listening to a digitized voice for 18 minutes gets monotonous, so he chose not one but four others (including the computer) to speak for him. "Multisensory" includes multiple voices. I find it ironic that Ebert said listening to a digitized voice is monotonous since many speakers speak in a monotonous tone and sound far less animated than Ebert's computer-generated voice!

In chapter 7, I said an 18- or 20-minute presentation always trumps a 60-minute one. The majority of my keynote speeches last about an hour. Am I being hypocritical? Not at all. Like Ebert did, I share the stage. In my presentations I introduce multiple voices through video clips of inspiring leaders. Video gives me the opportunity to engage two senses at once—visual and auditory.

Feel It

The holy grail of a presentation is to transport the audience to another place. The visual display of information helps them to see it, but if the audience cannot physically touch something, how do we complete the journey? Again, think about a presentation as a Broadway play. An award-winning play has a wonderful story, intriguing characters, and relevant props. Great presentations have each of those elements, including simple props that give the audience a feel for what it's like to be in the scene.

A Musician Gets a Standing Ovation Without Playing One Note

You might recall punk rocker Amanda Palmer from chapter 3. I mentioned that Palmer's TED 2013 video received more than one million views within one week of being posted online.

Palmer's theme was simple and straightforward—don't make people pay for music. Since digital content is already available and shareable, Palmer suggests artists should ask for support directly from their fans. Most of the people who watch her presentation probably never have experienced life on the streets as a struggling musician, but Palmer takes them there.

Without saying a word, Palmer walked onstage and placed a milk crate on the floor. She stepped on the crate, draped a veil across her left arm, and held out a flower in her right hand. She slowly took in two deep breaths, posed motionless for several seconds, and spoke:

> So I didn't always make my living from music. For about the five years after graduating from an upstanding liberal arts university, this was my day job. I was a self-employed living statue called the 8-Foot Bride, and I love telling people I did this for a job, because everybody always wants to know, who are these freaks in real life? Hello. I painted myself white one day, stood on a box, put a hat or a can at my feet, and when someone came by and dropped in money, I handed them a flower and some intense eye contact. And if they didn't take the flower, I threw in a gesture of sadness and longing as they walked away.[20]

Palmer delivered the first three minutes of her presentation while standing on the crate, reliving her experiences and the people who gave her money. "I had no idea how perfect a real education I was getting for the music business on this box." Eventually, her band earned enough money and she quit being a street performer. As soon as Palmer told the audience she had quit being a statue, she walked off the box. The box remained on the stage as Palmer delivered her presentation, its presence acting as a metaphor for her narrative:

I decide I'm just going to give away my music for free online whenever possible . . . I'm going to encourage downloading, sharing, but I'm going to ask for help, because I saw it work on the street.

My music career has been spent trying to encounter people on the Internet the way I could on the box, so blogging and tweeting not just about my tour dates and my new video but about our work and our art and our fears and our hangovers, our mistakes, and how we see each other. And I think when we really see each other we want to help each other.

Palmer concluded her presentation with this challenge: I think people have been obsessed with the wrong question, which is, "How do we make people pay for music?" What if we started asking, "How do we let people pay for music?" As she said thank you, Palmer pulled out the flower that she had used to open her presentation, extended the flower to her listeners with an outstretched hand, and threw it into the audience. The audience jumped to its feet for a sustained 15-second standing ovation. Palmer the musician had given the performance of her life and hadn't played a note.

The TED.com page where Palmer's video had been posted received more than 500 comments in one week. Jody Murray commented, "I'm disappointed in my own skeptical inner voice wanting to dislike this talk but in the end it was not possible to. Amazing presentation and examples of such beautiful ideas realized."

Can you recall ever seeing an "amazing" business presentation with beautifully realized ideas? They don't happen very often in corporate boardrooms, do they? Yet, Amanda Palmer was delivering a business case for giving songs away for free, a very controversial subject in the music industry, and she did it in a way that her listeners could really feel and experience.

Feeling the Pain of Slow Downloads

Palmer stood on a prop—a milk crate— to help people "feel" the pain of being a struggling musician. Props and demonstrations are useful multisensory tools to help the audience tangibly grasp your idea and the problem it solves.

For example, I worked with tech-company executives to introduce an extremely fast USB drive for computers. The product had a "read/write speed of 190/170 megabytes per second." The description itself is not very interesting or tactile in any way, yet in a simple demo we found a way to get the audience to "feel" their current pain and to contrast that pain with the joy they'd feel by using the new product.

After a brief introduction and explanation of the product, the speaker walked to stage left, where a laptop computer was sitting on a chest-high table. He pulled the new product—a USB drive— from his pocket, plugged it into the computer, and handed a stopwatch to someone in the audience. He asked the audience member to start the clock as he moved a 1.5 GB movie file from the computer to the drive. The total time that elapsed was 10.5 seconds. He then asked the audience member to start the clock again, and this time as he transferred the file using a competitor's product. Without saying a word, the executive and the audience watched as the transfer happened. They waited. And waited. And waited. More than 40 seconds later the transfer was complete. "Not all USB drives are created equal," he concluded. If the executive had talked through the demonstration, time would have gone faster for the people in the audience. Instead he was silent, drawing out the pain of slow downloads.

The Feather and the Blowtorch

"I'm a pediatrician and an anesthesiologist so I put children to sleep for a living. And I'm an academic so I put audiences to sleep for free."[21] That's how Dr. Elliot Krane, who runs the pain-management service at Packard Children's Hospital at Stanford, opened his TED presentation in 2011. Pain is usually a symptom of something wrong. For some children, the pain doesn't go away and becomes the disease.

Krane explained that before he showed the TED audience how this type of pain happens and how it's treated, he wanted to show them how it *feels*.

> Imagine that I'm stroking your arm with this feather [Krane gently swipes a yellow feather up and down his left arm]. Now I want you to imagine that I'm stroking it with this [He ignites a blowtorch and puts it near his arm. People laugh uncomfortably because they know what it must feel like]. What does it have to do with chronic pain? Imagine what your life would be like if I were to stroke it with this feather but your brain was telling you that this [picks up the blowtorch] is what you were feeling. That is my experience with patients with chronic pain. Imagine something even worse. Imagine I was stroking your child's arm with this feather and your brain was telling them they were feeling this hot torch.

The kinesthetic sense (touch) is sometimes difficult to incorporate into a presentation if the topic is about an idea (or, in Krane's case, a medical condition) instead of a physical product. But as Krane demonstrates, it can be done with a little imagination.

Once he put the blowtorch down, Krane transitioned to the visual sense, showing a photograph of one of his patients, a 16-year-old aspiring dancer who had sprained her wrist and, after it healed, continued to live with excruciating pain in the injured arm. "Chandler" had allodynia, a medical condition whereby the slightest touch causes indescribable, burning pain.

Medical conferences are infamous for having some of the dull-

8.4: Dr. Elliot Krane using a blowtorch in his TED 2011 presentation. Corutesy James Duncan Davidson/TED (http://duncandavidson.com).

est presentations of any event. It's not just my opinion. Ask any doctor. They'll tell you the majority of presentations are boring and poorly prepared. I know. I work with many doctors and executives who run pharmaceuticals, medical-device companies, and health-care organizations. Interestingly, but not surprising, if you do a Google search for "how to give a better medical presentation," the first link takes you to TED.

The bottom line is this: people remember information more vividly when more than one sense is stimulated. The next time you design a presentation, be imaginative about "touching" the five senses through the stories you tell (auditory), the photographs or slides you show (visual), and the props you use (feel).

Not What You Would Expect from a Blue Tiffany Gift Box

Stacey Kramer survived a cancerous brain tumor. An average speaker would have started her presentation with that revelation.

Instead, Kramer took an imaginative multisensory approach to her topic. The audience saw a photo of a beautifully wrapped Tiffany blue box as Kramer said:

> Imagine, if you will—a gift. I'd like for you to picture it in your mind. It's not too big—about the size of a golf ball. So envision what it looks like all wrapped up. But before I show you what's inside, I will tell you, it's going to do incredible things for you. It will bring all of your family together. You will feel loved and appreciated like never before and reconnect with friends and acquaintances you haven't heard from in years. Adoration and admiration will overwhelm you. It will recalibrate what's most important in your life.[22]

Kramer drew out the story of the gift before revealing the startling conclusion. "By now I know you're dying to know what it is and where you can get one. Does Amazon carry it? Does it have the Apple logo on it? Is there a waiting list? Not likely. This gift came to me about five months ago. It looked more like this when it was all wrapped up—not quite so pretty [photo of a red plastic bag with the word *biohazard* written on it]. And this, and then this [photos of the x-ray showing her tumor and the long scar on the back of her head where the doctors had removed it]. It was a rare gem—a brain tumor, hemangioblastoma—the gift that keeps on giving."

The contrast between the lovely Tiffany box at the beginning of Kramer's presentation and the unpleasant photos at the end create a striking sensory experience for Kramer's audience. Kramer ended her presentation with a positive message and a lesson from the event that nearly took her life: "And while I'm okay now, I wouldn't wish this gift for you. I'm not sure you'd want it. But I wouldn't change my experience. It profoundly altered my life in ways I didn't expect in all the ways I just shared with you. So the next time you're faced with something that's unexpected, unwanted and uncertain, consider that it just may be a gift."

TEDnote

HELP THE AUDIENCE TO "FEEL" YOUR PRESENTATION. Step outside the slides every once in a while. Build in demonstrations, show products, ask the audience to participate. If you're launching a product, it's fairly easy to do this because you can show people a physical product to see and touch. But what if your content is pure idea or concept? You can still create multisensory experiences. In one of my keynote presentations on the topic of customer service, I talk about a chain of soap stores called Lush. It's expensive soap. I hold a bar up and ask how many people would pay $37 a pound for it. Nobody's hand goes up. I walk into the audience and ask for a volunteer to smell and feel the soap. I ask the question again. If they still say they wouldn't pay for it, I give them the bar "for free." I continue to build the story and to give away soap. Soon the audience realizes that the more they learn about the soap, the more likely they are to pay for it. It's a fun way to get the audience involved while helping them improve brand communications and the customer experience.

Secret #8: Paint a Mental Picture with Multisensory Experiences

What Kramer did took courage, and that's why you don't see great presentations every day. It takes courage to make your story so simple that a seventh-grader can understand it. It takes courage to build a slide with one word on it, as Bono did. It takes courage to show photographs instead of filling your slides with bullets points and text. It takes courage to pull out a feather and a blowtorch as Dr. Krane did without feeling silly. Metaphorically, it takes courage to stand on a milk crate for three minutes as Amanda Palmer did.

Courage stands out. Courage gets noticed. Courage wins hearts and minds. Courage is what you need to deliver the talk of your life. I know you have courage. Find it, celebrate it, and revel in it. Courageous public speaking will transform your life and the lives of the people who listen to you. You have ideas that were meant to be seen, felt, and heard. Use your voice to astonish people, inspire them, and to change the world.

Stay in Your Lane

I don't think of work as work and play as play.

It's all living.

—SIR RICHARD BRANSON

IN DECEMBER 2010, FACEBOOK CHIEF operating officer Sheryl Sandberg was waiting offstage to address a TED audience. "The day before, I had dropped my daughter off at preschool and told her I was flying off to the East Coast so I wouldn't see her that night. She clung to my leg and begged me not to leave. I couldn't shake that image and, at the last minute, asked Pat [Paley Center CEO] if I should add it to my speech. 'Absolutely tell that story,' said Pat."[1]

Sandberg realized that she could help other women only by being honest about her own challenges and feelings. "I took a deep breath and stepped onstage. I tried to be authentic and shared my truth. I announced to the room—and basically everyone on the Internet—that I fall very short of doing it all. It felt really good not just to admit this to myself, but to share it with others."[2]

Secret #9: Stay in Your Lane

Be authentic, open, and transparent.

Why it works: Most people can spot a phony. If you try to be something or someone you're not, you'll fail to gain the trust of your audience.

PUBLIC SPEAKING IS CONSIDERED AN art form. I hope this book has demonstrated that the artful element of persuasion is backed by credible science. Now I'd like you to set aside the techniques and the science and speak from the heart. That's right, everything we've discussed will be meaningless if you are putting on an act.

YOU CAN LEARN FROM OTHERS and how they achieved success in public speaking, but you'll never make a lasting impression on people unless you leave your own mark. I remember listening to Oprah Winfrey respond to a young woman who had said that she wanted to be the next Oprah. "No, you don't," Oprah said. Ms. Winfrey explained that people should identify what lane they should be in, and to stay in their lane. She said that successful people identify their life's core purpose and relentlessly follow that purpose to become the best representation of themselves that they can become.

It takes courage to stay in your lane. As Dr. Jill was crafting her now famous "My Stroke of Insight" presentation, she had a decision to make. Although the first 12 minutes of her presentation were engrossing, there was nothing "vulnerable" or "personal" about it. Dr. Jill told me she needed a conclusion that would "bust it out to the universe."

One week before her TED talk, Dr. Jill's best friend told her that the presentation didn't work. "Jill, you take us to this incredibly vulnerable space and you take us on this journey. We go with you, we are wide open, we are all yours, and then you're going to teach us [about stroke]? You should hold the space."[3] Holding the space meant being vulnerable, expressing the raw emotion of the stroke and what it had taught her.

Dr. Jill got the message and changed her conclusion one week before the TED conference. Here is how she ended the presentation: "My spirit soared free, like a great whale gliding through the sea of silent euphoria. Nirvana. I found Nirvana . . . and if I have found Nirvana and I'm still alive, then everyone who is alive can find Nirvana. And I pictured a world filled with beautiful, peaceful, compassionate, loving people who knew that they could come to this space at any time . . . then I realized what a tremendous gift this experience could be, what a stroke of insight this could be to how we live our lives."

Most scientists wouldn't dare go to the place where Dr. Jill took her audience. Even if their "spirit soared free like a gliding whale," they wouldn't tell anyone about it. Dr. Jill realized that the story of her spiritual transformation had a lot more meaning than the story of a stroke. When her left hemisphere shut down, the ego part of her brain, she experienced a spiritual enlightenment. She no longer felt separate from the universe but a part of it. She informed the audience and educated them about stroke. If she had ended there, it would have made a good presentation. Dr. Jill took it one step further. She inspired and enlightened. The presentation went from good to remarkable. It took courage for Dr. Jill to stay in her lane, but it made all the difference.

On an episode of ABC's *Grey's Anatomy*, the character Dr. Callie Torres was preparing to give a TED talk. Torres, an orthopedic surgeon, wasn't happy with the presentation she had prepared because it seemed boring compared to what she'd seen on the TED stage. "Who wants to hear about cartilage?" she said. Due to the mayhem in the hospital, Callie missed her flight to

TED and she thought she was off the hook. But at the last minute her colleagues set up a remote satellite feed so that Callie could still deliver her presentation to a live audience (you can do that on a hit TV show).

Callie sat down nervously with a stack of note cards. "Just talk," said another doctor. "Just be who you are." The doctor was instructing Callie to stay in her lane. Callie set the notes aside, took a deep breath, and said, "Hi. I'm Dr. Callie Torres and I've had a pretty bad year. I was almost killed in a car wreck . . . an accident claimed the life of my best friend and father of my child. I'm an orthopedic surgeon by trade and I work with cartilage so I've spent a lot of time thinking about what holds us together when things fall apart . . ."

Although *Grey's Anatomy* is a fictional medical drama, it strikes me that when the writers of the show wanted to build a story line around TED, they realized that the real magic of a memorable TED presentation relies on the speaker setting aside her notes and speaking from the heart, letting her audience get a peek of her soul. Screenwriters are storytellers and they intuitively understand that the magic of TED lies deeper than the topic of a presentation. An inspiring speaker should move his or her listeners to think differently about their lives, careers, or businesses. A great speaker makes you want to be a better person.

I chose the Richard Branson quote that opens this chapter because I think many speakers separate their true selves from the persona they show to others. Branson, whom I've met and interviewed more than once, doesn't put on an act. He's real. He's the same person on and off camera. Work is not separate from play and play is not separate from work. "It's all living," Branson feels.

Many executives whom I meet act and speak one way in the privacy of our conversation, only to sound completely different when they deliver a presentation. They act, look, and sound like two different people. They're not comfortable in their lane. They want to be in somebody else's lane.

I can't tell you how many times I've met leaders who are passionate, humorous, enthusiastic, and inspiring, only to discover that the minute they get onstage they become soulless, stiff, boring, and humorless. When I ask why, some respond, "Because I'm giving a presentation."

Please keep this in mind. When you deliver a presentation, your goal should not be to "deliver a presentation." It should be to inspire your audience, to move them, and to encourage them to dream bigger. You cannot move people if they don't think you're real. You'll never convince your audience of anything if they don't trust, admire, and genuinely like you.

TEDnote

PRESENT YOUR CONTENT TO A DIFFERENT AUDIENCE. One way I help clients to be more authentic when they are "on" is to have them present their content to a friend or spouse before they have to present it to the intended audience. They are more likely to let some of their "real" self come out when delivering the information to someone they have a relationship with than to a group of listeners they don't necessarily have a close connection with.

In Sheryl Sandberg's talk, "Why We Have Too Few Women Leaders," she says that women often underestimate their abilities in the workplace. I would argue that the same lack of confidence affects many people—men and women—when it comes to their ability to give inspiring presentations. I've heard all the excuses: I'm shy; I'm not good at public speaking; I get nervous; kids made fun of me in elementary school; my content is complicated; etc. These reasons—or a variation of them—may very well explain why you're not confident about giving a presentation, but in no way do they define your potential as a public speaker.

I can assure you that many people, even great communicators, are insecure about their public speaking ability. The internationally famous pastor Joel Osteen said he was "scared to death" before his first sermon in October 1999. Ten years later he hit a home run, preaching to a sold-out crowd at the new Yankee Stadium. It took him ten years and hundreds of sermons to master the craft of public speaking, but today Osteen is considered one of the most inspirational spiritual leaders in the world.

Richard Branson said he nearly got sick when he was asked to speak early in his career. "My mind went blank when I took the microphone. I mumbled incoherently for a bit before leaving the podium. It was one of the most embarrassing moments of my life, and my face glowed red as the Virgin logo,"[4] he said.

Branson committed himself to becoming a better speaker. He practiced relentlessly. "Good speakers aren't just lucky or talented—they work hard." Branson also learned to be himself, to be authentic. "To be an impressive public speaker, you have to believe in what you are saying. And if you speak with conviction and you're passionate about your subject, your audience will be far more forgiving of your mistakes because they'll have faith that you are telling the truth. Prepare, then take your time and relax. Speak from the heart."

Billionaire investor Warren Buffett was "terrified" of public speaking. He was so nervous, in fact, that he would arrange and choose his college classes to avoid having to get up in front of people. He even enrolled in a public speaking course but dropped out before it even started. "I lost my nerve," he said. At the age of 21, Buffett started his career in the securities business in Omaha and decided that to reach his full potential he had to overcome his fear of public speaking.

Buffett enrolled in a Dale Carnegie course with 30 other people who, like him, were "terrified of getting up and saying our names." Buffett revealed his early insecurity in an interview for a

Web site aimed at helping young women find career success. The host asked Buffett, "What habits did you cultivate in your 20s and 30s that you see as the foundation of success?"[5] Buffett answered, "You've got to be able to communicate in life and it's enormously important. Schools, to some extent, underemphasize that. If you can't communicate and talk to other people and get across your ideas, you're giving up your potential." Very prestigious business schools fall short when it comes to making communication skills a vital part of their programs. I've lost count of how many brilliant MBAs I've coached at large corporations who tell me, "We don't get this stuff in school but it's so important for what I do."

TEDnote

PUT IN TIME. Do you remember locking your car door when you left it this morning? You many not remember it but of course you did. You need to practice communicating your content every day at every opportunity so that the mechanics of giving your presentation don't monopolize your attention and focus. You don't want to be the dancer counting the steps out loud. Repetition frees your mind to tell your "story" in a way that is interesting, dynamic, and, more important—authentic.

I've worked with corporate leaders who are worth millions of dollars and run some of the world's largest brands, representing products and services that touch your life every day. Many have privately admitted to me that they are not confident about public speaking. My job is to bring out their confidence so that they can captivate their audiences. I do so by helping them to identify their "lane" and why they're passionate about that lane. Then, once we craft, visualize, and rehearse the presentation, it's time to let go and, as Branson suggested, speak from the heart. This approach has never failed.

Secret #9: Stay in Your Lane

The next time you deliver a presentation, you'll be compared to TED speakers. Your audience will be aware that there's a fresh, bold style of delivering information; a style that lifts their spirits, fills their souls, and inspires them to think differently about the world and their roles in it.

Today, people around the globe have viewed TED presentations more than one billion times online via the TED site, YouTube, or embedded in countless blogs. Even the TED presenters themselves are getting better and better every year, an observation that TED curator Chris Anderson made at TED 2013.

The TED style permeates much of our popular culture. When former president Bill Clinton appeared on Stephen Colbert's show on Comedy Central, Colbert suggested that Clinton combine his conference, the Clinton Global Initiative, with TED and call it "Bill and Ted's excellent initiative!" It got the biggest laugh of the interview, but the joke would have bombed had the audience not known about TED or the type of presentations it's known for.

While the TED style is infusing our culture—and, as we've discussed in the eight previous chapters, TED speakers do share techniques in common—each person must find his or her own passion about the topic to make an authentic connection with the audience. Above all, do not try to be Tony Robbins, Dr. Jill, Bono, Sheryl Sandberg, Richard Branson, or any of the other people you've read about in this book. They carved out a lane for themselves and drove in it exceptionally well. Stay in your lane. Hold the space. Be true to your authentic self—the best representation of yourself that you can possibly be.

AUTHOR'S NOTE

If you're like most people, you're capable of so much more than you've imagined for your life. You have the capacity to move people, to inspire them, to provide hope to the despondent and direction to the lost. You have the ability to educate and electrify, inform and inspire, *but only if you believe in your ability to do so.*

Don't let negative labels hold you back from achieving your destiny. Some people might tell you that you're not good enough, that you don't have what it takes to make a compelling business pitch or to give a great presentation. Often the worst labels are those we place on ourselves. I find that leaders who are nervous about speaking in public say the most awful things to themselves— words that they would never say to anyone else. I've heard leaders say:

I'm terrible at giving presentations.

I got nervous once and it ruined me. I'm a horrible public speaker.

Nobody wants to listen to me. I'm boring.

If these are the type of phrases you repeat to yourself day after day, it's no wonder you get nervous! You can't control what other people say about you but you can control how you frame those comments and you can most certainly control the things you tell yourself. Instead of replaying negative thoughts over and over again, reframe your thoughts and replace those negative labels with words of encouragement, empowerment, and strength.

Remember, ideas are the currency of the twenty-first century. Your ideas will change the direction of your life and potentially change the world. Don't let anything—including negative labels—stand in your way.

At the end of my interview with TED speaker Larry Smith, he said, "I wish you success." Smith doesn't say "Good luck" because luck has little to do with your success. You don't need luck to be an inspiring speaker. You need examples, techniques, passion, and practice. You also need courage—the courage to follow your passion, articulate your ideas simply, and express what makes your heart sing.

Wishing you success,
Carmine Gallo

NOTES

Introduction: Ideas Are the Currency of the Twenty-first Century

1. Julie Coe, "TED's Chris Anderson," Departures.com, March/April 2012, http://www.departures.com/articles/teds-chris-anderson (accessed April 11, 2013).

2. Daphne Zuniga, "The Future We Will Create Inside the World of TED," documentary, New Video Group, Inc., 2007.

3. Stanford University, "'You've Got to Find What You Love,' Jobs Says," Stanford Report, June 14, 2005, Steve Jobs's Commencement Address, delivered on June 12, 2005, http://news-service.stanford.edu/news/2005/june15/jobs-061505.html (accessed April 11, 2013).

4. Daniel Pink, *To Sell Is Human* (New York: Riverhead Books, 2012), 2.

5. Robert Greene, *Mastery*, (New York: Viking, 2012), 12.

6. Tony Robbins, "Why We Do What We Do," TED.com, June 2006, http://www.ted.com/talks/tony_robbins_asks_why_we_do_what_we_do.html (accessed April 11, 2013).

1. Unleash the Master Within

1. Aimee Mullins, "It's Not Fair Having 12 Pairs of Legs," TED.com, March 2009, http://www.ted.com/talks/aimee_mullins_prosthetic_aesthetics .html (accessed April 11, 2013).

2. Cameron Russell, "Looks Aren't Everything. Believe Me, I'm a Model," TED.com, January 2013, http://www.ted.com/talks/cameron_russell _looks_aren_t_everything_believe_me_i_m_a_model.html (accessed April 11, 2013).

3. Robert Greene, *Mastery*, (New York: Viking, 2012), 12.

4. *Daily News*, "Buddhist Monk Is the World's Happiest Man," October 29, 2012, http://india.nydailynews.com/newsarticle/7b470adb0a9b6c32e19e16a08 df13f3d/buddhist-monk-is-the-worlds-happiest-man#ixzz2ILd7tSGa (accessed April 11, 2013).

5. Matthieu Ricard, "The Happiest Person in the World?", Matthieu Ricard blog post, November 12, 2012, http://www.matthieuricard.org/en/index.php /blog/255_the_happiest_person_in_the_world/ (accessed April 11, 2013).

6. Matthieu Ricard, Buddhist monk, in discussion with the author, March 16, 2013.

7. Larry Smith, Professor of Economics of Waterloo, Canada, in discussion with the author, June 26, 2012.

8. Melissa S. Cardon, Joakim Wincent, Jagdip Singh, and Mateja Drnovsek, "The Nature and Experience of Entrepreneurial Passion," *Academy of Management Review*, vol. 34, no. 3 (2009), 511–532.

9. Richard Branson, "Richard Branson: Life at 30,000 Feet," TED.com, October 2007, http://www.ted.com/talks/richard_branson_s_life_at_30_000 _feet.html (accessed April 11, 2013).

10. Cheryl Mitteness, Richard Sudek, and Melissa S. Cardon, "Angel investor characteristics that determine whether perceived passion leads to higher evaluations of funding potential," *Journal of Business Venturing*, vol. 27 (2012), 592–606.

11. Jill Bolte Taylor, "Jill Bolte Taylor's Stroke of Insight," TED.com, March 2008, http://www.ted.com/talks/jill_bolte_taylor_s_powerful_stroke_of_insight .html (accessed May 18, 2013).

12. Jill Bolte Taylor, "Does Our Planet Need a Stroke of Insight?", Huffington Post, TED Weekends: Reset Your Brain, January 4, 2013, http://www .huffingtonpost.com/dr-jill-boltetaylor/neuroscience_b_2404554.html (accessed April 11, 2013).

13. Pascal Michelon, adjunct professor at Washington University in St. Louis, in discussion with the author, January 22, 2013.

14. Howard Friedman and Leslie Martin, "The Longevity Project: Surprising Discoveries for Health and Long Life from the Landmark Eight-Decade Study" (New York: Hudson Street Press, 2011), 28.

15. Joyce E. Bono and Remus Ilies, "Charisma, Positive Emotions and Mood Contagion," *Science Direct*, The Leadership Quarterly, vol. 17 (2006), 317–334.

16. Richard St. John, "Richard St. John's 8 Secrets of Success," TED.com, December 2006, http://www.ted.com/talks/richard_st_john_s_8_secrets_of _success.html (accessed April 24, 2013).

17. Ernesto Sirolli, "Ernesto Sirolli: Want to Help Someone? Shut Up and Listen!" TED.com, November 2012, http://www.ted.com/talks/ernesto _sirolli_want_to_help_someone_shut_up_and_listen.html (accessed April 11, 2013).

2. Master the Art of Storytelling

1. Bryan Stevenson, "Bryan Stevenson: We Need to Talk about an Injustice," TED.com, March 2012, http://www.ted.com/talks/bryan_stevenson_we _need_to_talk_about_an_injustice.html (accessed April 24, 2013).

2. Bryan Stevenson, founder and director of the Equal Justice Initiative, in discussion with the author, December 17, 2012.

3. Ben Affleck, "Ben Affleck: 8 Talks that Amazed Me," TED.com, http:// www.ted.com/playlists/32/ben_affleck_8_talks_that_amaz.html (accessed April 24, 2013).

4. Uri Hasson, Asif A. Ghazanfar, Bruno Galantucci, Simon Garrod, and Christian Keysers, "Brain-to-Brain Coupling: A Mechanism for Creating and Sharing a Social World," Neuroscience Institute, Princeton University, 2012, http://psych.princeton.edu/psychology/research/hasson/pubs/Hasson_et_al_ TiCS_2012.pdf (accessed April 11, 2013).

5. Greg J. Stephens, Lauren J. Silbert, and Uri Hasson, "Speaker-Listener Neural Coupling Underlies Successful Communication," Proceedings of the National Academy of Sciences of the United States of America, July 26, 2010, http://www.ncbi.nlm.nih.gov/pmc/articles/PMC2922522/ (accessed April 11, 2013).

6. Brené Brown, "Brené Brown: The Power of Vulnerability," TED.com, December 2010, http://www.ted.com/talks/brene_brown_on_vulnerability.html (accessed April 24, 2014).

7. Andrew Stanton, "Andrew Stanton: The Clues to a Great Story," TED. com, March 2012, http://www.ted.com/talks/andrew_stanton_the_clues_to_a _great_story.html (accessed April 24, 2013).

8. Dan Ariely, "Dan Ariely: Our Buggy Moral Code," TED.com, March 2009, http://www.ted.com/talks/dan_ariely_on_our_buggy_moral_code.html (accessed April 24, 2013).

9. Chip Heath and Dan Heath, *Made to Stick: Why Some Ideas Survive and Others Die* (New York: Random House, 2007), 64.

10. Ibid., 84.

11. Ken Robinson, "Ken Robinson Says Schools Kill Creativity," TED.com, June 2006, http://www.ted.com/talks/ken_robinson_says_schools_kill_creativ ity.html?qsha=1&utm_expid=166907-20&utm_referrer=http%3A%2F%2F www.ted.com%2Fsearch%3Fcat%3Dss_all%26q%3Dken%2Brobinson (accessed May 18, 1013).

12. YouTube.com, "Apr 29-Joel Osteen-Yes Is in Your Future," YouTube .com, May 12, 2012, http://www.youtube.com/watch?v=VJiW_H3_0S4 (accessed May 18, 2013).

13. Bono, "8 Talks That Give Me Hope," TED.com, http://www.ted .com/playlists/53/bono_8_talks_that_give_me_hop.html (accessed May 18, 2013).

14. Seth Godin, "Seth Godin: How to Get Your Ideas to Spread," TED.com, April 2007, http://www.ted.com/talks/seth_godin_on_sliced_bread.html (accessed April 24, 2013).

15. Ludwick Marishane, "Ludwick Marishane: A Bath without Water," TED.com, December 2012, http://www.ted.com/talks/ludwick_marishane_a _bath_without_water.html (accessed May 18, 2013).

16. Jonah Sachs, *Winning the Story Wars: Why Those Who Tell the Best Stories Will Rule the Future* (Boston, MA: Harvard Business Review Press, 2012), 14.

17. Malcolm Gladwell, "Malcolm Gladwell: Choice, Happiness and Spaghetti Sauce," TED.com, September 2006, http://www.ted.com/talks/malcolm_glad well_on_spaghetti_sauce.html (accessed May 18, 2013).

18. Peter Guber, *Tell to Win: Connect, Persuade, and Triumph with the Hidden Power of Stories* (New York: Crown Business, 2011), vii.

19. Ibid, 9.

20. Ibid, 33.

21. Annie Murphy Paul, "Your Brain on Fiction," *The New York Times*, Sunday Review/The Opinion Pages, March 17, 2012, http://www.nytimes.com/2012

/03/18/opinion/sunday/the-neuroscience-of-your-brain-on-fiction.html ?pagewanted=all&_r=1& (accessed April 11, 2013).

22. Significantobjects.com, About page, http://significantobjects.com/about/ (accessed May 18, 2013).

23. YouTube.com, "Kurt Vonnegut on the Shapes of Stories," YouTube.com, October 30, 2010, http://www.youtube.com/watch?v=oP3c1h8v2ZQ (accessed May 18, 2013).

24. Isabel Allende, "Isabel Allende: Tales of Passion," TED.com, January 2008, http://www.ted.com/talks/isabel_allende_tells_tales_of_passion.html (accessed May 18, 2013).

3. Have a Conversation

1. Amanda Palmer, "The Epic TED Blog, Part One: It Takes a Village to Write a TED Talk," Amanda Palmer and the Grand Theft Orchestra, March 7, 2012, http://amandapalmer.net/blog/20130307/ (accessed April 11, 2013).

2. James R. Williams, "Guidelines for the Use of Multimedia in Instruction," Proceedings of the Human Factors and Ergonomics Society 42nd Annual Meeting, vol. 42, no. 20 (1998), 1447–1451, Sage Journals online, http://pro.sagepub.com/content/42/20/1447 (accessed May 18, 2013).

3. Lisa Kristine, "Lisa Kristine: Photos that Bear Witness to Modern Slavery," TED.com, August 2012, http://www.ted.com/talks/lisa_kristine_glimpses_of_modern_day_slavery.html (accessed May 18, 2013).

4. YouTube.com, Taylor, "The Neuroanatomical Transformation of the Teenage Brain: Jill Bolte Taylor at TEDxYouth@Indianapolis," YouTube.com, February 21, 2013, http://www.youtube.com/watch?v=PzT_SBl31-s (accessed May 19, 2013).

5. Morgan Wright, Chief Crime Fighter, Washington D.C. Metro Area, in discussion with the author, April 4, 2013.

6. Colin Powell, "Colin Powell: Kids Need Structure," TED.com, January 2013, http://www.ted.com/talks/colin_powell_kids_need_structure.html (accessed May 19, 2013).

7. Colin Powell, *It Worked for Me: In Life and Leadership* (New York: Harper, 2012), 243.

8. Ernesto Sirolli, "Ernesto Sirolli: Want to Help Someone? Shut Up and Listen!" TED.com, November 2012, http://www.ted.com/talks/ernesto_sirolli_want_to_help_someone_shut_up_and_listen.html (accessed April 11, 2013).

9. Jennifer Granholm, "Jennifer Granholm: A Clean Energy Proposal—

Race to the Top," TED.com, February 2013, http://www.ted.com/talks/jennifer
_granholm_a_clean_energy_proposal_race_to_the_top.html (accessed May 18,
2013).

10. Bob M. Fennis and Marielle Stel, "The Pantomime of Persuasion: Fit
Between Non Verbal Communication and Influence Strategies," *Journal of
Experimental Social Psychology*, vol. 47 (2011), 806–810.

11. Amy Cuddy, "Amy Cuddy: Your Body Language Shapes Who You Are,"
October 2012, http://www.ted.com/talks/amy_cuddy_your_body_language
_shapes_who_you_are.html (accessed May 18, 2013).

12. Janine Shepherd, "Janine Shepherd: A Broken Body Isn't a Broken Person," TED.com, November 2012, http://www.ted.com/talks/janine_shepherd
_a_broken_body_isn_t_a_broken_person.html (accessed May 19, 2013).

4. Teach Me Something New

1. Robert Ballard, "Robert Ballard on Exploring the Ocean," TED.com,
May 2008, http://www.ted.com/talks/robert_ballard_on_exploring_the_oceans
.html (accessed May 18, 2013).

2. Robert Ballard, *Titanic* explorer, in discussion with the author, February
18, 2013.

3. James Cameron, "James Cameron: Before Avatar . . . a Curious Boy,"
TED.com, March 2010, http://www.ted.com/talks/james_cameron_before_ava
tar_a_curious_boy.html (accessed April 11, 2013).

4. Ibid.

5. John Medina, *Brain Rules* (Seattle, WA: Pear Press, 2008), 32.

6. Ibid, 265.

7. Martha Burns, "Dopamine and Learning," Indigo Learning, September
21, 2012, http://www.indigolearning.co.za/dopamine-and-learning-by-martha
-burns-phd/ (accessed April 11, 2013).

8. Ibid.

9. Martha Burns, "Dopamine and Learning: What the Brain's Reward
Center Can Teach Educators," Scientific Learning, September 18, 2012,http://
www.scilearn.com/blog/dopamine-learning-brains-reward-center-teach-edu
cators.php (accessed April 11, 2013).

10. Hans Rosling, "Hans Rosling: Stats that Reshape Your Worldview," TED
.com, June 2006, http://www.ted.com/talks/hans_rosling_shows_the_best_stats
_you_ve_ever_seen.html?qshb=1&utm_expid=166907-19&utm_referrer=http
%3A%2F%2Fwww.ted.com%2Fsearch%3Fcat%3Dss_all%26q%3Drosling
(accessed May 19, 2013).

11. Ibid.

12. Nicholas A. Christakis, "The World's 100 Most Influential People: 2012," *TIME*, April 18, 2012, http://www.time.com/time/specials/pack ages /article/0,28804,2111975_2111976_2112170,00.html (accessed April 11, 2013).

13. Susan Cain, "Susan Cain: The Power of Introverts," TED.com, March 2012, http://www.ted.com/talks/susan_cain_the_power_of_introverts.html (accessed April 24, 2013).

14. 14. Revolution.com, About Revolution Web site page, http://revolution .com/ourstory/about-revolution (accessed May 19, 2013).

15. Fast Company Staff, "Twitter's Biz Stone and Ev Williams and Charlie Rose: The Long and Short of Creative Conversations," *Fast Company* online, http://www.fastcompany.com/welcome.html?destination=http://www.fast company.com/3004361/a-conversation-charlie-rose-biz-stone-ev-williams (accessed May 19, 2013).

16. Seth Godin, "Seth Godin: How to Get Your Ideas to Spread," TED. com, April 2007, http://www.ted.com/talks/seth_godin_on_sliced_bread.html (accessed April 24, 2013).

17. Gregory Berns, *Iconoclast*, (Boston, MA: Harvard Business Press, 2008), 25.

18. Vivienne Walt, "A Mayoral Makeover," *TIME*, October 2, 2005, http:// www.time.com/time/magazine/article/0,9171,1112793,00.html#ixzz2KpjEAsKp (accessed April 11, 2013).

19. James Flynn, Michael F. Shaughnessy, and Susan W. Fulgham, "An Interview with Jim Flynn about the Flynn Effect," Academic journal article from *North American Journal of Psychology*, vol. 14, no. 1, http://www.questia.com/ library/1G1-281111803/an-interview-with-jim-flynn-about-the-flynn-effect (accessed April 11, 2013).

20. Nicholas D. Kristof, "It's a Smart, Smart, Smart World," *The New York Times*, The Opinion Pages, December 12, 2012, http://www.nytimes.com/2012 /12/13/opinion/kristof-its-a-smart-smart-smart-world.html?_r=0 (accessed April 11, 2013).

21. Dan Pink, author, in discussion with the author, February 13, 2013.

22. John Medina, affiliate Professor of Bioengineering at the University of Washington School of Medicine, in discussion with the author, June 27, 2008.

23. Docurama Films, "TED: The Future We Will Create Inside the World of TED," 2007, produced and directed by Steven Latham and Daphne Zuniga.

24. Ben Saunders, "Ben Saunders: Why Bother Leaving the House?", TED .com, December 2012, http://www.ted.com/talks/ben_saunders_why_bother _leaving_the_house.html (accessed April 11, 2013).

5. Deliver Jaw-Dropping Moments

1. YouTube, "Bill Gates Releases Malaria Mosquitoes TED!! Must See," YouTube, February 6, 2009, http://www.youtube.com/watch?v=tWjpVJ8YNtk (accessed April 11, 2013).

2. *NBC Nightly News with Brian Williams*, "Bill Gates Bugs Out," original premiere February 5, 2009, http://bigdonald.com/nbc-nightly-news-with-brian -williams-bill-gates-bugs-out/gait19 (accessed April 24, 2013).

3. John Medina, *Brain Rules* (Seattle, WA: Pear Press, 2008), 80.

4. Ibid., 81.

5. Rebecca Todd, psychology professor at the University of Toronto, in discussion with the author, February 25, 2013.

6. Ibid.

7. Jill Bolte Taylor, "Jill Bolte Taylor's Stroke of Insight," TED.com, March 2008, http://www.ted.com/talks/jill_bolte_taylor_s_powerful_stroke_of_insight .html (accessed April 24, 2013).

8. YouTube, "The Neuroanatomical Transformation of the Teenage Brain: Jill Bolte Taylor at TEDxYouth@Indianapolis," YouTube, February 21, 2013, http://www.youtube.com/watch?v=PzT_SBl31-s (accessed April 11, 2013).

9. YouTube, "The Lost 1984 Video (The Original 1984 Macintosh Introduction)," YouTube, http://www.youtube.com/watch?v=2B-XwPjn9YY (accessed January 30, 2009).

10. YouTube, "The Microsoft Deal—Macworld Boston (1997)," YouTube, December 21, 2012, http://www.youtube.com/watch?v=PjT19XTxZaU (accessed April 11, 2013).

11. YouTube, "Apple Music Event 2001-The First Ever iPod Introduction," YouTube, http://www.youtube.com/watch?v=kN0SVBCJqLs&feature=related (accessed January 30, 2009).

12. Apple, "Macworld San Francisco 2007 Keynote Address," Apple, http:// www.apple.com/quicktime/qtv/mwsf07/ (accessed January 30, 2009).

13. Raghava KK, "Raghava KK: My 5 Lives as an Artist," TED.com, February 2010, http://www.ted.com/talks/raghava_kk_five_lives_of_an_artist.html (accessed May 19, 2013).

14. Freeman Hrabowski, "Freeman Hrabowski: 4 Pillars of College Success in

Science," TED.com, April 2013, http://www.ted.com/talks/freeman_hrabowski
_4_pillars_of_college_success_in_science.html (accessed May 19, 2013).

6. Lighten Up

1. Ken Robinson, "Ken Robinson Says Schools Kill Creativity," TED.com, June 2006, http://www.ted.com/talks/ken_robinson_says_schools_kill_creativity .html?qsha=1&utm_expid=166907-20&utm_referrer=http%3A%2F%2Fwww .ted.com%2Fsearch%3Fcat%3Dss_all%26q%3Dken%2Brobinson (accessed May 18, 1013).

2. A. K. Pradeep, *The Buying Brain: Secrets for Selling to the Subconscious Mind* (Hoboken, NJ: John Wiley & Sons, 2010), 29.

3. Rod A. Martin, *The Psychology of Humor: An Integrative Approach* (Burlington, MA: Elsevier Academic Press, 2007), 120.

4. Ibid.

5. Ibid., 128.

6. Fabio Sala, "Laughing All the Way to the Bank," *Harvard Business Review*, September 2003, http://hbr.org/2003/09/laughing-all-the-way-to-the-bank/ar/1 (accessed April 11, 2013).

7. YouTube, "Jerry Seinfeld on How to Write a Joke," YouTube.com, December 20, 2012, http://www.youtube.com/watch?v=itWxXyCfW5s (accessed May 19, 2013).

8. Dan Pallotta, "Dan Pallotta: The Way We Think about Charity is Dead Wrong," TED.com, March 2013, http://www.ted.com/talks/dan_pallotta_the _way_we_think_about_charity_is_dead_wrong.html (accessed May 19, 2013).

9. Jill Bolte Taylor, "Jill Bolte Taylor's Stroke of Insight," TED.com, March 2008, http://www.ted.com/talks/jill_bolte_taylor_s_powerful_stroke_of_insight .html (accessed May 18, 2013).

10. John McWhorter, "John McWhorter: Txtng Is Killing Language. JK!!!", TED.com, April 2013, http://www.ted.com/talks/john_mcwhorter_txtng_is _killing_language_jk.html (accessed May 18, 2013).

11. Juan Enriquez, "Juan Enriquez: The Next Species of Human," TED. com, February 2009, http://www.ted.com/talks/juan_enriquez_shares_mind boggling_new_science.html (accessed May 19, 2013).

12. Chris Bliss, "Chris Bliss: Comedy Is Translation," TED.com, February 2012, http://www.ted.com/talks/chris_bliss_comedy_is_translation.html (accessed May 19, 2013).

13. Rose George, "Rose George: Let's Talk Crap. Seriously," TED.com, April

2013, http://www.ted.com/talks/rose_george_let_s_talk_crap_seriously.html (accessed May 19, 2013).

14. YouTube.com, "Jim Carrey and Stephen Hawking on Late Night with Conan O'B," YouTube.com, February 26, 2010, http://www.youtube.com/watch?v=sRO4fAevMZQ (accessed May 19, 2013).

15. Stephen Hawking, "Stephen Hawking: Questioning the Universe," TED.com, April 2008, http://www.ted.com/talks/stephen_hawking_asks_big_questions_about_the_universe.html (accessed May 19, 2013).

7. Stick to the 18-Minute Rule

1. Larry Smith, Professor of Economics at University of Waterloo, Canada, in discussion with the author, June 26, 2012.

2. Amit Agarwal, "Why Are TED Talks 18 Minutes Long?" Digital Inspiration, February 15, 2010, http://www.labnol.org/tech/ted-talk-18-minutes/12755 / (accessed May 18, 2013).

3. Paul E. King, Professor and Chair, Department of Communication Studies, in discussion with the author, December 3, 2012.

4. Roy Baumeister, *Willpower: Rediscovering the Greatest Human Strength* (paperback) (New York: Penguin Books, 2012), 48.

5. Matthew May, *The Laws of Subtraction: 6 Simple Rules for Winning in the Age of Excess Everything* (New York: McGraw-Hill, 2012), xiv.

6. David Christian, Anglo-American historian and scholar of Russian history, and creator of an interdisciplinary approach known as Big History, in discussion with the author, December 13, 2012.

7. Neil Pasricha, "Neil Pasricha: The 3 A's of Awesome," TED.com, January 2011, http://www.ted.com/talks/neil_pasricha_the_3_a_s_of_awesome.html (accessed May 19, 2013).

8. Kevin Allocca, "Kevin Allocca: Why Videos Go Viral," TED.com, February 2012, http://www.ted.com/talks/kevin_allocca_why_videos_go_viral.html (accessed May 19, 2013).

9. Majora Carter, "Majora Carter: 3 Stories of Local Eco-Entrepreneurship," TED.com, December 2010, http://www.ted.com/talks/majora_carter_3_stories _of_ecoactivism.html (accessed September 30, 2013).

10. Carmine Gallo, "How to Pitch Anything in 15 Seconds [Video]," *Forbes*, Leadership, July 17, 2012, http://www.forbes.com/sites/carminegallo/2012/07 /17/how-to-pitch-anything-in-15-seconds/ (accessed April 11, 2013).

8. Paint a Mental Picture with Multisensory Experiences

1. Michael Pritchard, "Michael Pritchard: How to Make Filthy Water Drinkable," TED.com, August, 2009, http://www.ted.com/talks/michael_pritchard _invents_a_water_filter.html (accessed April 11, 2013).

2. Richard Mayer, "Cognitive Theory of Multimedia Learning (Mayer)," Learning-Theories.com, posted in Cognitive Theories, Learning Theories & Models, http://www.learning-theories.com/cognitive-theory-of-multimedia-learning -mayer.html (accessed May 18, 2013).

3. Emily McManus, "TEDsters Talk about Al Gore's Impact," TED.com, October 12, 2007, http://blog.ted.com/2007/10/12/i_was_actually/ (accessed April 11, 2013).

4. Elizabeth Blair, "Laurie David: One Seriously 'Inconvenient' Woman," NPR, Special Series Profiles, May 7, 2007, http://www.npr.org/templates/story /story.php?storyId=9969008 (accessed April 19, 2013).

5. Carmine Gallo, "Richard Branson: If It Can't Fit on the Back of an Envelope, It's Rubbish (An Interview)" Forbes.com, October 22, 2012, http://www .forbes.com/sites/carminegallo/2012/10/22/richard-branson-if-it-cant-fit-on -the-back-of-an-envelope-its-rubbish-interview/ (accessed May 18, 2013).

6. YouTube, "An Inconvenient Truth (1/10) Movie Clip—Science of Global Warming (2006) HD," YouTube, October 8, 2011, http://www.youtube.com /watch?v=NXMarwAusY4 (accessed April 11, 2013).

7. Nancy Duarte, "Nancy Duarte: The Secret Structure of Great Talks," TED.com, February 2012, http://www.ted.com/talks/nancy_duarte_the_secret _structure_of_great_talks.html (accessed May 19, 2013).

8. John Medina, *Brain Rules* (Seattle, WA: Pear Press, 2008), 84.

9. Ibid., p.233.

10. Bill Gates, "Bill Gates on Energy: Innovating to Zero!", TED.com, February 2010, http://www.ted.com/talks/bill_gates.html (accessed May 19, 2013).

11. David Christian, "David Christian: The History of Our World in 18 Minutes," TED.com, April 2011, http://www.ted.com/talks/david_christian_big _history.html (accessed May 19, 2013).

12. Bono, "Bono: The Good News on Poverty (Yes, There's Good News)," TED.com, March 2013, http://www.ted.com/talks/bono_the_good_news_on _poverty_yes_there_s_good_news.html (accessed May 19, 2013).

13. Chris Jordan, "Chris Jordan: Turning Powerful Stats into Art," TED.com, June 2008, http://www.ted.com/talks/chris_jordan_pictures_some_shocking _stats.html (accessed April 11, 2013).

14. Lisa Kristine, "Lisa Kristine: Photos that Bear Witness to Modern Slavery," TED.com, August 2012, http://www.ted.com/talks/lisa_kristine_glimpses _of_modern_day_slavery.html (accessed May 18, 2013).

15. Pascale Michelon, Director of The Memory Practice and Adjunct Professor at the Washington University in St. Louis, in discussion with the author, January 22, 2013.

16. Janine Shepherd, "Janine Shepherd: A Broken Body Isn't a Broken Person," TED.com, November 2012, http://www.ted.com/talks/janine_shepherd _a_broken_body_isn_t_a_broken_person.html (accessed May 19, 2013).

17. Cesar Kuriyama, "Cesar Kuriyama: One Second Every Day," February 2013, http://www.ted.com/talks/cesar_kuriyama_one_second_every_day.html (accessed May 19, 2013).

18. Bono, "Bono: The Good News on Poverty (Yes, There's Good News)," TED.com, March 2013, http://www.ted.com/talks/bono_the_good_news_on _poverty_yes_there_s_good_news.html (accessed May 19, 2013).

19. Roger Ebert, "Roger Ebert: Remaking My Voice," TED.com, April 2011, http://www.ted.com/talks/roger_ebert_remaking_my_voice.html (accessed May 19, 2013).

20. Amanda Palmer, "Amanda Palmer: The Art of Asking," TED.com, March 2013, http://www.ted.com/talks/amanda_palmer_the_art_of_asking. html (accessed May 2013).

21. Elliot Krane, "Elliot Krane: The Mystery of Cronic Pain," TED.com, May 2011, http://www.ted.com/talks/elliot_krane_the_mystery_of_chronic_pain .html (accessed May 19, 2013).

22. Stacey Kramer, "Stacey Kramer: The Best Gift I Ever Survived," TED .com, October 2010, http://www.ted.com/talks/stacey_kramer_the_best_gift _i_ever_survived.html (accessed May 19, 2013).

9. Stay in Your Lane

1. Sheryl Sandberg, *Lean In: Women, Work, and the Will to Lead* (New York: Alfred A. Knopf, 2013), 139.

2. Ibid.

3. Jill Bolte Taylor, president of the Greater Bloomington Affiliate of NAMI in Bloomington, Indiana, and national spokesperson for the Harvard Brain Tissue Resource Center, in discussion with the author, March 19, 2013.

4. Richard Branson, "Richard Branson on the Art of Public Speaking,"

Entrepreneur, February 4, 2013, http://www.entrepreneur.com/article/225627 (accessed April 11, 2013).

5. Meredith Lepore, "6 Essential Tips for Work and Life from Warren Buffet ," Levoleague.com, May 8, 2013, http://www.levoleague.com/career -advice/warren-buffett-life-tips (accessed May 19, 2013).

INDEX